REINVIGORATING FINANCING APPROACHES FOR SUSTAINABLE AND RESILIENT INFRASTRUCTURE IN ASEAN+3

MAY 2023

ASIAN DEVELOPMENT BANK

ADB

CONTENTS

Tables, Figures, and Boxes — v

Foreword — vi

Acknowledgments — vii

Abbreviations — viii

Executive Summary — ix

I   Introduction — 1

II Infrastructure Landscape and Opportunities — 4

III Issues and Challenges — 9

IV Innovative Financing Mechanisms — 17

V Summary Actions and Conclusions — 63

Appendix: Case Studies — 67

1   Blended Finance — 67

2   Blended Finance — 71

3   Asset Recycling — 74

4   Asset Securitization — 76

5   Convertible Debt and/or Grant Structure — 80

6   Municipal Bonds — 83

7   Sustainable Bonds — 86

8   Green Bonds — 89

9   Government Green Fund — 93

10 Green Transition Financing — 95

11 Public–Private Partnership — 97

12 Climate Risk and Catastrophe Insurance — 100

13 Crowdfunded Impact Investments — 103

14 Land Value Capture — 106

15 Debt-for-Climate/Nature Swap — 109

TABLES, FIGURES, AND BOXES

Tables

ES1	Summary of Innovative Financing Mechanisms	xiii
1	Barriers to Infrastructure Allocations by Institutional Investors	2
2	Financiers	18
3	Blended Finance Instruments	22
4	Types of Green Bonds	37
5	Crowdfunding Models	52
6	Land Value Capture Tools	56
A1	Financing Products for Eligible Investees	69
A2	Indonesia's Green Sukuk 2018 Issuance	90

Figures

ES1	Mechanics of Innovative Finance	xii
1	Innovative Financing Models	19
2	Blended Finance Barriers and Interventions	21
3	Asset Recycling Process	26
4	How Securitization Works	29
5	Financing Model Framework	32
6	Financing Model	34
7	Outline of the Bond Labeling Process	37
8	Use of Proceeds	38
9	Allocation of Green Bonds Investments in Association of Southeast Asian Nations	39
10	Green Bond Financing Framework	40
11	Green Fund Mechanism	43
12	Green Fund Issuance—Key Steps	44
13	Typical Public–Private Partnership Structure	48
14	The Virtuous Cycle of Value Capture	55
15	Debt-for-Nature Swap Process	58

A1   Different Tranches of Shares Issued   67
A2   Operational Structure   68
A3   Shareholding and Financing Structure   70
A4   Overarching Goals and Objectives of Advance Market Commitment   71
A5   National Highways Authority of India Stakeholder Role and Responsibilities   75
A6   Portfolio Breakdown by Geographical Location and Sector   76
A7   Portfolio Breakdown by Asset Type   77
A8   The Take-Out Facility Value Proposition   78
A9   Take-Out Facility Shareholders   79
A10   Convertible Grants   80
A11   Exploration Risk at Different Stages of the Value Chain   81
A12   Stakeholder Role and Responsibilities   82
A13   Pune Municipal Bond Stakeholders   84
A14   Alignment of Eligible Green and Social Projects, Assets, and Expenditures   87
      with Sustainable Development Goals
A15   Eligible Sectors under the Green Bond and Green Sukuk Framework   89
A16   Green Sukuk Issuance and Monitoring Process   90
A17   Green Municipal Fund Stakeholders   94
A18   Green Transition Financing Model   95
A19   Umbulan Spring Project Transaction Scheme   98
A20   Securite Crowdfunding Investment Model   103
A21   Hong Kong, China—Land Value Capture Model   107
A22   Seychelles—Debt-for-Nature Swap Model   109

Boxes

1   Global Finance Facility of the International Finance Corporation   20
2   Australia—Asset Recycling   25
3   Project Finance Collateralized Debt Obligation   28
4   Global Green Bond Issues   38
5   Green Fund Market   43
6   Sustainable Development Goals Indonesia One Green Finance Facility   45
7   Energy Transition Mechanism   46

FOREWORD

In the region defined by the Association of Southeast Asian Nations along with the People's Republic of China, Japan, and the Republic of Korea (ASEAN+3), infrastructure development, supported by traditional sources of financing such as government revenue and debt financing, has been a key pillar of economic growth and development over the past 5 decades. Institutional partners, including multilateral development banks such as the Asian Development Bank, have supported the economic transformation of the ASEAN+3 region from being mostly agricultural economies in the early 1970s to becoming some of the most active export manufacturers and fastest growing economies in the world today. Between 1970 and 2020, loans and grants from the Asian Development Bank to Southeast Asian economies amounted to $107 billion, with bilateral and multilateral donors, trust funds, and other partners contributing about $26.9 billion in sovereign co-financing during the same period.

As the ASEAN+3 region emerges from the COVID-19 pandemic, infrastructure demand will only continue to grow as economies look to address the gaps in healthcare, education, digital, and social infrastructure exposed by the COVID-19 pandemic; and to rebuild in a more sustainable and inclusive manner in alignment with the Sustainable Development Goals. At the same time, the region will have to address the increasingly devastating effects of climate change, while striking the right balance between addressing energy transition needs and continued economic transformation. It is clear that the widening infrastructure financing gap can no longer be met by traditional sources of financing. There is, hence, a pressing need to identify new ways to encourage greater private sector participation in financing infrastructure development in the region, which has thus far been limited to the traditional models of public–private partnerships.

This report systematically presents various innovative models of merging public, private, institutional, and other forms of capital to deliver resilient, sustainable, and future-ready infrastructure in the ASEAN+3 region. From blended finance and asset securitization to municipal and green bonds, and from crowd finance to carbon credit markets, the report examines how innovative finance can become a magnet for the private and institutional funds needed to back public–private infrastructure partnerships. It summarizes critical success factors from actual case studies, from within and outside the ASEAN+3 region, that can be adapted, replicated, and upscaled in the ASEAN+3 context for successful implementation. If done well, these solutions can turn large, lofty, and complex designs into doable, bankable investments that are sustainable, inclusive, and climate friendly.

However, more work remains to be done: our task is not just to build infrastructure quickly, but to build infrastructure that is resilient, sustainable, and future-ready. Therefore, we must unite to strengthen the infrastructure financing ecosystem and forge new partnerships to build a greener, more sustainable, and inclusive future for our children and successive generations.

Ahmed Muneeb Saeed
Vice-President (Operations 2) for East Asia, Southeast Asia, and the Pacific
Asian Development Bank

ACKNOWLEDGMENTS

This publication was prepared by the Regional Cooperation and Operations Coordination Division (SERC) of the Southeast Asia Department (SERD) of the Asian Development Bank (ADB). It was financed by ADB under the Knowledge and Support Technical Assistance (TA)-9964 Policy Advice for COVID-19 Economic Recovery in Southeast Asia.

This report was written by Kewal Thapar and James Villafuerte. The authors are grateful for PwC Singapore and all members of the ASEAN+3 Finance Process, in particular members of the ASEAN+3 Working Group on Infrastructure Finance—Ministry of Finance, Government of the People's Republic of China; People's Bank of China; Hong Kong Monetary Authority; Ministry of Finance, Government of Indonesia; Ministry of Finance, Government of Japan; Ministry of Economy and Finance, Government of the Republic of Korea; Department of Finance, Government of the Philippines; Ministry of Finance, Government of Singapore; and Bank of Thailand—for their contributions to this report, in particular through the provision of valuable case studies.

James Villafuerte, principal economist and Dulce Zara, senior regional cooperation officer of SERC led the preparation of this report under the supervision of Alfredo Perdiguero, director of SERC. Mae Hyacinth Kiocho and Joyce Marie Lagac provided technical support, while Melissa May Ebarvia extended administrative assistance.

The authors are also grateful for the valuable comments and suggestions from all peer reviewers from ADB's Macroeconomics Research Division, Office of the Chief Economist and Director General, Regional Cooperation and Integration Division of the Economic Research and Regional Cooperation Department; Office of Public–Private Partnership; Private Sector Operations Department; and the Environment, Natural Resources, and Agriculture Division, Office of the Director General, and Thailand Resident Mission of the Southeast Asia Department; and Sustainable Development and Climate Change Department.

Shreemoyee Patra anchored the editing, typesetting, proofreading, and cover designing of the publication. ADB's Support Division of the Department of Communications facilitated the publishing of this report.

ABBREVIATIONS

AATIF	Africa Agriculture Trade and Investment Fund
ACGF	ASEAN Catalytic Green Finance Facility
ADB	Asian Development Bank
AMBIF	ASEAN+3 Multicurrency Bond Issuance Framework
AMC	Advance Market Commitment
ASEAN	Association of Southeast Asian Nations
ASEAN+3	ASEAN plus the People's Republic of China, Japan, and the Republic of Korea
BIM	Bayfront Infrastructure Management
CCRIF	Caribbean Catastrophe Risk Insurance Facility
CDM	Clean Development Mechanism
COVID-19	Coronavirus disease
DFNS	debt-for-nature-swap
ESG	environmental, social, and governance
EU	European Union
GDF	Geothermal Development Facility
GDP	gross domestic product
GHG	greenhouse gas
GMF	Green Municipal Fund
IFC	International Finance Corporation
JBIC	Japan Bank for International Cooperation
KI	Keppel International Holding
MTRC	Metro Transit Railway Corporation
NHAI	National Highways Authority of India
PCV	pneumococcal conjugate vaccines
PMC	Pune Municipal Corporation
PPP	public–private partnership
PUB	National Water Agency
RMBS	residential mortgage-backed securities
SDG	Sustainable Development Goal
SEADRIF	Southeast Asia Disaster Risk Insurance Facility
SERD	PT Supreme Energy Rantau Dedap
SeyCCAT	Seychelles Conservation and Climate Adaptation Trust
SME	small and medium-sized enterprise
SPV	special purpose vehicle
TFG	Thaifoods Group
TOT	toll–operate–transfer
US	United States
WAL	weighted average life

EXECUTIVE SUMMARY

Infrastructure lays the foundation for economic development and growth. It supports the provision of goods and services that enhance the quality of life, enables businesses, and improves productivity. It underpins all vital aspects of economic activity and is the key to national prosperity in a competitive global environment. Underinvestment in infrastructure slows down the economy and subjects the society and businesses to higher levels of pecuniary and environmental stress. The coronavirus disease (COVID-19) pandemic (2019–2021) led to a massive global supply chain disruption that brought the world economy to a grinding halt, in turn, initiating recessionary conditions.

Geopolitical tensions have since impacted food and energy security leading to inflationary trends, forcing governments to allocate substantial resources to alternate procurement patterns and social protection programs aimed at continuance of essential services and reducing vulnerability of its populations. Market volatility, financial contraction, and uncertain and unreliable supply chains coupled with the higher cost of capital (increased interest rates) have contributed to reduced investor appetite as viability and return on investment is suspect. There is, therefore, an urgent need to de-risk project financing and widen the investment funding pool by actively engaging with institutional investors and the private sector through the use of innovative financing mechanisms.

Despite country-level variations and global headwinds, the Association of South East Asian Nations (ASEAN) region has shown remarkable resilience, and is leading the economic recovery by being one of fastest growing regions in the world in 2022. The Asian Development Bank (ADB) has forecasted that Southeast Asia's gross domestic product (GDP) will grow by 4.7% in 2023 and 5% in 2024. These figures are higher than the GDP growth rates of most developed world economies. Additionally, the inflation rate for Southeast Asia is expected to be moderate at 4.4% in 2023 and 3.3% in 2024, gradually returning to pre-pandemic averages. At present, Asia's share of global GDP is over 45% while Europe and North America combined account for about 44%. With the reopening of the People's Republic of China and the abatement of inflationary pressures, Asia is poised to be the growth engine of the global economy by increasing its share of global GDP to over 50% by 2030.

Rapid economic development, urbanization, and population growth in the region have resulted in an ever-widening gap between current spending and finances required to meet the increasing demand for infrastructure. In addition to current inflationary conditions, the COVID-19 pandemic, weather-related disasters, and adverse impacts of climate change have further exacerbated the demand for and the cost of developing sustainable infrastructure. Closing the infrastructure gap is critical for ASEAN plus the People's Republic of China, Japan, and the Republic of Korea (ASEAN+3) to fulfill their commitments toward Sustainable Development Goals (SDGs), improve competitiveness, and address environmental challenges.

According to ADB, developing Asia will need to invest $13.8 trillion or $1.7 trillion annually from 2023 to 2030 to sustain economic growth, reduce poverty, and respond to climate change (climate-adjusted estimate). For ASEAN, the total infrastructure investment need is estimated at $2.8 trillion (baseline estimate) and $3.1 trillion (climate-adjusted estimate), placing the annual investment need at $184 billion and $210 billion, respectively. The infrastructure gap figures do not include the additional expenditure associated with disasters and extreme weather events that increasingly impact existing infrastructure in Southeast Asia. According to the long-term climate risk index for 2000–2019, the Philippines, Myanmar, and Thailand rank amongst the 10 countries most affected by weather-related loss events and are most vulnerable to climate-linked risks.

Public and social infrastructure development in the region has traditionally been almost entirely financed by public resources (up to 92%) but is unable to bridge the widening deficit between requirements and mobilized capital. More recently, constrained public finances on account of increased energy costs and reallocation of funds to social protection and food security programs have further curtailed government spending on infrastructure development. As infrastructure financing requirements are extremely large and finite public funds do not permit large-scale investments on a continuing basis, a paradigm shift is necessary in the sourcing and mobilization of capital resources. Member countries of ASEAN have not been able to gainfully tap foreign direct investments and though foreign investments have returned to pre-pandemic levels, the region receives only 11% of total global foreign direct investments inflows. The perception that infrastructure funding is a public responsibility and an investment domain for public funding keeps private investors at bay as few participation opportunities are made available to them. In addition, political instability, weak governance, inadequate regulatory capacity, and the absence of a robust pipeline of viable investment-ready projects contribute to underinvestment in infrastructure. These projects often involve high up-front capital cost, long gestation periods, risk of uncertain return, and a social benefit that may not meet the financial risk–return appetite of private investors. These obstacles and perceptions adversely impact the mobilization of vital funds resulting in the deferment of investment decisions.

As climate-induced extreme events increase in intensity and frequency, populations and ageing infrastructure become more compromised and vulnerable. Urgent adaptation and mitigation measures have to be adopted to make communities more resilient. Also, disaster risk reduction norms and standards have to be mainstreamed in the design and planning of all infrastructure works. The SDGs need to be integrated into the development architecture to ensure that investments in sustainable infrastructure are a pre-requisite to undertaking any developmental activity. Adequate financial and implementation support can then attain a "triple win," building infrastructure that reduces emissions and climate risk, stimulates economic development, and increases returns for investors.

The SDGs have provoked a fundamental shift in the outlook and process to developing infrastructure toward a holistic and transformative approach that combines different means of implementation and integrates the economic, social, and environmental dimensions of sustainable development. The choice of infrastructure will now determine the commitment to: clean water, renewable energy, reduced greenhouse gas emissions, and low carbon footprint, and to building resilience to extreme weather and other natural hazard events. Though this will impact the incremental capital cost of infrastructure, it will reduce direct losses as well as the indirect costs of disruption. As resilient and sustainable infrastructure involves incremental cost, creative funding and collaborations are required to address systemic risks and apply risk-informed management strategies for sustainable development to close the infrastructure gap.

In a post-pandemic world, disruptive conditions have triggered once-solved issues and reversed decades of progress, leading to a low growth–low investment era, rife with risks relating to unbridled inflation, cost of living crises, geopolitical tensions, debt-stressed economies, and decline in human development. There is a growing realization that the target to limit global warming to 1.5°C by 2030 will be missed if timelines are not shrunk for emission reduction interventions. Together, these risks and prevailing conditions create an uncertain and unstable environment that is inimical to mobilizing investments for development projects. Member countries of ASEAN that want to meet investment needs over the next decade and beyond will have to employ innovative financing approaches to attract funds from global institutional and private sector investors.

The pandemic, geopolitical tensions, and increased national indebtedness have combined to expose the weak links in the globalization chain and accelerated a shift toward regionalization. The ASEAN+3 is now a closer-knit economic bloc securing their collective future and economic growth. The concepts of self-sustenance and self-sufficiency are being increasingly adopted by developing domestic industries to replace imports in order to reduce supply chain disruptions and lessen the reliance on international trading partners. Most industries are seeking multiple suppliers to ensure continuance of goods and services, and reduce supplier non-performance risk. This has acted as a catalyst for ASEAN+3 countries that depend on food imports to invest more in agriculture and food self-sufficiency by developing infrastructure for climate-smart crop production, small-scale food processing, and high-tech agribusiness. The energy crisis has hastened the transition to renewable energy as ASEAN+3 countries seek to meet demand by investing in solar and wind energy plants and reducing reliance on fossil fuels. There is improved planning and investment attention on healthcare infrastructure and social protection programs. Member states are increasingly sharing knowledge to mitigate and be better prepared for similar catastrophic events by embracing universal healthcare as a shared key capability.

The taxonomy of infrastructure has now been expanded to include digital infrastructure that is multidimensional in application as it cuts across sectors as well as economic and social inequalities. It represents the new ubiquitous soft infrastructure that is becoming the backbone and lifeline for the delivery of all goods and services. Digitalization has been the vital link during the pandemic; the Consolidated Strategy on the Fourth Industrial Revolution for ASEAN (2021) provides policy guidance in building an ASEAN digital community. The ASEAN Digital Masterplan 2025 outlines interventions to upgrade digital infrastructure and expand network coverage to rural areas. The Masterplan on ASEAN Connectivity 2025 promotes the adoption of digital technology by micro, small, and medium-sized enterprises to enhance their participation in the digital economy.

The future of infrastructure will be shaped by making new infrastructure sustainable and existing infrastructure resilient to the impacts of climate change. Both policy emphasis and investment are being directed at the development of social infrastructure such as healthcare and education facilities in recognition of the fact that as society evolves and becomes interconnected, there is a greater need for these services.

Closing the infrastructure-financing gap is difficult, but not impossible. While there are wide-ranging constraints currently limiting infrastructure development, innovative finance provides novel approaches that could mobilize increased capital investment to bridge the infrastructure gap. Currently more than $200 trillion of private capital is invested in global capital markets. Innovative finance mechanisms, therefore, need to be devised and curated to catalyze private and institutional finance for the infrastructure sector. An investment-enabled environment enriched by innovative financing solutions and undergirded by the right technology can mobilize these resources to help bridge the infrastructure gap.

Innovative finance mechanisms can be defined as new and evolving models beyond commercial debt finance that are able to attract private and institutional capital, along with public funds, for developmental activities. More importantly, innovative finance is primarily focused on the delivery of positive social and environmental outcomes through market-based financing instruments rather than on resource mobilization through ingenious fundraising approaches. It employs public funds to catalyze private and institutional financing by reducing risk, creating an enabling investment environment, and providing an opportunity to collaborate on sustainable outcomes.

Innovative financing essentially targets the private sector and large institutional funds by creating investment opportunities for collaboration on sustainable infrastructure projects that are usually outside the ambit of their existing investment portfolio. It provides new sectors for investment through a combination of risk distribution, liquidity enhancement, volatility reduction, capital timeliness and adequacy, and positive risk-adjusted returns. It fosters collaboration between private, public, and institutional donors to inject much-needed capital into social and environmentally sustainable projects not considered by capital markets that traditionally view them with a return-on-investment lens. Innovative finance thus acts as a magnet to attract private and institutional finance for sustainable development. Some inventive mechanisms also crowd-in small investors for local projects that are unable to raise capital from traditional sources.

Good governance (in terms of a conducive investment environment backed by a supportive regulatory framework) and innovative finance mechanisms comprise the twin drivers for financing sustainable development infrastructure. Together they form the nucleus that can utilize limited public funds to provide the charge and momentum for private and institutional investors to infuse capital into economic and social projects by meeting their expectations, both in terms of an enabling environment as well as risk-adjusted returns. The mechanics and interdependencies of this approach are schematically presented in Figure ES1.

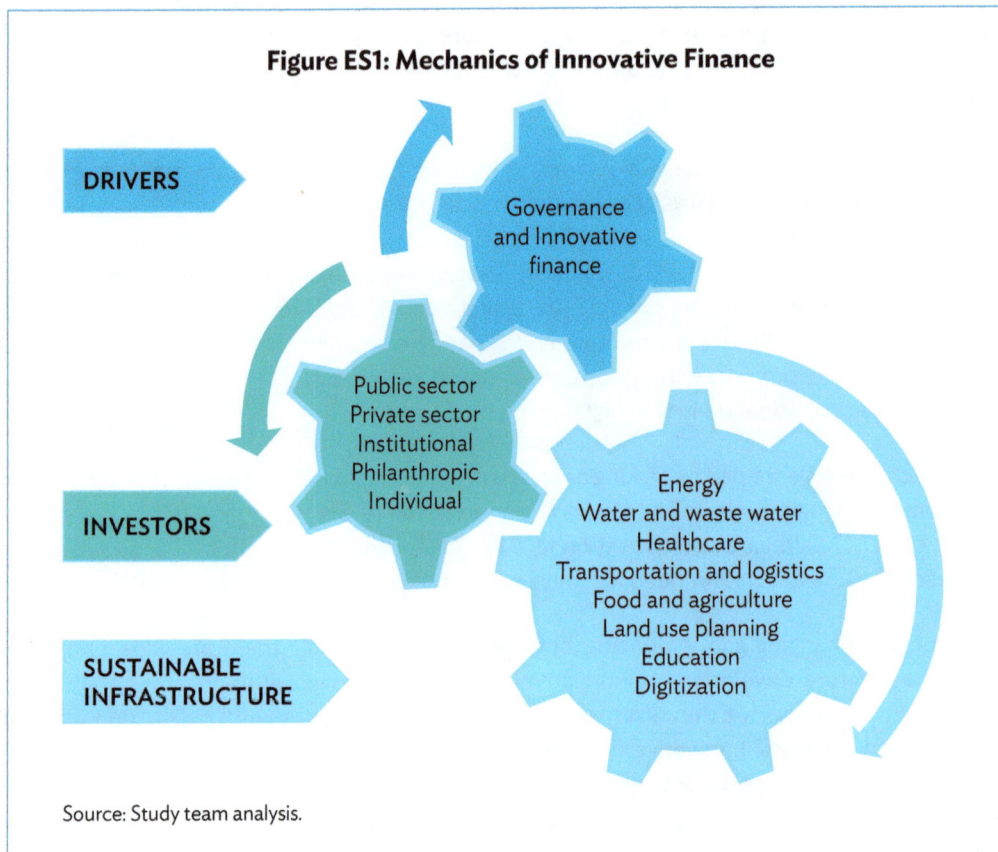

Figure ES1: Mechanics of Innovative Finance

DRIVERS

Governance and Innovative finance

Public sector
Private sector
Institutional
Philanthropic
Individual

INVESTORS

Energy
Water and waste water
Healthcare
Transportation and logistics
Food and agriculture
Land use planning
Education
Digitization

SUSTAINABLE INFRASTRUCTURE

Source: Study team analysis.

This report is intended as a knowledge publication to promote the use of creative financing models by the public sector and multilateral organizations to catalyze infrastructure investments in the ASEAN+3 region, taking into consideration their unique socio-economic circumstances. It seeks to provide companies, investors, policy makers, and financing agencies a range of innovative financing mechanisms and approaches to stimulate sustainable infrastructure development. Several successfully implemented business models have been illustrated to demonstrate how novel financing instruments and structuring mechanisms can be adopted to de-risk infrastructure investments and enable collaboration between the private sector, public agencies, and financial institutions to achieve developmental goals. The report highlights the importance of blending different financing instruments to provide flexibility and a new dimension to resource mobilization so that potentially viable projects receive the required capital investment. It provides alternatives for public–private partnerships (PPPs) and strategic employment of public funds to attract private investment, accomplish key development goals, and meet shareholder expectations for investment returns through the effective use of these approaches. The report also offers an "ASEAN+3 voice" to the international discourse on infrastructure financing, focusing on the needs of developing Asian economies. Table ES1 below provides a summary of the innovative finance models discussed.

Table ES1: Summary of Innovative Financing Mechanisms

Financing Model	Sector or Project Fit	Key Users/Providers of Finance
Blended finance	**Project:** For social or economic projects which are unable to secure commercial bank financing	Multilateral development banks (MDBs)
	Sectors: Applicable to all sectors	Private investors such as private equity funds, pension funds, and banks
Asset recycling	**Project:** For assets that are owned by the government but could be better developed by the private sector to enhance economic returns	Government to be responsible for identifying suitable assets
	Sectors: Applicable to all sectors	Private investors participate in the sale/lease of the assets
Asset securitization	**Project:** For income-producing assets which are separable from the originator	Originator to convert their assets into marketable securities for sale
	Sectors: Applicable to all sectors	Private/institutional investors are the purchasers of such securities
Convertible debt structures	**Project:** Used to help mitigate risk on higher risk projects	Private and/or institutional investors are usually the purchaser of convertible debt
	Sectors: Applicable to all sectors	
Municipal bonds	**Project:** Typically used for public projects with robust cash flows	Purchasers of these bonds can be MDBs or private investors such as pension funds, institutional investors, or banks
	Sectors: Applicable to all sectors	
Green bonds	**Project:** Projects which follow the International Capital Market Association's Green Bond Principles	Issuers can be either governments, MDBs, or from the private sector
	Sectors: Typically, applicable to energy but has potential for use in other sectors such as transport, water, and waste management	Investors are typically institutional investors such as pension funds, insurance companies, and sovereign wealth funds
Government green funds and/or transition funds	**Project:** Projects which follow a combination of environmental and social themes	Funds usually set up by the government
	Sectors: Popular in the water and renewable energy sector	Investors are typically private and/or institutional investors or MDBs
Public–private partnerships	**Projects:** Large capital-intensive infrastructure projects requiring private sector managerial and technical expertise	Funds from commercial and institutional lenders plus equity contribution by private and public sector
	Sectors: Industry, public services	
Insurance-linked products	**Projects:** Safeguard against extreme weather and natural hazard events	Premiums partially financed by public funds or subsidized
	Sectors: Agriculture, health	
Crowd financing	**Projects:** Start-ups, small and medium-sized enterprises, projects that cannot access or obtain traditional financing or afford cost of funding	Small private investors, venture capital investors or funds, angel investors, and family offices
	Sectors: Local public infrastructure, technology, and small businesses	
Debt-for-climate and/or nature swaps	**Projects:** Support environmental management, climate action, and nature preservation	Environment funds, bilateral and/or governments, conservation agencies, and philanthropic foundations
	Sectors: Marine and coastal conservation, land management, sustainable agriculture, renewable energy, reforestation, etc.	
Carbon credit markets	**Projects:** Reduction in emission of greenhouse gases	Emitters of greenhouse gases and projects that provide carbon offsets
	Sectors: Carbon sequestration, renewable energy	

Source: Study team analysis.

These mechanisms (blended finance and asset securitization, in particular) help to mitigate and better allocate risks between the public and private sector. Green bonds and government green funds can help to attract funding from private sector to support infrastructure investments that are environmentally sustainable. Debt-for-nature swaps could provide some relief to foreign debt-stressed economies while ensuring that their natural resource conservation and environmental programs are adequately funded. It is important that policy makers and infrastructure development stakeholders understand the characteristics and critical success factors of each financing model before determining its applicability for an infrastructure project. Some of the mechanisms can be implemented independently, in tandem or sequentially during the life cycle of a project to ensure capital adequacy.

The role and influence of philanthropic investors cannot be underestimated and should be channeled to leverage substantial private sector investments. Philanthropic funding is catalytic capital that is risk tolerant, concessionary, and flexible. Funding from institutions such as Bill and Melinda Gates Foundation and The Rockefeller Foundation have been able to raise private capital in double-digit ratio multiples in comparison to the sums invested by them while ensuring maximum social impact that aligns with the SDGs.

The imperative to build resilient and sustainable infrastructure in ASEAN is being increasingly realized as the impacts of climate change are now manifested by the frequency of floods, droughts, storm surges, and typhoons. Scarce government resources are being diverted to emergency rescue, relief, and rebuilding activities. Governments and aid agencies end up spending billions of dollars in responding to crises and undertaking recovery and reconstruction activities than they would have spent in prevention had resilience been mainstreamed into developmental activities. Resilient infrastructure can generate a quantifiable benefit that could finance the additional costs of building all-weather and disaster-resistant infrastructure. *The Asia-Pacific Disaster Report 2022*, which captures the complexity of disaster risk by including direct and indirect losses, reveals that the annual average losses in the region are more than four times the previous estimate (2017), reaching $91 billion—a substantial proportion of which is attributed to agricultural drought losses. *The World Risk Report 2022* assesses 192 countries in terms of their exposure to disasters, extreme weather-related events, susceptibility and vulnerability of the population, and lack of coping and adaptive capacities. The report ranks six ASEAN countries as among the top 35 most vulnerable and high-risk nations. The Philippines is first on the list, followed by Indonesia at 3rd, Myanmar at 6th, Viet Nam at 12th, Thailand at 23rd, and Malaysia at 35th. With the increase in intensity and frequency of extreme weather events, disaster risk reduction measures need to be adopted in conjunction with developing resilient infrastructure.

Members of ASEAN have also committed to reduction in greenhouse gas emissions in order to transition to a net-zero economy. ADB recently established an Energy Transition Mechanism—piloted in Indonesia and the Philippines—to help the region become net zero by 2050. The Energy Transition Mechanism is designed to leverage the power of blended finance to accelerate retiring or repurposing coal-fired power plants, helping support a country's transition to a green economy. ADB hopes this will become the model for retiring coal plants across the region and massively reducing carbon dioxide emissions.

The monetization of social and environmental co-benefits that may result from sustainable infrastructure is currently unrealized as financial markets do not quantify or attribute any value to these benefits. Some pathways to consider these benefits using cost–benefit and life cycle assessments have been adopted, and there is growing acceptance that benefits accruing from initiatives could be monetized through innovative financing models that could provide valuable cash flows. Impact investors as well corporate and institutional investors now include environmental, social, and governance criteria while evaluating investment options.

The effectiveness and success of innovative financing models is largely dependent upon the willingness and adaptability of policy makers to foster a sustainable infrastructure investment environment. Governance is a key driver and together with innovative financing mechanism it will be able to catalyze and unleash private investment. Member countries of ASEAN+3 have a pivotal role to play and should work to

(i)   improve regulatory frameworks and create a private sector centric investment-enabling stable environment that ensures transparency and dispute resolution;

(ii)   promote credit enhancement and de-risking tools;

(iii)   explore the possibility and potential to secure an investment grade rating for the project;

(iv)   conduct innovative finance pilots in different sectors to demonstrate potential and viability;

(v)   build capacity and create awareness of innovative finance approaches across ASEAN+3;

(vi)   set up project development units or infrastructure accelerators;

(vii)   provide project development funding to translate concepts into projects;

(viii) tap large philanthropic organizations with a strong global footprint and local organizations with avowed environmental, social, and governance objectives;

(ix)   tap multilateral development financing institutions to access concessional finance, grants, aid, etc.;

(x)   create an enabling environment for PPPs by enacting laws, streamlining procurement and bidding processes, and introducing conditional de-risking mechanisms; explore and undertake new approaches beyond traditional PPP;

(xi)   leverage capital, sectoral, and technical expertise of the private sector through partnerships;

(xii)   implement effective project management measures to ensure projects are completed in time, within budgets, and compliant with established legal, financial, and environmental norms;

(xiii) mainstream disaster risk management as an integral component of developing sustainable infrastructure;

(xiv)   improve the effectiveness and efficiency of how infrastructure investment is utilized; and

(xv)   build smart sustainable infrastructure that is cost effective, less polluting, and resilient to climate variability impacts.

Capital constraints pose a serious challenge to maintaining economic growth and avoiding stagnation and, therefore, require a menu of innovative financing solutions that can unlock private and institutional capital to bridge the funding gap. The development of investment-ready project pipeline supported by innovative financing structures that are cost effective, ensure delivery efficiency, and provide expected risk-adjusted returns is critical to widening the existing pool of investors. Public and private financial intermediaries need to rethink investment strategies to shift from the crowded landscape of $100 million ticket funds, which account for about 80% of the market, to large billion-dollar blended funds offering a diverse portfolio of sustainable assets and risk adjusted returns.

ADB continues to be a strong and committed partner of the ASEAN+3 region in adopting innovative financing solutions through project identification, structuring and financing, and supporting capacity building. It provides loans, grants, and technical assistance to its developing member countries and to the private sector for building and maintenance of infrastructure in water, energy, transport, urban development, and information and communications technology.

In summary, the critical success factors and key design features for innovative finance mechanisms are: attractiveness to investors based on risk-adjusted returns; true and standardized solutions; scalability; replicability; digital economy enablement; and a fundamental change in mindset from grant and aid-dependency to a commercially viable model.

The innovative financing market is now beyond the nascent stage but is still evolving to meet the multiple development challenges that confront both developed and developing nations. Some of the innovation financing models such as guarantees, bonds, and PPPs have already proved successful in catalyzing private capital and have been scaled and replicated in ASEAN across sectors. For the successful development of innovative finance, effective action and collaboration of all stakeholders in the infrastructure project life cycle is critical. This should promote increased private sector participation at scale in large capital-intensive projects that have a significant economic, environmental, and social impact and ensure sustainable development

Public funds need to leverage their investment by mobilizing finance from the private and institutional sectors in multiples far beyond the current average of 1:3. They should aim for early double-digit ratios if not at least doubling fund sourcing. This will be *the tipping point* where public, private, and institutional capital can provide adequate resources to reduce the infrastructure investment gap and work toward their commitments in accomplishing their sustainable development goals.

I INTRODUCTION

1.1 Economic Performance and Outlook

The Southeast Asian economies have shown remarkable resilience to the adverse effects of the pandemic and other economic shocks. This is largely attributed to the lessons learned from previous crises and their adoption of prudent macro-economic policies, which have resulted in sustainable growth. The reopening of the People's Republic of China (PRC), an increase in remittances, resumption of tourism, and weakening of commodity and energy prices have all played a significant role in the region's economic recovery. The Asian Development Bank (ADB) has forecasted that Southeast Asia's gross domestic product (GDP) will grow by 4.7% in 2023 and 5% in 2024. These figures are higher than the GDP growth rates of most developed world economies. The inflation rate for Southeast Asia is expected to be moderate at 4.4% in 2023 and 3.3% in 2024, gradually returning to pre-pandemic averages.[1] At present, Asia's share of global GDP is over 45% while Europe and North America combined account for about 44%. With the reopening of PRC and the abatement of inflationary pressures, Asia is poised to be the growth engine of the global economy by increasing its share of global GDP to over 50% by 2030.[2]

1.2 Infrastructure Snapshot

Since 2014, the Group of 20 (G20) has emphasized the role of infrastructure in promoting economic growth and reducing poverty.[3] Generally, the availability of transport, communication, electricity, safe water and sanitation, health infrastructure, and other basic facilities has a tremendous impact on improving the quality of life and well-being. Infrastructure facilities and services are also ingredients of efficient production, transport, and trade that spur economic growth and help reduce poverty. Furthermore, where roads and transport system are well developed, businesses will be encouraged to set up shops as they have convenient access to supplies, inputs, and other products, and at the same time, gain better access to major outlets, markets, and trading centers, enhancing the development of backward and forward linkages in the economy.

While the economic effects of infrastructure may vary, the employment and production effects are clear. These impacts differ by sector as well as over time. In Japan, for instance, infrastructure showed greater benefits in urban than rural areas and overall, it produced greater manufacturing benefits in 1990 than in 2010. Similarly, in Thailand too, infrastructure benefited manufacturing more than services. In the Philippines, on the other hand, highways had more impact on business tax revenues and regulatory fees than property tax revenues.

The wide global infrastructure investment gap is, therefore, a matter of concern. The global infrastructure financing gap has been variously estimated to range from $5.5 trillion to as much as $15 trillion by 2040. Adopting McKinsey's gap estimate of $3.7 trillion[4] (for economic infrastructure) as the base, adding 30% for meeting the Sustainable Development Goal (SDG) targets, and providing for other infrastructure and climate and disasters, there is at least a $6 trillion spending gap between now and 2035 with regional variations.

---

[1] Asian Development Bank. *Asian Development Outlook*. April 2023. https://www.adb.org/sites/default/files/publication/863591/asian-development-outlook-april-2023.pdf.

[2] World Economics. 2023. *The Future is Asian*. February. https://www.worldeconomics.com/Thoughts/The-future-is-asian.aspx.

[3] The G20 is the premier forum for international economic cooperation. It plays an important role in shaping and strengthening global architecture and governance on all major international economic issues. https://www.g20.org/en/about-g20/#overview.

[4] J. Woetzel et al. 2017. *Bridging infrastructure gaps: Has the world made progress*. Mckinsey Global Institute. https://www.mckinsey.com/capabilities/operations/our-insights/bridging-infrastructure-gaps-has-the-world-made-progress.

There are sufficient savings to finance infrastructure investment in Asia. For example, there are about $4.4 trillion in pension funds and $5.1 trillion with insurers in the region.[5] Linking infrastructure demand with these institutional funds searching for yield could offer huge benefits for the region.

However, there are barriers and risks for long-term institutional funds to invest in infrastructure (Table 1). Asia suffers from a global investment bias—Asian investors usually prefer to invest in "safer" European Union (EU) and United States (US) assets. Asia's domestic investors are often concerned about political risk, weak regulatory systems and legal enforcement, bureaucracy, governance standards, capital markets with low liquidity, and currency risk. There are widespread qualitative and quantitative investment restrictions, especially in Asian emerging markets. There is a major intermediation challenge with most pension funds and insurers preferring low-risk assets.

Private participation in infrastructure investment is critical. The ratio of public-to-private finance in infrastructure is roughly 1:2 in developed countries but 2:1 in developing economies. Private participation is about 0.6%–0.8% of GDP in emerging markets, and about 0.1%–0.2% of GDP in East Asia and the Pacific. For total investment in infrastructure, not one developing economy in Asia spends the 6% of GDP or higher level required to maintain robust growth.[6]

Table 1: Barriers to Infrastructure Allocations by Institutional Investors

Issues with government support for infrastructure projects	Lack of political commitment over the long-term
	Lack of infrastructure project pipeline
	Fragmentation of the market among different levels of government
	Regulatory instability
	High bidding costs
Lack of investor capability	Lack of expertise in the infrastructure sector
	Problem of scale of pension funds
	Regulatory barriers
	Short-termism of investors
Issues with investment	Negative perception of the value of infrastructure investments
	Lack of transparency in the infrastructure sector
	Misalignment of interests between infrastructure funds and pension funds
	Shortage of data on infrastructure projects

Source: Study team analysis.

Private financing could become a viable alternative for many projects in Asia. Experience from certain developed economies demonstrates how public–private partnerships (PPP) may be leveraged to finance infrastructure across transport, water, education, health, communications, and housing, among others. Translating this success to Asia remains a major challenge, given the relatively low private participation in infrastructure investment.

Private participation requires strong institutions and consistent policies. Consistency in national and regional infrastructure plans is essential and retrospective regulatory changes are particularly harmful. Building confidence is central in attracting institutional investors. This takes time and requires project success. Any increase in private financing of infrastructure would require an adequate supply of risk-managed asset and investment vehicles. And it helps when PPPs can attract investors through value added or indirect economic effects such as promoting tourism, manufacturing, agriculture, or services—Japan's railway development is a good historical example.

---

5   *ADB Briefs No. 85. September 2017.* https://www.adb.org/sites/default/files/publication/367226/adb-brief-85.pdf.
6   ADB Economic Research and Regional Cooperation Department. 2015. Asia's Growth and Development Challenges: Relevant Themes for the APEC Finance Ministers Meeting. Unpublished.

Attract and leverage foreign direct investment (FDI). In 2021, FDI inflows into the Association of Southeast Asian Nations (ASEAN) region (excluding PRC), hit a record high of $175 billion, matching the pre-pandemic levels seen in 2019. This increase was driven by multinational companies diversifying their manufacturing supply chains and investing in rapidly growing consumer markets in ASEAN to take advantage of the fast expanding consumer markets. Strong inflows of FDI into electronics manufacturing and electric vehicle projects were significant contributors. However, the ASEAN member countries have not been able to fully leverage FDI at the macro level, as the region only receives 11% of total global FDI inflows.[7]

However, infrastructure projects must heed social and environmental effects as well. There is a need to establish safeguards for the environment (pollution, for example) and involuntary settlement (orderly land acquisitions and rights protection).

1.3 Organization of the Report

This report provides an overview of the infrastructure investment landscape and analyzes issues, challenges, and opportunities related to financing of infrastructure in the Association of Southeast Asian Nations region plus the PRC, Japan and the Republic of Korea (ASEAN+3). The objective is to provide an introduction to key innovative financing concepts; outline the structures, stakeholders, and sector application; and summarize the critical success factors for implementation. The report is by no means an exhaustive list of all financing mechanisms or their variations. The intention is to present successful innovative financial mechanisms that can be adapted, replicated, and upscaled in the ASEAN+3 context. The purpose is to identify lessons learned and present select case studies as reference material for policy makers in the region so that they can serve as important blueprints to address development financing challenges. More importantly, the policy brief serves to create awareness on structuring project financing, strategic use of public funds, de-risking of investments, and creating an investment-enabled environment.

The report comprises of five sections. After this brief introduction, the paper reviews in section 2 the infrastructure landscape that has emerged in region since the coronavirus disease (COVID-19) pandemic by summarizing benefits from infrastructure investment, recent trends, the infrastructure gap, as well as new infrastructure domains; section 3 discusses issues and challenges facing infrastructure financing in the region, including the fiscal bind that the public sector faces in infrastructure; challenges of shallow capital markets and limited intermediated credit available for infrastructure; institutional and policy hurdles that limit private participation; and issues related to governance, project preparation capacity, and the delivery of green and resilient infrastructure. Section 4 provides an overview of relevant financial models or solutions that can finance infrastructure projects and mitigate some of the challenges identified in the previous section. The report's final section recommends policy and regulatory initiatives and suggests project development structures as key enablers to unlock the potential of innovative financing mechanisms. The section also highlights critical success factors that can revitalize infrastructure development and ensure its resiliency and sustainability, underscoring the importance of these factors in achieving successful infrastructure outcomes in a post-COVID world. Case studies of actual projects that are representative of the financing mechanisms are attached as an appendix, to provide more granular information in terms of innovative financing solutions available to ASEAN+3 economies. The financing mechanisms and their linked case studies share ingenious financial approaches that have been adopted in different geographies, including ASEAN+3 economies, to illustrate how traditional financial systems have been remodeled to achieve project objectives.

---

[7]   United Nations Conference on Trade and Development (UNCTAD). 2022. *World Investment Report 2022*. https://unctad.org/system/files/official-document/wir2022_en.pdf.

II INFRASTRUCTURE LANDSCAPE AND OPPORTUNITIES

2.1 Infrastructure to Restore Economies Post-Pandemic

Economic and social infrastructure provided huge benefits during the pandemic. Economic infrastructure including utilities, transport, logistics, flood control, communication networks, and financial systems directly generates economic growth through the provision of goods and services. On the other hand, social infrastructure helps deliver public services such as those for health and education, sports and recreation centers, parks and art museums, and community and safety centers. During the pandemic, both these types of infrastructure were helpful in coping with and mitigating its impact. For instance, transport systems and communications infrastructure were relied upon to deliver the medical goods and services and relay the latest advisories to health professionals and the population.

Infrastructure investment can help avoid economic stagnation in the post-pandemic period. Even before the pandemic, the infrastructure gap in the region has been substantial. Expectedly, this gap has widened during the pandemic as infrastructure investment and maintenance upkeep took a back seat in favor of pandemic-related expenditure on health, education, and social protection assistance. In the post-pandemic world, some governments in the region are delivering recovery budget plans that involve infrastructure rebuilding. This trend stems from the strong correlation between infrastructure investment and economic benefits. A study by the Economic Policy Institute suggests that for every $100 spent on infrastructure, private-sector output was boosted by $13 (median) and $17 (average) in the long run. Furthermore, each $100 billion in infrastructure spending would also boost job growth by roughly $1 million full-time equivalents.[8] Policy makers are well aware of the nexus between infrastructure spending, economic growth, and job creation. The pandemic has forced economies into a downward spiral, with lockdowns and movement restrictions suppressing output, disrupting supply chains, and choking demand for goods and services. Expectedly, in the post-pandemic period, despite the current recessionary trends, infrastructure investment could become a prominent and effective tool to fast-track economic recovery.

2.2 Infrastructure to Reinforce Sustainability and Resilience

Infrastructure investment can also help deliver the SDGs and lay the foundation for sustainable and resilient development. Due to the extensive negative impact of the COVID-19 pandemic, it is critical to accelerate SDG progress. According to World Bank estimates, the pandemic has pushed 150 million people into extreme poverty (earning less than $1.90 per day), and 8 out of the 10 "new poor" will be in middle income countries.[9] In Southeast Asia, ADB estimated that 4.7 million people were pushed into extreme poverty in 2021 as over 9.3 million jobs were lost.[10] In its recent report, the United Nations (UN) stated that more than 4 years of progress against poverty had been erased by the pandemic and that conflict, COVID-19, climate change, and growing inequalities are converging to undermine food security and health systems in addition to deepening a global learning crisis.[11] Investments in sustainable infrastructure are a prerequisite to accelerating the delivery of many SDGs. The focus on SDGs means that attaining poverty reduction and economic growth must be linked and incorporated with strategies that improve health and education, reduce inequality, and spur economic growth while tackling climate change and working to preserve

8   J. Bevans. Economic Policy Institute. 2017. *The potential microeconomic benefits of increasing infrastructure investment.* https://www.epi.org/publication/the-potential-macroeconomic-benefits-from-increasing-infrastructure-investment/.
9   The World Bank. Press Release. 2020. *COVID-19 to Add as Many as 150 Million Extreme Poor by 2021.* https://www.worldbank.org/en/news/press-release/2020/10/07/covid-19-to-add-as-many-as-150-million-extreme-poor-by-2021.
10   ADB. 2022. *Southeast Asia Rising from the Pandemic.* Manila. https://www.adb.org/sites/default/files/publication/779416/southeast-asia-rising-pandemic.pdf.
11   United Nations. 2022. *The Sustainable Development Goals Report.* New York. https://unstats.un.org/sdgs/report/2022/The-Sustainable-Development-Goals-Report-2022.pdf.

our ecosystems and biodiversity. The drive toward a sustainable and resilient transition also means developing an infrastructure pipeline—roads, buildings, energy, and water projects—with due consideration to economic, social, and environmental implications. This approach includes, among others, (i) reducing carbon and environmental footprint; (ii) protecting biodiversity; (iii) developing resilience to climate change; (iv) moving beyond basic compliance on core labor and human rights standards; and (v) increasing inclusivity, diversity, and opportunities for communities, and prioritizing local recruitment. This will require fortifying these project platforms to drive local economic development and capacity building, and more broadly improve the quality of life in the surrounding community and region. Infrastructure also forms the basis of building resilient societies. For example, due to their critical nature, the delivery of communications, healthcare, transportation, energy, and water and sanitation services is vital in times of crises.

Quality infrastructure is central to delivering sustainable development. When countries build infrastructure assets to produce electricity, provide safe drinking water, or facilitate transport, these assets must be economically efficient in view of life-cycle costs to support sustainable development. They also need to be resilient to the risks of potential damages from climate change and disasters. And most importantly, they must be accessible and inclusive to benefit everyone, including women, remote communities, disadvantaged, and marginalized groups.

However, infrastructure can also damage the environment and greening the infrastructure is an important future priority. Infrastructure projects such as the building of dams, construction of road networks, and development of power plants pose environmental risks relating to loss of biodiversity, displacement of communities, greenhouse gas emissions, and pollution. In this regard, the adoption of the SDGs provided the direction to encourage investments in sustainable infrastructure as a prerequisite for undertaking any developmental activity. Sustainable infrastructure has been defined as infrastructure that is socially inclusive, low carbon, and resilient. Therefore, new infrastructure projects must be designed to promote environmental sustainability and help meet the global climate targets. This will require the greening of infrastructure through investments in renewable electricity, energy efficiency, charging infrastructure for electric vehicles, climate-smart urban transport systems, or emerging green hydrogen supply chains which are cost-effective options that simultaneously abate carbon dioxide emissions, and create jobs.

2.3 The Infrastructure Gap

Rapid economic progress and population growth has generated a significant demand for infrastructure in the region. It has also contributed to an ever-widening gap between current spending and required financing to the growing infrastructure demand in the region. Shrinking public budgets, political and economic instability in some countries, weak capacity, and inadequate regulatory frameworks all contribute to underinvestment in infrastructure in the region. The pandemic has further restricted financial and fiscal space, increased debt burden, and stymied progress in key priority areas for ASEAN+3 economies. It is now imperative that governments continuously reflect on the infrastructure needs and wants of their citizens to be truly responsive and effective. Citizens' needs are changing, and their expectations of government are also higher than in the past. Therefore, governments must step up and deliver infrastructure to its citizens so that their trust is maintained, and the preparedness of society for future crises enhanced.

According to ADB, developing Asia will need to invest $13.8 trillion or $1.7 trillion annually from 2023 to 2030 to sustain economic growth, reduce poverty, and respond to climate change (climate-adjusted figure).[12] As a percentage of GDP, Southeast Asia requires investments at 5.7% and East Asia at 5.2%. For ASEAN, the total infrastructure investment need is estimated at $2.8 trillion (baseline estimate) and $3.1 trillion (climate-adjusted estimate), placing the annual investment need at $184 billion and $210 billion, respectively.

---

[12]   Asian Development Bank. 2017. *Meeting Asia's Infrastructure Needs.* https://www.adb.org/sites/default/files/publication/227496/special-report-infrastructure.pdf.

The COVID-19 pandemic crisis brought renewed focus on digital or soft connectivity infrastructure, which is usually overshadowed by traditional infrastructure such as roads, energy, and transportation. The pandemic exposed inadequacies in investment priorities, operating systems, and handling crises. One of the most visible trends during the pandemic was the reliance on communication infrastructure (such as telecommunications and broadband services) and the deployment of digital or technology solutions and online channels. This has led to the expansion of digital content, transformation into digital format, and shift to online or contactless markets. Compared to the pre-pandemic period, operators experienced as much as 60% increase in internet traffic.[13] Data traffic in emerging economies also increased by as much as 25%–50% as more and more activities moved online. Increased data consumption with end users adopting cloud and streaming technologies has strengthened the demand for digital data infrastructure. Investment in new technology and digital infrastructure is key to making our societies more resilient to crisis. Digital technologies and online solutions also enable greater efficiency and lower cost, aside from generating large network externalities and agglomeration benefits. Despite the surge in digital connectivity during the pandemic, as of 2021, about 2.9 billion people remain offline, as the digital divide continues to lead to serious inequities in development outcomes. Therefore, significant investments to upgrade digital infrastructure are required that will also involve technology upskilling of users.

Digitalization has been the vital link during the pandemic; the Consolidated Strategy on the Fourth Industrial Revolution for ASEAN provides policy guidance in building a Digital ASEAN Community through three focus areas: technological governance and cybersecurity; digital economy; and digital transformation of society.[14] The ASEAN Digital Masterplan 2025 outlines interventions to upgrade digital infrastructure and expand network coverage to rural areas. The Master Plan on ASEAN Connectivity 2025 promotes the adoption of digital technology by micro, small, and medium-sized enterprises to enhance their participation in the digital economy. It recognizes the need for high quality and widespread connectivity throughout ASEAN— delivered through robust telecommunications infrastructure that can improve existing infrastructure and extend connectivity to underserved areas and unconnected regions.[15]

The pandemic has also raised the demand for social infrastructure such as health, education, and social protection. In particular, the pandemic has revealed that a deficit in basic healthcare facilities exists in many economies in the region. Social infrastructure comprises health facilities such as hospitals, research and testing laboratories, mobile health, vaccination centers, quarantine facilities; education facilities and tools such as universities, classrooms, online classes, downloadable lessons, Massive Open Online Courses, mobile phones and tablets, and radio and TV programs; and social protection services such as community pantries, food kitchens, shelters for the homeless, and cash transfer programs. These services or programs have become a lifeline to vulnerable populations who are ill-prepared to withstand the effects of COVID-19. However, most developing economies have limited resources to invest in modernizing their health, education, and social protection infrastructure.

The Asia and Pacific region needs $13.8 trillion from 2023 to 2030 or $1.7 trillion per year to meet its social infrastructure requirements over the next 15 years.[16] This figure is equivalent to 4.6% of the projected GDP, lower than ADB's projection on physical infrastructure needs by 5.7% of GDP. The social infrastructure investment needs are concentrated in the lower middle and upper middle-income countries, which account for 95% of the total investment needed. The sectors of public housing for urban slum population and health dominate the investment needs, accounting for 2.3% and 1.1% of GDP, respectively. This is followed by education and government building needs at 1% and 0.2% of GDP, respectively.

---

[13]   Organisation for Economic Co-operation and Development (OECD). 2020. *Digital Transformation in the Age of COVID-19: Building Resilience and Bridging Divides.* Digital Economy Outlook 2020 Supplement. OECD, Paris. www.oecd.org/digital/digital-economy-outlook-covid.pdf.

[14]   ASEAN. 2021. *Consolidated Strategy on the Fourth Industrial Revolution for ASEAN.* https://asean.org/wp-content/uploads/2021/10/6.-Consolidated-Strategy-on-the-4IR-for-ASEAN.pdf.

[15]   ASEAN. 2022. *Driving Inclusive and Sustainable Digital Transformation in ASEAN.* Issue 23. https://asean.org/wp-content/uploads/2021/09/ASEAN-Digital-Masterplan-EDITED.pdf.

[16]   Institute for Economic and Social Research, Faculty of Economics and Business Universities Indonesia and Japan International Cooperation Agency. 2020. *Estimating Social Infrastructure Needs in Diverse and Dynamic Asia.* https://www.jica.go.jp/jica-ri/publication/booksandreports/l75nbg000019iphd-att/report_20200923.pdf.

While the pandemic has stalled existing infrastructure development, it has also raised the demand for new infrastructure assets that are needed to cope with new challenges in the post-pandemic period. For instance, airports have been significantly impacted by the pandemic with airline capacities dropping 70%–80% at the height of lockdowns and travel restrictions. To minimize physical contact as passengers move through check-in counters, security checkpoints, and customs clearance, the use of contactless digital technologies in airports needs to be factored in while developing new airport designs. The widespread work-from-home arrangements affect commuting patterns and city transportation system schedules. More people working from home or closer to home in shared work environments may shift demand to localized areas where people live, rather than centralized places where people work. Alternative transportation for short distances such as bicycles, scooters, and motorcycles have become prevalent post-pandemic, which calls for greater investments or enhancements of infrastructures. Cities will need to evaluate space for walking, cycling, and use of other light means for transportation.

The adverse impacts of climate change and weather-related disasters have further exacerbated the costs and demand for developing sustainable infrastructure. In 2020, the ASEAN region was hit by 405 disaster events which affected 19.3 million people, displaced 2.4 million, and resulted in damages of over $227 million.[17] *The Asia-Pacific Disaster Report 2022*, which captures the complexity of disaster risk by including direct and indirect losses, reveals that the annual average losses in the region are more than four times the previous estimate (2017), reaching $91 billion—a substantial proportion of which is attributed to agricultural drought losses. Southeast Asian countries were confronted with the dual challenge of managing the COVID-19 pandemic while also contending with disasters, particularly typhoons and floods. With climate change intensifying and biological threats persisting, the region is expected to face even more complex hazards. According to estimates by the Economic and Social Commission for Asia and the Pacific (ESCAP), the cumulative risks from multiple cascading hazards could result in losses equivalent to 4.32% of Southeast Asia's regional GDP in the worst case climate scenario.[18] The infrastructure gap figures do not include expenditure on recovery from disasters and extreme weather events. Cambodia, the Philippines, Myanmar, Viet Nam, and Thailand rank among 14 countries most affected by weather-related loss events (Long-Term Climate Risk Index 2000–2019) and are extremely vulnerable to climate-linked risks.[19] *The World Risk Report 2022* evaluates 192 countries based on their likelihood of facing natural hazard events, extreme weather events, susceptibility and vulnerability of their populations, and inadequacy of coping and adaptation measures. Among the most vulnerable and high-risk nations, six ASEAN countries are ranked within the top 35. The Philippines is identified as the most vulnerable and is ranked first on the list, followed by Indonesia at 3rd, Myanmar at 6th, Viet Nam at 12th, Thailand at 23rd, and Malaysia at 35th.[20] As climate-induced extreme events increase in intensity and frequency, populations and aging infrastructure become more compromised and vulnerable. Resilient and sustainable infrastructure needs to be developed that reduces emissions and climate risk, stimulates economic development, and increases returns for investors. This will involve incremental cost and creative funding. Regional collaborations will be required to address systemic risks and apply risk-informed management strategies to close the infrastructure protection gap to mitigate climate action failures, build resilience to extreme weather events, and strengthen coping capacities.

Closing the infrastructure gap has become more important than ever, to reinvigorate growth, enhance economic development, and deliver on the SDGs. The United Nations Conference on Trade and Development (UNCTAD) estimated a requirement between $3.3 trillion to $4.5 trillion a year to achieve the SDGs in developing countries alone.[21] Current levels of public and private financing of SDGs cover $1.4 trillion, leaving a gap of $2.5 trillion to be bridged. About 30% may be bridged by public resources, leaving at least 70% to be covered by private capital. ADB

[17] ASEAN Secretariat. 2021. *ASEAN Disaster Resilience Outlook. Preparing for a future beyond 2025.* Jakarta. https://asean.org/wp-content/uploads/2021/10/ASEAN-Disaster-Resilience-Outlook-Preparing-for-the-Future-Beyond-2021-FINAL.pdf.

[18] ESCAP. 2022. *Pathways to Adaptation and Resilience in Southeast Asia. Asia-Pacific Disaster Report 2022 for ESCAP Subregions.* https://www.unescap.org/kp/2022/asia-pacific-disaster-report-2022-escap-subregions-summary-policymakers.

[19] David Eckstein, Vera Künzel, Laura Schäfer. 2021. *Global Climate Risk Index 2021.* Germanwatch. www.germanwatch.org.

[20] Bündnis Entwicklung Hilft. 2022. *World Risk Report 2022.* https://weltrisikobericht.de/wp-content/uploads/2022/09/WorldRiskReport-2022_Online.pdf.

[21] UNCTAD. 2014. *World Investment Report.* Geneva. https://unctad.org/system/files/official-document/wir2014_en.pdf.

estimates that its 45 developing member countries from Asia and the Pacific require $26 trillion to meet SDGs by 2030 or about $1.7 trillion per year. But only about $880 billion is invested in infrastructure per year.[22] The prevailing disruptive environment requires a fresh approach to tackling fiscal needs and challenges. It requires engaging new investors and reducing the financial burden of the public sector for infrastructure development. The impacts of the COVID-19 pandemic are likely to sharpen focus on key infrastructure trends that will entail changing business models for "challenged assets," reassessing risks sharing to ensure equitable allocation and reduce risk asymmetry, making changes to PPP legal frameworks to provide greater flexibility to external partners, and adopting performance-based and collaborative contracting models.[23] There is an increasing move toward self-reliance, as countries seek to build domestic capacities, redesign supply chains to build resilience to global shocks, and shift to multiple suppliers. As energy transition and digitization are the core sectors receiving the most interest from investors, it is an opportune moment to accelerate the adoption of green technologies and materials by embedding sustainability and resilience criteria into project life cycles.

At the same time, the financial landscape has become more restrictive with rising debt levels and increasingly limited fiscal resources, constraining the ability of governments in the region to fund new infrastructure needs. The ASEAN+3 comprises developed, developing, and least developed countries with different political and economic structures. As a consequence, the impact of the pandemic has been varied. The path to economic recovery is dependent on a country's fiscal health; the sectors affected by the pandemic (such as tourism, construction, mining, and transportation); reliance on international trade; and skills of its labor force. Unsurprisingly, two divergent growth scenarios are emerging— more buoyant growth is expected for Indonesia, Malaysia, the Philippines, and Singapore, and fragmented and slow growth for Brunei Darussalam, Cambodia, Lao People's Democratic Republic (Lao PDR), Thailand, and Viet Nam. The pandemic laid bare the fiscal vulnerabilities of countries and highlighted their strengths and timely measures that reduced its impact. Fiscal spending as a share of GDP was higher for Singapore, Indonesia, Malaysia, and the Philippines, ranging from 15%–41% of their respective 2020 GDP, while the fiscal response of the rest of the countries in the region averaged below 10% of 2020 GDP.[24] The ASEAN+3 governments have implemented a wide range of measures from health systems and social protection programs to subsidies to firms and tax deferrals. Despite the efforts of the central banks across the ASEAN region, some countries continue to face challenges due to disrupted trade links, risk of credit rating downgrade, currency risk caused by a strengthening US dollar, inflation risk, and inability to restructure debts or obtain waivers. The resultant resource crunch has limited the capacity of the government to fund infrastructure projects.

Innovative financing models could help encourage private participation and collaboration with the government to deliver these critical infrastructure assets. An investment-enabled environment coupled with innovative financing solutions underpinned by technology can help bridge the infrastructure gap by tapping into global capital markets. Strategies for changing the current trajectory of investments will, therefore, have to be private- and institutional-finance centric. Innovative finance mechanisms that support development projects beyond debt finance and curated solutions that can catalyze private and institutional capital to bridge the infrastructure-financing gap will be critical to mobilize investments. These mechanisms are focused on the delivery of positive social and environmental outcomes through market-based financing instruments rather than on resource mobilization through ingenious fundraising approaches. They provide new sectors and opportunities for investment through a combination of risk distribution, increased liquidity, reduced volatility, assured capital adequacy, and positive risk-adjusted returns. More importantly, new forms of partnerships and recalibrated financing mechanisms are designed to reduce debt burden, de-risk investments, reinvigorate competitiveness, and ensure resilient and sustainable development.

---

[22]   ADB. 2017. *Meeting Asia's Infrastructure Needs*. Manila. https://www.adb.org/sites/default/files/publication/227496/special-report-infrastructure.pdf.

[23]   PricewaterhouseCoopers. 2020. *The global forces shaping the future of infrastructure. Global Infrastructure trends.* https://www.pwc.com/gx/en/industries/capital-projects-infrastructure/publications/infrastructure-trends.html.

[24]   Footnote 10.

III ISSUES AND CHALLENGES

3.1 Background

The importance of infrastructure for economic growth and the ever-widening gap between infrastructure demand and supply have been extensively emphasized in the context of sustainable development. The economic and social impacts of the COVID-19 pandemic, the heightened geopolitical tensions, energy and food insecurity, and a spate of severe climate-induced disasters have further underscored the urgent need to bridge the infrastructure gap. The existing level of infrastructure development has been unable to match the requirements of a growing population, keep pace with technological advances, and build adequate resilience to counter the adverse impacts of climate change and disasters. The main challenge for post-pandemic economic recovery is mobilizing finance to fund key infrastructure projects to revive industries, build better, provide livelihood opportunities, and improve social and health-related services.

The pandemic reduced a once vibrant $90 trillion global economy to a slow and stuttering pace as most countries witnessed a downward spiral of economic activity following forced lockdowns, lower production, disrupted supply chains, and a significant fall in the demand of goods and services. The risks of a major economic recession are now real, as economies contract and public spending is channeled to social protection schemes and emergency health and relief payments. Government fiscal and monetary policies are more focused on interventions to rein-in runaway inflation. Policy makers are faced with multiple challenges of prioritizing scarce resources. On the one hand, it is critical to provide immediate relief, balance budgets, and limit fiscal deficits, while on the other, it is also important to provide stimulus packages, financial incentives, and monetary interventions to stabilize markets, ease access to credit, increase spending, and generate employment opportunities.

Debt-burdened and resource-constrained developing and emerging economies are unable to make financial allocations for infrastructure development and are further pressured by their commitments toward achieving their SDGs to address the issues of poverty, inequality, food and energy insecurity, and environmental degradation. Reduced trade and supply chain disruptions have further hobbled and constrained economies as both exports and imports of vital goods and commodities have been affected. Travel restrictions have severely impacted a once burgeoning and thriving transport and hospitality industry, leaving a trail of underutilized infrastructure and loss of livelihood. It is against this challenging economic backdrop that infrastructure financing has to be mobilized by adopting innovative mechanisms and fiscal policies that leverage scarce public resources to crowd-in private and institutional investment.

Historically, the public sector has been responsible for developing a sizeable proportion of the large-scale projects especially in water, energy, transportation, and social infrastructure, so much so that financing of some of the sectors is often viewed as a public responsibility and an investment domain for public funding. With the increased opportunities for private sector involvement in energy, water, and communications projects, the allocations of public funding for these sectors have been reduced. However, the quantum of private and institutional funding for infrastructure is inadequate to meet the increasing demand. Infrastructure projects often involve a high capital cost up-front, long gestation period, risk of uncertain returns, and a social benefit that may not appear to meet the investment and risk-to-return criteria of private investors. These obstacles and perceptions adversely impact the mobilization of vital funds resulting in the deferment of investment decisions and the passing on of a larger infrastructure deficit burden to future generations, thereby leading to economic stagnation, loss of competitive edge, and inadequate public services. The COVID-19 pandemic has necessitated the reallocation of public funds to social protection schemes and management of critical debt and deficit budget issues. Rising interest rates to control inflation have increased the cost of raising capital thus discouraging private investors.

3.2 Demographic Change and Urbanization

The population of ASEAN countries in 2023 is estimated to be about 680 million of which over 50% comprise urban residents. According to projections, the proportion of the urban population in the region is expected to increase to 55.7% by 2030. This means that out of a total population of almost 726 million people, nearly 405 million people are estimated to reside in urban areas by that time.[25] Changes in population demographics and spatial density due to urban migration have contributed to increasing exposure in vulnerable locations adding to catastrophe risk. Increased household wealth in the ASEAN region is expected to create increased demand for infrastructure in the energy, water and sanitation, transportation, and social infrastructure sectors (health, education, and public amenities), thus contributing to a widening of the infrastructure gap. In the region's four most populated economies—Indonesia, the Philippines, Thailand, and Viet Nam—the mass affluent class (estimated to increase by 8% per year between 2017 and 2030) is expected to replace the middle class (estimated to grow at 4%) as the driver of economic growth. The affluent population in these four countries will increase from 46 million to 125 million and their share of the population is projected to be as much as 21%.[26] The aging of populations in Southeast Asia (Singapore and Japan) will also necessitate additional investments in healthcare and social welfare infrastructure.

3.3 Increased Mobility

In developing Southeast Asian economies, an increase in transport infrastructure investment is expected. The increasing wealth and requirement for nationwide connectivity leads to a demand in vehicle ownership, which, in turn, creates a significant demand for improved higher capacity road networks. Governments also need to invest significantly in other transport infrastructure such as rail, ports, and airports, and in communications networks to ensure efficient logistics and connectivity.

As environmental degradation and unpredictable weather patterns linked to climate change have crippled rice production, leading to loss of cultivable land and reduced yields, increased rural–urban migration for livelihoods is mounting pressure on urban infrastructure in ASEAN countries. According to a 2020 study by the Bank of Thailand's Puey Ungphakorn Institute for Economic Research, over 9.5 million people from farming households were working outside the farm sector.[27] The study found that 76% of farming households are forced to rely on nonfarm income. It is projected that the Lower Mekong subregion comprising Cambodia, Lao PDR, Myanmar, Thailand, and Viet Nam will have 6.3 million climate migrants representing 2.7% of the total population of the region. The World Bank has estimated that as many 216 million people could move due to the slow onset of climate change from areas with lower water availability and crop productivity and from areas affected by sea rise and storm surges.[28] Increased allocations will need to be earmarked for improving agricultural production, weather forecast and catastrophe, and weather-indexed climate insurance to safeguard smallholder farmers.

3.4 Banks Cannot Meet Infrastructure Financing Requirements

The financial sector in the ASEAN+3 region is narrow, being largely dominated by banks. Pension funds and insurance companies comprise a second level and the share of capital markets, though growing, is small. Therefore, banks are more often than not the main source of finance for projects and businesses. Since banks can provide only short-term financing as they are constrained by their liabilities (deposits), any allocation to long-term investments leads to a maturity mismatch. Asian banks are largely risk averse to infrastructure projects because of the tightening regulations on credit lending, including credit risk measurement as stipulated by the Basel Committee on Banking Supervision. In the absence of venture capital or its inadequacy and limited government funding, it is difficult to finance capital-

---

25 ASEAN Secretariat. 2022. *ASEAN Sustainable Urbanization Report 2022. Sustainable Cities towards 2025 and Beyond.* https://unhabitat.org/sites/default/files/2022/12/asean_sustainable_urbanisation_report_final_dec_2022.pdf.

26 Aparna Bharadwaj, Justine Tasiaux, and Vaishali Rastogi. 2018. *Beyond the "Crazy Rich": The Mass Affluent of Southeast Asia.* Boston Consulting Group. https://www.bcg.com/publications/2018/beyond-crazy-rich-mass-affluent-southeast-asia.

27 S. Chantarat et al. 2020. *Thai agricultural households in the COVID-19 crisis.* Puey Ungphakorn Institute for Economic Research. https://www.pier.or.th/en/abridged/2020/11/.

28 V. Clement et al. 2021. *Groundswell Part 2: Acting on Internal Climate Migration.* World Bank. Washington, DC. https://openknowledge. worldbank.org/entities/publication/2c9150df-52c3-58ed-9075-d78ea56c3267.

intensive infrastructure projects. As a consequence, there is heavy reliance on credit intermediated form of financing. This is both an insufficient and expensive modality for infrastructure financing. In the case of green energy projects, it is even more difficult to obtain financing; this serves as a disincentive for parties that wish to undertake projects that seek to advance the expansion of green renewable energy. Insurance firms and pension funds are the only other available source for large long-term infrastructure projects.

3.5 Asset Class

Traditional financing mechanisms do not recognize public infrastructure as an investment asset class, thus depriving the sector of vital funds. The common barriers to the emergence of infrastructure as a separate asset class is the heterogeneity in the setup of the projects, the lack of a critical mass of bankable projects, and insufficient data to track asset performance.[29] Infrastructure projects, even within a country, are diverse in nature (economic, social, and digital), differ in contractual structures and regulatory frameworks (building permissions, environmental requirements, licensing, etc.), and have discrete risk return profiles. This makes harmonization difficult as investors often do not have the necessary information to properly assess an infrastructure project.[30] Rapid urbanization, climate change, and the need for technologically and environmentally sustainable infrastructure have increased the demand for specific infrastructure, depending upon the economic development of a country. Developing nations are focused on building basic infrastructure and attracting foreign capital investment while developed countries face the challenge of replacing their aging infrastructure with new technologically advanced systems. The latter is particularly true in the case of the communications sector where most developing nations leapfrogged to digital and internet-based systems while more developed economies struggled with legacy systems.

Since infrastructure equity has performed well and infrastructure debt funds have seen historically low default rates, institutional and private investors are increasingly diversifying into new asset classes that offer strong long-term returns. The economic outlook post pandemic and the heightened geopolitical tensions (due to food and energy insecurity and market uncertainty) have also kindled interest in investments that have lower volatility and are less disrupted by technology and state-influenced tariff policies.

The G20 recognized the importance of developing infrastructure as an asset class and in 2018 began work on four work streams: (i) contractual standardization, (ii) financial standardization, (iii) project preparation, and (iv) bridging the data gap. The report highlights that while the private long-term savings in the hands of institutional investors is at an all-time high of over $80 trillion, there are barriers to be addressed in the emergence of infrastructure as an asset class.[31]

3.6 Shyness of Private and Institutional Investment

One of the principal reasons that the private sector is not interested in entering long-term financing of infrastructure projects, including green projects, is the low rate of return and the associated risks. In most cases, the reluctance of private sector or institutional investment participation stems from the lack of bankable, investment-ready pipeline of infrastructure projects. This is considered to be one of the major bottlenecks in attracting private capital to infrastructure.

Inadequate and weak capacity to prepare infrastructure projects especially in the developing and least developed economies of the ASEAN region is another challenge. Project preparation is a critical enabler of infrastructure development and involves the conceptualization, prioritization, feasibility and socioeconomic impact assessments, and financial and contractual structuring. The costs of project preparation have increased (roughly between 5%–10% of total project investment), driven by the increased complexity of projects, the need to satisfy regulatory requirements,

29   OECD. *Roadmap to Infrastructure as an Asset Class.*https://www.oecd.org/g20/roadmap_to_infrastructure_as_an_asset_class_argentina_ presidency_1_0.pdf.
30   T. Ehlers. 2014. Understanding the challenges for infrastructure finance. *BIS Working Papers* No. 454. https://www.bis.org/publ/work454.htm.
31   KPMG. 2020. *Pandemic and the Future of Infrastructure as an Asset Class. Investor Insights for the Asia Pacific.* https://assets.kpmg.com/content/ dam/kpmg/sg/pdf/2020/06/pandemic-and-the-future-of-infrastructure-as-an-asset-class-062020.pdf.

and independent validation, as well as factoring in the relevant SDGs. However, it is critical that project preparation be regarded as an investment to avoid future inefficiencies, and to better achieve the intended goals of infrastructure projects.[32]

The lack of capacity to develop a well-researched, validated, and bankable project has limited investment grade (rated) opportunities in the infrastructure financing space of emerging markets. The paucity of verifiable and viable investment opportunities has led to low private sector participation. Large fund management financial institutions find it difficult to build a diversified portfolio of infrastructure assets without a large capital allocation. Smaller financial entities lack resources and capacity for credit analyses and active portfolio management of infrastructure.

Private sector participation is further constrained by limited liquidity in the secondary loan market, especially for infrastructure project debt. The lack of de-risking mechanisms and investment incentives and guarantees also deter and discourage private sector investment. The perceived risk of low returns and the expectation that risk-adjusted returns should match or be higher than conventional investments (that is, equity-type returns with bond-type risk) is both unfair and untenable. A comparative evaluation of risk-adjusted return of infrastructure investments needs to take into account its low sensitivity to market swings, long-term stable and predictable cash flows, hedge against inflation, and low default rates.

3.7 Climate-Resilient Infrastructure Investments for Meeting Sustainable Development Goals

Rapid economic growth, impacts of climate change, adverse weather events, and compromised energy, water, and transportation systems all compel an intensified focus to develop resilient and sustainable infrastructure that meets economic, environmental, and social goals. Achieving the SDGs involves scaling up financing of investments that will ensure environmental and social benefits. Estimates obtained by summing up data from the UNCTAD and International Energy Agency show that about $2.6 trillion will be required annually through 2030 to meet the SDGs and stay on the path of a net-zero strategy by 2050. An analysis of the pipeline of greenfield projects in emerging markets and developing economies on industry databases estimated a pipeline of approximately $1.2 trillion in "investable" infrastructure projects across sustainable infrastructure.[33] Most of these projects will not be fully developed for quite some time, thus the availability of investment-ready projects is far below the estimated $2.6 trillion annual requirement. It is important to consider that the infrastructure financing gap is not only driven by a lack of investor involvement or poor access to capital or the want of innovative financial mechanisms but also by the absence of a robust and bankable infrastructure pipeline.

Financial barriers continue to be the main obstacle to the development of clean energy and green projects in Asia. Infrastructure projects are already capital-intensive and incorporating climate-smart, resilient, and sustainable features add further costs. This explains why most banks are reluctant to finance renewable energy projects. To mitigate the higher cost, adoption of newer technologies could help lower the initial set up costs and guarantee revenue stream. Along with government incentives, these can help encourage bank lending to these projects. Preliminary evidence shows that sustainable infrastructure investments performed better than other infrastructure sector investments. Wind and solar equities have generated a compound annual return of 16%, which is higher than those of listed and unlisted infrastructure equities.[34]

Natural hazard events and climate risks have increasingly destroyed infrastructure assets in the region, and ASEAN+3 countries need to develop approaches and solutions to protect infrastructure assets, build resilience, and develop sustainable projects. Global economic loss from disasters in 2022 was estimated at $3,13 billion, of which over 95% was attributed to extreme weather-related events.[35] Resilient and sustainable infrastructure involves incremental cost

---

[32]   Global Infrastructure Hub. 2021. *Infrastructure Monitor 2021.* https://cdn.gihub.org/umbraco/media/4740/gihub_v10.pdf

[33]   D. Zelikow and F. Savas. 2022. Mind the gap: Time to rethink infrastructure finance. World Bank Blogs. 20 May. https://blogs.worldbank.org/ppps/mind-gap-time-rethink-infrastructure-finance.

[34]   Footnote 32.

[35]   AON. 2023. *Weather, Climate and Catastrophe Insight.* https://www.aon.com/getmedia/f34ec133-3175-406c-9e0b-25cea768c5cf/20230125-weather-climate-catastrophe-insight.pdf.

and creative funding. There is an urgent need to build sustainable and resilient infrastructure assets and to mainstream environmental conservation into all construction and project activity. Green infrastructure development is critical to deliver a wide range of ecosystem services such as water purification, air quality, and climate mitigation and adaptation, and achieve global climate and development commitments (including nationally determined contributions) in this "decade for delivery." It will also be critical to sustain socioeconomic development during the COVID-19 pandemic recovery period.

As ASEAN+3 countries plot their economic recovery from the impacts of the pandemic toward a more sustainable development phase, they will need to ensure an equitable and balanced transition to support their manufacturing and urbanization requirements. The widely differing levels of socioeconomic development among the member states together with the prevailing global situation of rising inflation and interest rates, energy insecurity, food insecurity, conflict, and related geopolitical issues make it difficult to secure investments. A survey of key financial stakeholders (borrowers, lenders, and market influencers) conducted by Economic Research Institute for ASEAN and East Asia found that market-based risks (currency and interest rates and regulatory environment), lack of grid connectivity for power generation, inadequate and fragmented supply chains, and lack of access to information about carbon emission reduction potential of projects were the major barriers to investment in low-carbon activities.[36]

A need for a taxonomy was identified as a key enabler to increase the participation of all existing and potential stakeholders by harmonizing the definition of green and sustainable activities across ASEAN. The main objective of a taxonomy is to mobilize all forms of finance to support the achievement of sustainable development (including transition to net-zero carbon emissions) and "a common language by which the degree of sustainability of a project or investment can be measured."[37] This is necessary as investors (especially multilateral development banks, pension funds, bilateral funding institutions, and philanthropic foundations), are increasingly committed to investing in sustainable projects.

To support ASEAN's commitment to sustainability, a regional taxonomy was developed as a common building block, to enable an orderly transition and foster sustainable finance adoption. It was important that the economic growth and development of each ASEAN country be considered while framing the regional taxonomy. The ASEAN Taxonomy is a sustainable finance tool that is "intended as a reference point for sustainable projects and activities in ASEAN to help issuers and investors understand the sustainability impact of a project or economic activity."[38] The ASEAN Taxonomy has been designed as a multitiered concept comprising of a Foundation Framework and a Plus Standard. The Foundation Framework, which is applicable to all ASEAN countries, sets out the environmental objectives and essential criteria; economic activities must fulfill at least one of the environmental objectives and all essential criteria. The Plus Standard provides guidance to further qualify and benchmark eligible green activities and investments as also activity-level criteria and thresholds to determine if an activity contributes to the environmental objectives of the taxonomy.

In a related development, the Hongkong and Shanghai Banking Corporation (HSBC), the International Finance Corporation (IFC), the Organisation for Economic Co-operation and Development, the Global Infrastructure Facility, and the Climate Policy Initiative came together to establish an industry-led PPP called "Finance to Accelerate Sustainable Transition-Infrastructure (FAST-Infra)" to develop a consistent, globally applicable labeling system for investments in sustainable infrastructure assets. The labeling system will provide assurance to investors that their investments are contributing to meeting environmental and social resiliency and governance (ESG) objectives that contribute to the SDGs and meet their own ESG standards. The FAST-Infra plans targeted financial interventions

36   ERIA Discussion Paper Series 313. *Unlocking the Potentials of Private Financing for Low-carbon Energy Transition:Ideas and Solutions from ASEAN Markets*. https://www.eria.org/uploads/media/discussion-papers/Unlocking-the-Potentials-of-Private-Financing-for-Low-cabon-Energy-Transistion-Ideas-and-Solutions-from-ASEAN-Markets.pdf.

37   EU-ASEAN Business Council. *The ASEAN Taxonomy: The Need for Further Enhancements to Attract Sustainable Finance*. https://www.eu-asean.eu/wp-content/uploads/2022/04/ASEAN-Taxonomy-Paper-For-Publication.pdf.

38   ASEAN Taxonomy Board. *ASEAN Taxonomy for Sustainable Finance; Version 1*. https://asean.org/book/asean-taxonomy-for-sustainable-finance/.

through a technology platform, a power purchase agreement or revenue guarantee, a modified "managed co-lending portfolio program," and a financing facility to lend to national development banks.[39]

3.8 Association of Southeast Asian Nations Bond Market

Recent years have witnessed a surge in sustainable bond markets, not only in terms of financing amounts but also in the form of innovative instruments. The expanding sustainable bond family now includes green bonds, social bonds, sustainability bonds, sustainability-linked bonds, and transition bonds. Asia is home to the second-largest regional sustainable bond market in the world after Europe, accounting for around 20% of global issuance. The ASEAN+3 markets dominate the sustainable bond market in Asia with the equivalent of $130 billion of sustainable bond issuance in the first six months of 2022 and $547.9 billion of sustainable bonds outstanding at the end of March.[40] Although ASEAN+3 has a larger conventional bond market than the EU, ASEAN+3 fell behind the EU in terms of sustainable bond market development. Sustainable bonds outstanding only account for 1.2% of the total bond market in ASEAN+3 whereas the share is 5.4% in the EU. The ASEAN+3 sustainable bond market has a shorter average maturity (less than 5 years) than the EU and has a lower share of rated sustainable bonds but a higher share of investment-grade bonds (that is, BBB and above) among rated bonds as compared to the EU. The shares of local currency denominated green, social, and sustainability bonds outstanding in ASEAN+3 were lower than in the EU.

There is a need for further development of the ASEAN+3 sustainable bond market—in particular, demand for longer-tenor and local currency-denominated sustainable bonds needs to be supported. There is also a tendency for investors in ASEAN+3 sustainable bond markets to demand quality, as indicated by the higher share of investment-grade bonds, which highlights the importance of boosting the supply of quality, or bankable, assets. To further develop the sustainable bond market in ASEAN+3, efforts are needed on both the demand and supply sides. On the demand side, despite an increasing awareness of sustainable investments around the world, current ESG investment practice in Asia remains relatively limited. According to Willis Towers Watson (2021), Asian asset owners only allocated an average of 10% of their portfolio to ESG-related strategies. This not only reflects weaker capacity in ESG investment in the region, but also weak standards and an underdeveloped ESG market ecosystem, along with a relatively small supply of sustainable assets in Asian markets.[41]

The benefits of issuing sustainable bonds to finance impact investments have been widely documented. They include positive investor recognition, a broadened potential investor base, greater resilience to shocks, more social capital, and lower financing costs over the negative "greenium."[42] Despite these benefits, however, the ASEAN+3 lacks a pipeline for sustainable projects and thus has a limited supply of sustainable bonds. This is partly driven by corporations' limited capacity to identify, manage, and report related sustainable investments. The lack of capacity is more pronounced in ASEAN economies where bond market development lags that of the PRC, Japan, and the Republic of Korea.

ADB's research highlighted that the main obstacles to investing in green bonds according to institutional investors were

- insufficient supply of green bonds, preventing the development of a green bond market in the region;
- lack of awareness of the clear benefits of green bonds over conventional bonds even in the more developed markets like Singapore, Malaysia, and Thailand;
- absence of policy guidance from regulators related to green bonds;

[39] M. Ridley. 2021. *FAST-Infra; A Public-Private Initiative to Raise Private Investment in Developing World Sustainable Infrastructure.* HSBC Centre of Sustainable Finance. January. https://www.sustainablefinance.hsbc.com/sustainable-infrastructure/fast-infra-a-public-private-initiative.

[40] K. Puongsophol, S. Tian, and S. Yamadera. 2022. Developing the Sustainable Bond Market in ASEAN+3: Challenges and Opportunities. *ADB Briefs* No. 234. Manila. https://www.adb.org/sites/default/files/publication/842741/adb-brief-234-sustainable-bond-market-asean3.pdf.

[41] Willis Towers Watson. 2021. *ESG Beliefs and Practices Survey 2021—Asian Asset Owners: Raising Their ESG Game.* https://www.wtwco.com/en-HK/Insights/2021/10/asian-asset-owners-raising-their-esg-game.

[42] ADB. 2021. *Asian Development Outlook 2021: Financing a Green and Inclusive Recovery.* Manila. https://www.adb.org/sites/default/files/publication/692111/ado2021.pdf.

- higher risk inherent in green bonds; and
- lack of internal guidance and resources for such investments.

In addition, underwriters also highlighted the lack of eligible project pipelines and that the majority of ASEAN investors preferred small ticket sizes, though underwriters were keener to work on bigger transactions.[43] Both institutional investors and underwriters were of the opinion that tax incentives could be an effective means of increasing the supply of and demand for green and sustainability bonds. Renewable energy was considered to be the most promising growth sector in ASEAN+3, both in terms of investment and the issuance of green bonds.

3.9 Risks

The COVID-19 pandemic, the recent market volatility on account of geopolitical events, and the economic repercussions of debt-burdened economies have together increased awareness about the "other risks" in infrastructure asset development. These include[44]

- construction risk,
- energy security,
- underdeveloped and disrupted supply chains,
- operational and management risk,
- business risk—demand and supply factors,
- leverage and interest rates,
- refinancing risk,
- legal and ownership risk,
- regulatory and fiduciary risk
- political and taxation risks,
- social risks (opposition from pressure group or corruption),
- illiquidity risk (immature secondary market),
- pricing risk (valuation basis),
- governance risks (such as conflict of interest or opacity),
- lack of experience with asset class and investment vehicle, and
- integration in asset-liability program and diversification on time.

In the context of current systems of carbon pricing, "carbon price risk" has emerged as a new form of political risk for both companies and investors. This risk is related to the probability of the emergence of future international climate agreements and changes in carbon-related national policies. The risk is technological as well as political, as there is uncertainty surrounding possible future technologies that might affect the speed and scope of the transition toward a low-carbon economy. This uncertainty further influences investors' ability to formulate long-term expectations about assets in which they could invest.[45] These risks need to be mitigated and planned for at the project development stage.

---

[43] Asian Development Bank and Global Green Growth Institute. 2022. *Survey on Green Bonds and Sustainable Finance in ASEAN. Insights on the Perspectives of Institutional Investors and Underwriters*. https://www.adb.org/sites/default/files/publication/840636/survey-green-bonds-sustainable-finance-asean.pdf.

[44] Adapted from Georg Inderst. *Infrastructure as an Asset Class. EIB Papers*. 15(1): pp. 70–105. https://papers.ssrn.com/sol3/papers.cfm?abstract_id=1860947.

[45] G. Gianfrate and G. Lorenzato. 2018. Stimulating non-bank financial institutions' participation in green investments. *ADBI Working Paper Series* No. 860. Tokyo. https://www.adb.org/sites/default/files/publication/445026/adbi-wp860.pdf.

3.10 Digital Transformation

Infrastructure is widely regarded as a more resilient sector but it was nevertheless impacted by the COVID-19 pandemic. The transport, construction, and hospitality sectors were most impacted while the communications and digital sectors performed well as the push toward enhanced adoption of technology meant that data center and technology infrastructure projects were quickly adopted. Technology now underpins and impacts all sectors and activities. It influences all aspects of asset and wealth management as exponential improvements in predictive analytics, artificial intelligence, and big data have simplified analysis and processing to facilitate objective investment decisions. The tardy expansion of digital infrastructure is slowing down growth in most sectors as the pace of innovation, together with increasing demand, has outstripped actual implementation. This has created pockets of inefficiency that still rely on legacy systems and are reluctant to transition.

Digital communications service, content providers, and manufacturers of hardware and software have a mutually dependent future but face serious issues even though they incur more than $300 billion a year of capital expenditure on infrastructure. The supply chain disruptions and bottlenecks due to the pandemic highlighted the need for manufacturing-intensive nations to invest in the production of critical components—semiconductor chips—to become more self-reliant.[46] There is a compelling requirement to transition to the next level of digital infrastructure that will reduce inefficiency and redundancy and enhance knowledge sharing. The digital value chain provides significant opportunities to improve productivity, reduce cost, minimize service delivery time, and increase employment. Digital infrastructure investments in upgrading existing networks and expanding its geographical spread with new equipment are critical to realize the full potential of the digital economy that has become the lifeline for all transactions and services. Without new approaches, these limitations will not be eased and will, thereby, slow down data access and analysis, threatening the growth of the digital economy.

3.11 Project Preparation and Management

Project preparation capacity in ASEAN countries is often weak. This is due to a range of factors, including inadequate human and financial resources, weak project management systems, and lack of access to technical and financial expertise. Some countries also lack policy and regulatory frameworks necessary to ensure effective project preparation. This lack of capacity has been a major barrier to the successful development of infrastructure projects in the region and has hindered the ability of ASEAN countries to attract and leverage FDI. Without adequate capacity and capability, countries are unable to properly assess the viability of projects, prepare sound business plans, and attract the necessary investments for these projects.

Multilateral development banks and bilateral funding agencies have helped to strengthen institutional capacity by providing technical assistance for projects through consultancy services and training programs in addition to establishing project management units and instituting monitoring, reporting, and evaluation systems. One of the barriers to getting infrastructure projects off the ground in the region is the lack of standard project finance loan documentation. Customized bespoke documents are time consuming and expensive to negotiate as legal vetting has to be done afresh. Non-standard clauses also lack certainty and precedent value in the event of disputes. Infrastructure Asia (InfraAsia), a facilitation office set up by Enterprise Singapore and the Monetary Authority of Singapore, has developed Standardized Core Project Loan Documents. The set of documents comprises the mandate letter, term sheet, and common terms agreement. The standardization of this core suite of project finance loan documents is an important step toward expediting and reducing the cost of project finance, and thereby narrowing the infrastructure investment gap for the region.[47]

---

[46]   The PRC, India, Japan and the Republic of Korea are setting up semi-conductor manufacturing facilities.

[47]   Infrastructure Asia. Standardised Core Project Finance Loan Documents. https://www.infrastructureasia.org/Media-Centre/Standardised-Core-Project-Finance-Loan-Documents.

IV INNOVATIVE FINANCING MECHANISMS

4.1 Introduction and Definition

Closing the infrastructure-financing gap is difficult, but not impossible. If a quarter of the net outflow of Asia's large savings pile were re-invested in infrastructure within the region, the financing gap would be filled as Asia invested $6.2 trillion in the rest of the world, while the rest of the world invested only $4.4 trillion in the region. "This nearly $2 trillion gap is at the heart of a conundrum that, if solved, could make up the shortfall for physical and soft infrastructure and unlock Asia's now obvious vast economic potential."[48] It is estimated that 40% of the infrastructure gap could be filled by public financial reforms, leaving the private sector to close the required investment deficit.

While there are wide-ranging constraints currently limiting infrastructure development, innovative finance provides novel approaches that could mobilize increased capital investment to bridge the infrastructure gap. Currently more than $200 trillion of private capital is invested in global capital markets. Innovative finance mechanisms, therefore, need to be devised and curated to catalyze private and institutional finance for the infrastructure sector.

Innovative finance mechanisms can be defined as new and evolving models beyond commercial debt finance that are able to attract private and institutional capital, along with public funds for developmental activities. More importantly, innovative finance is primarily focused on the delivery of positive social and environmental outcomes through market-based financing instruments rather than on resource mobilization through ingenuous fundraising approaches. It employs public funds as the trigger to catalyze private and institutional financing by reducing risk, creating an enabling investment environment, and providing an opportunity to collaborate on sustainable outcomes.

Innovative financing essentially targets the private and institutional sector by creating investment opportunities for collaboration on sustainable infrastructure projects that are usually outside their ambit or immediate zone of consideration. It provides new sectors for investment through a combination of risk distribution, increasing liquidity, reducing volatility, ensuring capital adequacy in a timely manner, and providing positive risk-adjusted returns. It fosters collaboration between private, public, and institutional donors to inject much needed capital into social and environmentally sustainable projects that are not considered by capital markets traditionally viewing them through a return-on-investment lens. Innovative finance thus acts as a magnet to attract private and institutional finance for sustainable development.

Besides broadening the funding base for infrastructure investments, innovative finance can create multiple benefits, such as diversification of sources of funds, reduced reliance on public debt, leveraging of private sector innovation and efficiency, and increased transparency and accountability of projects. It is a paradigm shift from the grant-based resource mobilization approach to solutions-focused financing mechanisms that seek to provide outlays for development projects. There is also an increasing emphasis on result-based financing structures such as performance-based contracts to stimulate private capital inflows.

The intended role of public finance is to act as a catalyst to crowd-in private and institutional capital. It should have a multiplier effect that can draw other investors often in double digit ratios, thereby ensuring that adequate capital is mobilized to achieve developmental goals.

---

[48] L. Zhigang and Ra, S. 2018. *How to Bridge the Financing Gap in Asian Infrastructure.* Asian Development Bank Blog. https://blogs.adb.org/blog/how-bridge-financing-gap-asian-infrastructure.

4.2 The Financiers

Prior to discussing innovative financial mechanisms, it is useful to enumerate the financiers and players that are currently involved and can potentially be crowded in for funding and investing in infrastructure projects (Table 2).

Table 2: Financiers

• National governments including municipalities and other local bodies	• Investment companies (including investment banks, asset managers, wealth managers, family and multifamily offices, investment trusts, and private equity funds)
• Multilateral development banks (ODA, loans, grants, and technical assistance)	• Insurance companies and private pension funds
• Bilateral funding by countries (ODA, loans, grants, and technical assistance)	• Public pension and superannuation plans
• Global development funds (GEF, Climate Fund, etc.)	• Sovereign wealth funds
• Development finance institutions (IFC, European Investment Bank, BII, DEG, etc.)	• Infrastructure operators and developers
• Global and regional development and economic cooperation programs (Belt and Road Initiative, Lancang–Mekong Cooperation, etc.)	• Endowments and philanthropic foundations
• Commercial and Export–Import Banks	• Large private corporates or individual investors (venture capital, angel investors, etc.)

BII= British International Investment, DEG = Deutsche Investitions-Und Entwicklungsgesellschaft MBH, GEF = Global Environment Facility, IFC = International Finance Corporation, ODA = official development assistance.
Source: Study team analysis.

From the list in Table 2, it is critical to identify financiers that have the capacity to invest at scale, over a longer term, and have conservative expectations of return on investment. Institutional investors comprising pension funds, insurance companies, and sovereign wealth funds represent the largest pool of investment capital as they control an estimated $91 trillion of assets under management. The extended gestation periods for infrastructure projects and long maturity and fixed nature of project bonds are an ideal match with their risk appetite and investment criterion.

4.3 Mechanics of Innovative Finance

The application of innovative financing approaches, instruments, and models requires a careful examination of resource requirements, existing and potential stakeholders, government policies and regulatory frameworks, scalability, and impact in terms of the economic and social value. Several critical questions need to be answered prior to initiating any investment process. Is the investment likely to have a positive economic and social cascading effect? Are national governments or local bodies supportive? Is the enabling environment stable and conducive to investment? What are the investment criteria and expectations of returns of potential investors? What can be done to de-risk the proposed investment or "sweeten the deal" to attract new private capital? What role can public finance play in catalyzing investment in sustainable infrastructure?

The combination of governance (in terms of a conducive investment environment that is backed by a supportive regulatory framework) and innovative finance mechanisms comprise the twin drivers for financing sustainable development infrastructure. Together, they form the nucleus that can utilize limited public funds to provide the charge and momentum to mobilize private and institutional investors for economic and social projects by meeting their expectations both in terms of an enabling environment as well as risk-adjusted returns.

Several innovative financial instruments and mechanisms that address market failures and institutional barriers have been devised and implemented to support positive developmental outcomes. Increased use of innovative financing models and approaches provides a means of attracting private sector capital that can make a significant contribution to bridge the infrastructure gap in ASEAN+3 economies. The various types of innovative financing models together with financial instruments and their potential application are discussed in the following subsections.

4.4 Innovative Financing Instruments and Mechanisms

This section describes successfully implemented innovative financing models (Figure 1) and illustrates each with a practical case study(ies) highlighting the sector, stakeholders, financing model framework, and critical success factors.

Figure 1: Innovative Financing Models

Blended finance is the strategic use of public, private, and philanthropic finance sources and development finance to mobilize additional private capital flows toward sustainable development in developing countries.

Asset recycling is the process of generating funds for the creation of new infrastructure by selling or leasing pre-existing infrastructure assets to the private sector and utilizing the proceeds received from the monetization.

Asset securitization is the transformation of infrastructure assets into marketable securities to sell in secondary capital markets (including to institutional investors).

Convertible debt structures include grants and loans that can be converted into loans or equity respectively, at certain milestones depending on the progress of an infrastructure development.

Municipal bonds represent debts that are issued by a state or local government, as well as its agencies or authorities, and one of their key characteristics is that the interest payments that investors receive are generally not subject to taxes.

Sustainable and green bonds are fixed income instruments that are designed to fund projects that provide favorable environmental outcomes and promote climate change resilience such as renewable energy, waste management, and clean transportation.

Government green funds and/or transition funds are a financial commitment to transit to a low-carbon, energy efficient, and green infrastructure-based economy by using a range of financial instruments, such as private, non-sovereign, and sovereign guaranteed loans; direct equity; and equity funds, to finance development outcomes that contribute to environmental sustainability.

Public–private partnership projects are collaboration ventures between the public and private sector, and both parties are bound by a contractual agreement stipulating the terms and conditions of their engagement and mutual responsibilities.

Climate risk and catastrophe insurance are financing mechanisms to mitigate risk, build resilience, and provide compensation, relief, rehabilitation, and reconstruction assistance against natural hazards and climate-induced extreme events.

Crowd funding is a mechanism that deploys social media and digital technology to collect small amounts of finance from a large number of individuals to finance new ventures or rehabilitate infrastructure or other projects where traditional financing is difficult.

Debt-for-nature/climate swap involves the purchase of the foreign debt, usually at a discount, and converting the debt into local currency. The proceeds are then utilized to fund environmental and conservation projects. The mechanism enables debt-stressed countries to free up resources to meet their development goals and fiscal obligations.

Carbon credit market mechanisms provide companies and governments a marketplace to buy carbon credits to offset their excess emissions and to sell emission reductions achieved through the use of clean technology, renewable energy, and carbon sequestration projects. Carbon credits incentivize entities to reduce emission by issuing tradable credits.

Source: Study team analysis.

4.4.1 Blended Finance

Key Objective

Blended finance, as defined by the Organisation for Economic Co-operation and Development, is the strategic use of development finance for the mobilization of additional funds to de-risk investments and reduce the cost of capital toward sustainable development in developing countries. It aims to address barriers to investment faced by private financiers across the investment lifecycle to attract additional finance to transactions that deliver development impact. Blended finance solutions can provide financial support to high impact projects that would not attract funding on strictly commercial terms because the risks are considered too high and returns are either unproven or are not commensurate with the level of risk (Box 1).

Description of the Financing Model

Blended finance has three characteristics:[49]

- Leverage: Use of development finance and philanthropic funds to attract private capital
- Impact: Investments that drive social, environmental, and economic progress
- Returns: Returns for private investors in line with market expectations based on perceived risk

---

Box 1: Global Finance Facility of the International Finance Corporation

The Global Finance Facility (GFF) of the International Finance Corporation (IFC) is a blended finance partnership focused on increasing access to finance for small and medium-sized enterprises (SMEs) in emerging markets by providing financial intermediaries with dedicated SME lending windows and by guaranteeing loans made to SMEs. This includes SMEs in fragile and conflict-affected markets, education, and healthcare. Established in 2012, the GFF blends commercial financing from the IFC and the European Investment Bank with donor funding from the Department for International Development (now Foreign, Commonwealth and Development Office) of the United Kingdom and the Netherlands. From 2012 to 2015, the GFF has supported its financial institution clients to lend $6.4 billion through more than 67,000 new SME loans.

Source: IFC. Destination: One Million New Jobs. Global SME Finance Facility Progress Report 2012-15. Washington, DC.

Sector and Project Fit

Blended finance solutions are typically employed in emerging markets for social or economic infrastructure projects that are not able to secure commercial bank financing on the basis of project cash flows (Figure 2). In such projects, capital providers require risk mitigation, facilitation, or partnerships with other financiers along the risk-capital spectrum.[50] Examples of blended finance include the use of public grants, loans, guarantees, and other instruments to leverage private capital to finance projects in sectors such as renewable energy, healthcare, education, and infrastructure. Blended finance can also be used to finance social programs such as microfinance or health insurance.

---

49   World Economic Forum and OECD. 2015. A How-to Guide to Blended Finance. World Economic Forum. Geneva. https://www.ethicalfinancehub.org/wp-content/uploads/2018/08/WEF_Blended_Finance_How_To_Guide.pdf.

50   John E. Morton and Astri Kimball. 2013. The Case for Capital Alignment to Drive Development Outcomes. Overseas Private Investment Corporation. *The 2013 Brookings Blum Roundtable Policy Briefs*. https://www.brookings.edu/wp-content/uploads/2016/06/2013-BBR-Capital-Alignment.pdf.

Figure 2: Blended Finance Barriers and Interventions

	Life Cycle of Projects				
	Preparing	**Pioneering**	**Facilitating**	**Anchoring**	**Transitioning**
Market Segment	High upfront costs; binary risk that a project will not happen	Early-stage projects with high business model risk; high transaction costs	Sectorial or project risks; returns below commercial rates	Macro or sectorial risks; liquidity, refinancing, and exit risks	Lack of local market knowledge and deal pipeline; inefficient markets
Public Sector Role	Funds upfront costs and activities reducing uncertainty, creating transparency, and building a pipeline of bankable projects	Little to no return expectations and absorbs costs, reduces business model risk and provides advisory services; can defer rights or enhance private returns	Takes a subordinate position with higher risk or provides low-cost leverage to enable private capital to meet their risk-return thresholds	Signaling effect and "stamp of approval" by achieving "first-close" or demonstrating viability to "crowd-in" private funds	Exit mature and sizeable investments that provide a pipeline for commercial actors
Direct Funding	Grants, repayable grants, highly flexible debt	Grants, repayable grants, junior equity, flexible debt	Equity, flexible debt	Market rate debt, equity	Market rate debt, equity

Technical assistance (technical/operational expertise): Advisory or preparatory services, assistance, and training to facilitate private investment in high-impact projects and enterprises to supplement the capacity of investees and more generally, lower the transaction costs

Risk underwriting (capital preservation): Risk reduction tools that fully or partially protect the investor against various forms of risk, effectively reducing their risk of capital losses

Market incentives (results-based financing and/or price guarantees): Guarantees of future payments contingent on performance in exchange for up-front investment in new or distressed markets, or to stimulate innovation around new products and services

Source: World Economic Forum, 2015.

Key Stakeholders

- Provider of junior equity, subordinated debt, or first loss capital
- Preferred equity and/or debt investors
- Fund manager
- Investee
- Provider of guarantee

Financing Model Framework

Blended finance can be provided by using a number of alternative financing approaches either as tools to facilitate capital inflows through **supporting mechanisms** (grants, guarantees) or as complementary **direct funding** (grants, equity, debt), depending on the type of capital needed at various stages of the investment life cycle (Table 3).

Table 3: Blended Finance Instruments

Grants	A financial award with no expected repayment or compensation over a fixed period of time
Guarantees	Protection from various forms of risk intended against capital losses for investors
Debt	Money lent for repayment at a later date, usually with interest.
	• Market rate debt, when rates and terms are determined based on capital markets prices and tenors, but can be subordinate to senior debt (i.e., mezzanine)
	• Flexible (concessional) debt, with favorable terms or rates for the borrower relative to market pricing
Equity	Ownership in a company—value determined at time of investment
	• Junior equity, accepts higher risk for lower financial returns in exchange for social, environmental, and economic impact, typically in a position to take the first losses

Source: World Economic Forum, 2015.

Blended finance aims to encourage investment and finance by enabling acceptable levels of risk-taking without disrupting normal market function, rather than providing excessive subsidies to private capital or completely eliminating risk. This is achieved by leveraging the willingness of development finance and philanthropic funders to assume greater risk exposure and accept non-commercial returns in exchange for development impact. One way to accomplish this is through a partial credit guarantee, which limits downside losses and improves the project's creditworthiness, thereby reducing the required level of risk for other investors. Pilots and project preparation facilities also help make projects more financially viable by offsetting high up-front transaction costs and reducing uncertainty around operational feasibility, which can attract new investors.

Based on a sample of blended finance transactions, the average mobilization ratio for concessionary finance to commercial capital is 3:1. It will be difficult to achieve this level of investment multiples initially, but blended finance will be able to provide adequate opportunities to "tip the scales" and be a game changer by enabling investment in new asset classes like infrastructure debt. The expected returns on blended finance vehicles range between 10% and 20% for institutional investors.

Multilateral development banks (MDBs) and development finance institutions (DFIs) play a key role in developing local capital markets by providing both direct and indirect support through their lending and technical assistance programs. They facilitate transactions through concessional financing (grants, low-interest loans, mezzanine debt, and other forms of financial support) to support blended finance projects. Direct financing is provided to local companies to help crowd-in private capital participation in the form of equity or debt investments. Technical assistance is also provided to attract private capital to these projects, as well as to assist with the structuring of the deals. The MDBs and DFIs also support local companies in accessing international capital markets by providing assistance on listing on stock exchanges, fundraising activities such as equity and bond issuance, and the development of local credit rating agencies and other financial intermediaries.

Critical Success Factors

- **Crowding-in and minimum concessionality.** Concessional finance crowds-in sustainable private investments if it is structured as an additionality to fill the gap in the overall financing that allows private projects to be financed commercially. The concessionality embedded in a financing package should not be greater than necessary to attract the required investment and maximize the leverage of private funding.[51]

- **High impact and commercial viability.** Impact achieved by each operation should aim to be commercially viable with a clear exit strategy on achieving financial sustainability. Blended finance should be designed to increase the mobilization of commercial finance and as driver to maximize development outcomes and impact.

- **Reinforcing markets.** Blended finance should address market failures effectively and efficiently minimize the risk of market distortion or crowding out of private finance. The phenomenon known as crowding out takes place when development funders invest in a project that could have secured complete private sector financing without any assistance from the public sector.

- **Promoting high standards.** Blended finance should promote adherence to high standards, including areas of corporate governance, environmental impact, integrity, transparency, and disclosure.[52] Transparency is particularly important when development finance and philanthropic funds are used to lower cost of capital and leverage private investments. Development and implementing agencies and/or bodies have to be accountable for the resources, have robust monitoring, and put systems in place to evaluate interventions on predefined metrics and performance indicators.

- **Focusing on national priorities and effective partnerships.** Blended finance mechanisms designed to support national priorities can promote an enabling environment for developing efficient local financial markets.[53] Stakeholders may be enabled to participate according to their investment and commercial objectives, thus creating effective partnerships based on balanced distribution of risk.

- **Potentially viable and bankable projects.** A pipeline of projects should be developed that can be scaled, and which offer investors cash flows in addition to demonstrating economic and social impact. Identifying risks and implementing blended finance mitigating solutions will attract and match the risk appetite of potential investors.

Case Studies

Several successful ASEAN+3 regional case studies demonstrate the functionality and scope of the blended finance approach. The Japan ASEAN Women Empowerment Fund (JAWEF) is a good example as it supports women entrepreneurs, thus fulfilling some of the SDGs. In ASEAN countries and others, the equity fund provides investments and loans to those microfinance institutions which support women entrepreneurs. A three-tiered blended finance structure mobilizes institutional investors to new areas through risk sharing. It leverages a first loss tranche and additional layer of mezzanine capital, provided on varying concessional terms to attract institutional investors to the senior tranche. As the first two tiers absorb losses before the other tiers, the risk is reduced for higher-level investors. The fund has raised $241 million and its investors include the Japan Bank for International Cooperation (JBIC), Japan International Cooperation Agency (JICA), Sumitomo Life Insurance Company, and the Sasakawa Peace Foundation. It has provided finance to over 250,000 microentrepreneurs by 2019 and JAWEF has helped in achieving financial inclusion.[54]

[51] DFI Working Group. 2018. *DFI Working Group on Blended Concessional Finance for Private Sector Projects: Joint Report Update.* https://www.adb.org/sites/default/files/institutional-document/457741/dfi-blended-concessional-fiance-report.pdf.

[52] *Blended Finance at IFC, Scaling up Private Sector Finance; Fact Sheet;* 14-15December, 2017. Vaasa.

[53] OECD. 2018. *DAC Blended Finance Principles for Unlocking Commercial Finance for the Sustainable Development Goals.* https://www.oecd.org/dac/financing-sustainable-development/blended-finances-principles/.

[54] Convergence Blending Global Finance. 2020. *Case Study: Japan ASEAN Women Empowerment Fund.* March. https://www.convergence.finance/resource/japan-asean-women-empowerment-fund-case-study/view.

In 2021, Cambodia's Ministry of Economy and Finance launched a $200 million credit guarantee scheme to provide access to loans for small and medium-sized enterprises (SMEs) to ensure business continuity and recovery during the COVID-19 pandemic. The Business Recovery Guarantee Scheme under the ministry's implementing arm—Credit Guarantee Corporation of Cambodia—provided collateral up to 70%–80%, thus de-risking the loan for private financial institutional lenders and reducing the contributory collateral amount required from SMEs.[55]

The International Finance Corporation (IFC) is an MDB that provides financial and technical assistance to private sector companies and projects in developing countries. In 2020, the IFC acted as an anchor investor in a green bond issuance of $561 million by the Indian renewable energy company Continuum Green Energy. The IFC provided a $200 million loan to the company, which was used to finance the issuance of the green bond, and it also subscribed to 10% of the bond issuance which further crowded-in private capital and resulted in the bond being oversubscribed seven times. This provided the company with the capital it needed to expand its renewable energy portfolio. The IFC also provided technical assistance to the company to support the issuance of the green bond, and to ensure that the project conformed with international standards for sustainability. This helped increase investor confidence in the project and attract more private capital.

Blended finance can also be provided as development guarantees that ensure that a subscribed project is aligned to the SDGs. The Sarulla Geothermal Power Project Indonesia was developed to reduce fossil fuel dependency by generating renewable energy. This infrastructure project, with co-financing of $1,170 million is one of the largest geothermal plants in the world that has been designed to save 1.3 million metric tons of carbon dioxide and provide local employment. The Government of Indonesia provided a 20-year Business Viability Guarantee letter and this, together with the risk guarantee and $492 million loan from JBIC, has enabled the project to mobilize co-financing from ADB; Mizuho Bank, Ltd.; The Bank of Tokyo-Mitsubishi UFJ, Ltd.; Sumitomo Mitsui Banking Corporation; Tokyo branches of Société Générale Bank; ING Bank N.V., and National Australia Bank Limited.[56]

GuarantCo is a DFI that provides partial credit guarantees for infrastructure projects in developing countries and was designed to develop blended finance solutions by receiving first loss equity contributions from public funds. Based on this funding, GuarantCo can provide guarantees up to three times the value of the equity contribution which, in turn, can, on average, mobilize up to four times private sector investment into infrastructure projects. Thus with $1 of public funding, GuarantCo can mobilize as much as $12 of private sector financing and given its high credit ratings (Fitch Rating AA- and Moody's A1), it has been successful in extending the tenor of the loans beyond the local capital market norms.[57] In 2020, GuarantCo provided a partial credit guarantee to EVNFinance, a Viet Nam renewable energy company, for its first onshore local currency verified green bond issuance. The guarantee helped to reduce the risk of the bond and attract more private capital, thus helping EVNFinance to finance its renewable energy projects. The bond was invested by institutional investors including Manulife and AIA. GuarantCo provided a partial guarantee of $50 million to a $75 million bond issuance which helped to reduce transaction costs and increase investor confidence by allowing EVNFinance to access capital at a lower cost. The guarantee covered up to 90% of the bond's principal amount and up to 50% of the interest payments for the first 5 years of the bond. It provided EVNFinance with access to lower interest rates and longer maturities. This helped to reduce the cost of capital for EVNFinance and attract more private capital, thus allowing the company to expand its renewable energy portfolio.

Appendix case studies 1 (Africa Agriculture and Trade Investment Fund) and 2 (Advanced Market Commitment) demonstrate the flexibility and the adaptability of blended finance approaches to different sectors, challenges, and scale at a global and regional level.

---

[55]   Centre for Asian Philanthropy and Society. *DECODED: Blended Finance in Action in Asia.* Hong Kong, China. https://wordpress.caps.org/topics/decoded/.

[56]   Information and data sourced from: JBIC. *Project Financing and Political Risk Guarantee for Sarulla Power Plant Project in Indonesia.* https://www.jbic.go.jp/en/information/press/press-2013/0331-19526.html and Mizuho. Geothermal Power Projects. https://thedocs.worldbank.org/en/doc/877101532398187778-0090022018/render/072018CIFSeminarHiroakiKanazawa.pdf.

[57]   OECD/ UN Capital Development Fund. 2020. *Blended Finance in the Least Developed Countries 2020: Supporting a Resilient COVID-19 Recovery.* OECD Publishing. Paris. https://www.oecd-ilibrary.org/development/blended-finance-in-the-least-developed-countries_57620d04-en.

4.4.2 Asset Recycling

📋 *Key Objective*

The key objectives of asset recycling are to monetize existing assets (by selling or leasing), fund future infrastructure developments with the goal of preventing additional public debt, and maintain or enhance current infrastructure provision.

💲 *Description of the Financing Model*

Asset recycling consists of three main components:

(i) review of public assets and identifying potential assets for monetization;

(ii) converting current infrastructure assets into liquid funds through the sale or lease to private entities; and

(iii) utilizing the proceeds obtained from the monetization of assets to invest in the development of new infrastructure.

Box 2: Australia—Asset Recycling
Australia was the first to implement a policy in 2014 to encourage state and local governments to engage in infrastructure asset recycling. The federal government offered grants of up to 15% of the proceeds from lease of existing facilities if the state or local government committed to using those proceeds for new infrastructure.
Net A\$20 billion (\$14.6 billion)* was realized from leases of existing infrastructure, generating an additional A\$6 billion (\$4.4 billion) in federal incentive grants. One example was the New South Wales government that leased electrical transmission system to a private partner and reinvested the proceeds and the federal grant in the Sydney Metro and other new road and rail projects.
* Conversion rate: \$1 = A\$1.37.   Sources: 1. US Department of Transportation, Federal Highway Administration, Center for Innovative Finance Support. Asset Recycling. https://www.fhwa.dot.gov/ipd/value_capture/defined/asset_recycling.aspx.   2. Marsh and McLennan Companies. 2018. *Infrastructure Asset Recycling*. https://www.marshmclennan.com/content/dam/oliver-wyman/v2/publications/infrastructure-asset-recycling-grc.pdf.

🏭 *Sector and Project Fit*

Asset recycling may not always be an appropriate approach to satisfy a country's infrastructure demands, and its adoption should entail an assessment of the government's financial capacity and future infrastructure requirements. One of the prerequisites for implementing this approach is that the government must possess an adequate amount of public assets that can be sold or leased. There may be national security concerns over privatizing certain assets to foreign investors.[58]

Which assets could be recycled?

(i) Brownfield assets provide an opportunity for the private sector to avoid the risks related to the construction phase and instead concentrate on maximizing the operational efficiency of the assets.

(ii) Unused or underutilized assets (e.g., land, facilities, etc.) may be recycled to improve returns.

(iii) Recycling of operating assets in need of a major overhaul or maintenance, where the private sector can bring significant improvement, can create higher economic return on the asset.

---

[58] Marsh and McLennan Companies. 2018. *Infrastructure Asset Recycling*. https://www.marshmclennan.com/content/dam/oliver-wyman/v2/publications/infrastructure-asset-recycling-grc.pdf.

Which assets should be invested in?

Proceeds received from asset monetization should be reinvested in the infrastructure sector and not be used to pay off public debt or social subsidy schemes. Proceeds should be targeted to infrastructure assets with greater social need or which yield higher economic returns.

Key Stakeholders

- **Government** (public) is responsible for identifying suitable assets for recycling and reinvestment.
- **Investor** (private) participates in sale or lease of asset from the government.
- **General public** (ultimate user of asset) engages in communication with the government on the benefits of such an arrangement.

Financing Model Framework

The asset recycling process is exhibited in Figure 3.

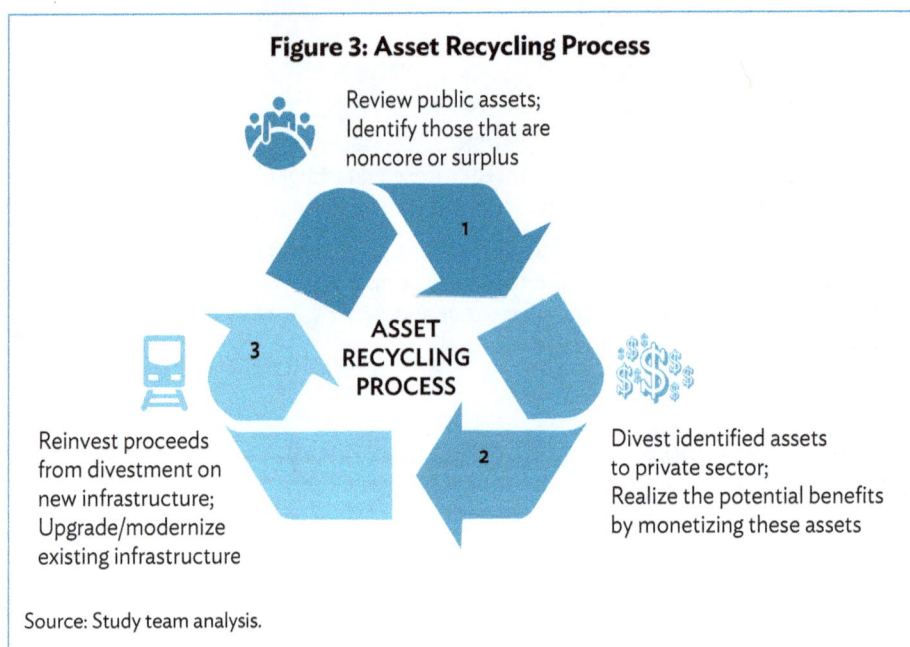

Figure 3: Asset Recycling Process

Review public assets; Identify those that are noncore or surplus

1

ASSET RECYCLING PROCESS

3

2

Reinvest proceeds from divestment on new infrastructure; Upgrade/modernize existing infrastructure

Divest identified assets to private sector; Realize the potential benefits by monetizing these assets

Source: Study team analysis.

Critical Success Factors

- **Clear policies on selecting suitable assets for recycling.** Efforts to identify assets for recycling will be more effective if there is a comprehensive life-cycle inventory of all public infrastructure assets. Thereafter, a consistent evaluation criterion should be applied when reviewing existing public assets. Governments can consider creating a register for critical infrastructure assets (e.g., electricity, ports, water and telecommunication related assets) to mitigate national security risks.
- **Ability to unlock the value of noncore and surplus assets.** For asset recycling to be viable, there must be significant private sector demand for the targeted assets, which should ensure that the sale or lease revenue is in line with the fair market value. If the returns do not justify the agreement, the government will be constrained in the reinvestment process, and public's perception of the sale or lease is likely to turn negative. Competition and a well-designed tender process can help to enhance returns.
- **Willingness of the public to accept private investment and management of infrastructure.** There are several factors that affect the successful implementation of an asset recycling initiative, including the willingness of the public to accept private investment and management of infrastructure. A crucial step

before launching such a scheme is to engage in regular public–private consultations. This dialogue is vital from a government perspective to garner strong public support and to ensure that there is sufficient private sector interest to generate a competitive bid. The public perception of the initiative can be managed through transparent terms and conditions that a prospective investor must meet if successful in their bid. These conditions should be defined when the asset is publicly identified for recycling and should include clear protection for government employees and end-users.[59]

- **Adequate oversight mechanisms over long-term leases.** If long-term lease agreements are a prerequisite to attracting private capital, public agencies will need technical capacity and expertise to incorporate performance metrics into the agreement and exercise oversight so as to ensure public benefit and protection of the public interest throughout the term of the lease.

- **Commitment to re-invest proceeds** (from the asset divestment) to develop new infrastructure or upgrade existing assets. For example, dedicated special purpose vehicles (SPVs) can be established to manage the proceeds and reinvestment.

- **Plan for change management** during the transition period as the organization structure, reward system, and work culture will change with new management and ownership.

Case Study

The privatization of the Manila Electric Company (MERALCO) by the Government of the Philippines was part of a larger effort to reduce the country's public debt. The government sold its shares in the company, raising approximately $1.1 billion in proceeds. The funds were used to pay down existing public debt, while allowing MERALCO to continue to provide reliable electricity services. The privatization also allowed MERALCO to pursue new investments and expand its reach to more communities in the country. In addition, the public was able to benefit from the sale of the shares through the reinvestment of the proceeds into infrastructure projects, such as the construction of new power plants, transmission lines, and distribution networks.

Asset recycling has been successfully implemented in Asia by both Indonesia and India in the transport sector (toll roads structured either as PPP or as state-owned enterprises). The Government of Indonesia is planning to monetize its cash flow positive operating assets to finance greenfield assets. A limited concession scheme (LCS) will provide investors with a 50-year concession to maintain and operate the toll roads in return for upfront payments that will be utilized to build new infrastructure. The LCS is loosely based on India's toll–operate–transfer mechanism that is detailed in the Appendix.

4.4.3 Asset Securitization

Key Objective

Asset securitization releases funds for public sector banks by converting their infrastructure assets into marketable securities to sell in secondary capital markets (including to institutional investors). It is also a means of transferring risk, and facilitates marketing of securities to investors with different risk appetites and investment time horizons.

Financing Model

- Asset securitization is the transformation of illiquid assets into a security—an instrument that is issued and can be traded in a capital market.

- Loans or other financial claims are assigned or sold to a third party, typically a special-purpose company or trust. This SPV, in turn, issues one or more debt instruments—asset-backed securities whose interest and principal payments are dependent on the cash flows from the underlying assets.

---

[59]   Footnote 58.

- Securitization of assets can lower risk, create liquidity to fund infrastructure assets, lower asset load on the balance sheet, and improve economic efficiency.

Project finance collateralized debt obligation is a type of structured finance product that combines the cash flows from a portfolio of project finance loans into a single security (see Box 3).

Box 3: Project Finance Collateralized Debt Obligation

A common structure for securitizing assets in **power, oil and gas, and energy** infrastructure projects is a project finance collateralized debt obligation (PF-CDO). A PF-CDO is collateralized by the cash flows generated by the underlying project finance loans. Investors in the PF-CDO receive payments from the cash flows generated by the projects, which are used to pay interest and principal on the PF-CDO. The PF-CDO may also be structured with various tranches, each with different levels of risk and return. The PF-CDOs provide a way for investors to gain exposure to a diversified portfolio of project finance loans, which can be an attractive investment for those seeking yield and diversification. The PF-CDOs are complex and may be subject to a variety of risks, including credit risk, liquidity risk, and market risk. The earliest PF-CDOs were cash securitization structures, in which the special purpose vehicle purchased loans as collateral for the CDO note issues. Project Funding Corp. I, sponsored by Credit Suisse First, was one of the earliest such cash PF-CDOs. Project Funding Corp. I issued about $617 million in debt and equity securities, collateralized by a portfolio of about 40 loans made primarily to United States infrastructure projects. It closed on 5 March 1998. The PF-CDO transactions rated by Moody's are a relatively well-structured finance asset class that invests in a range of project finance assets including public-private or private finance initiatives, regulated utilities, renewable energy projects, and large infrastructure sectors across Australia, the European Union, North America, and the United Kingdom.

Source: Asian Development Bank. 2017. *Securitization in India: Managing Capital Constraints and Creating Liquidity to Fund Infrastructure Assets.* Manila. http://dx.doi.org/10.22617/TCS179100-2.

Sector and Project Fit

While residential mortgage loans provide the core of the global asset-backed securities market, a wide range of other financial claims can and have been securitized. The US subprime mortgage crisis seriously dented investor confidence in this investment product following the increased issuance of mortgage-backed securities, interest-only lending, high interest rates, and the consequent fall in value of the underlying securitized assets. However, in principle, any income-producing asset with an adequate performance record and some diversification of credit risk can be securitized. Suitable assets are those separable from the originator and amenable to rigorous credit and statistical analysis.[60]

Key Stakeholders

- **Asset originator** (e.g., banks, finance companies, and corporations). The original lender and seller of the infrastructure assets.
- **Special purpose vehicle.** The entity that issues marketable securities.
- **Capital market investors.** Banks, insurance companies, mutual funds, pension funds, etc., that are the purchasers of securities.
- **Arranger.** Investment banks that are responsible for structuring the securities; they coordinate with other parties (such as investors, rating agencies, and legal counsel) to execute the transaction successfully.
- **Rating agency.** Analyzes risks associated with each transaction, monitors the performance of the transactions until maturity, and takes appropriate rating actions.
- **Credit enhancement provider.** Typically, the originator, as a facility that covers any shortfall in pool collections in relation to investor payouts. The enhancement can also be provided by a third party for a fee.

---

60 I.H. Giddy. 2000. *Asset Securitization in Asia.* New York: New York University.

⚙ *Financing Model Framework*

The asset securitization process, together with stakeholder responsibilities, is shown in Figure 4.

Figure 4: How Securitization Works

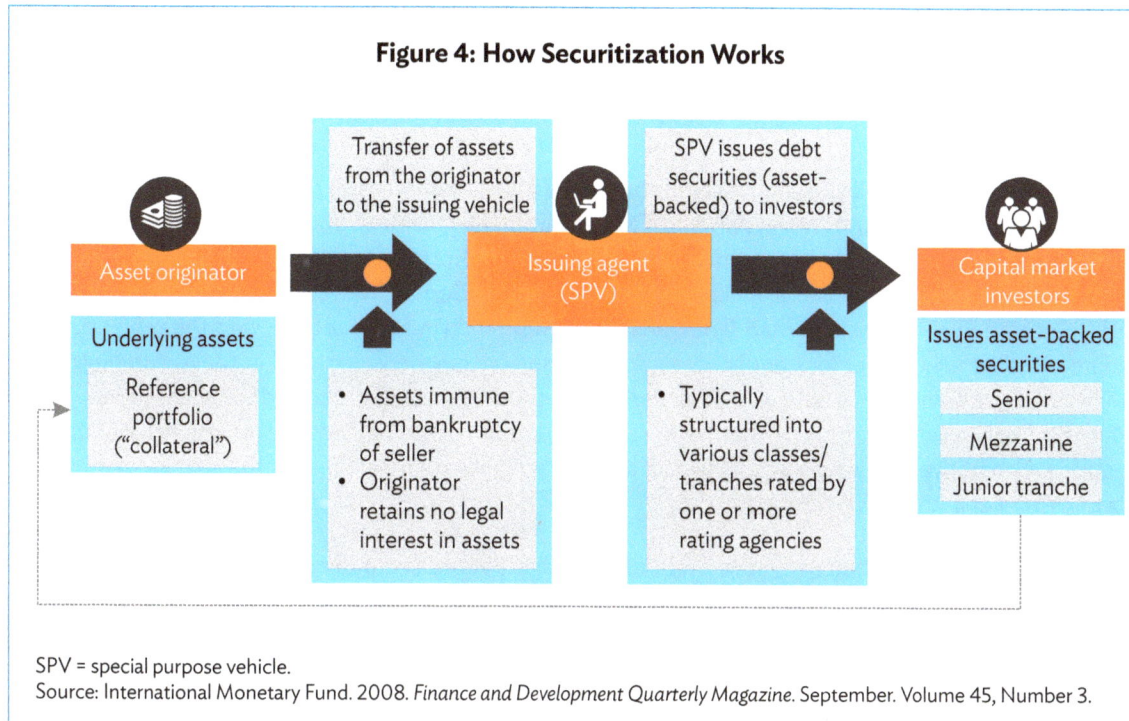

Transfer of assets from the originator to the issuing vehicle

SPV issues debt securities (asset-backed) to investors

Asset originator

Issuing agent (SPV)

Capital market investors

Underlying assets

Reference portfolio ("collateral")

- Assets immune from bankruptcy of seller
- Originator retains no legal interest in assets

- Typically structured into various classes/ tranches rated by one or more rating agencies

Issues asset-backed securities

Senior

Mezzanine

Junior tranche

SPV = special purpose vehicle.
Source: International Monetary Fund. 2008. *Finance and Development Quarterly Magazine.* September. Volume 45, Number 3.

👍 *Critical Success Factors*

- **Asset selection.** Assets selected should have the following identified attributes:
  - » operational assets, with a minimum of 1 year of stabilized operations, to provide adequate comfort to institutional investors;
  - » homogenous assets, in terms of the credit risk, tenure, and payment profile to ensure that payments to investors of securitized paper are made on time; and
  - » adequately sized asset pool, to ensure the marketability of a smaller pool and the built-in protection provided by a larger, more diversified pool, thus balancing risk and return trade-offs.
- **Risk management.** Since the SPV is normally structured to have no assets or business other than holding the securitized assets, the principal focus is on cash flows from assets. Early involvement of credit rating agencies in the risk-management process is essential to avoid defaults since investors rely heavily on their assessments. In addition, it is critical to manage reputation risk arising from negative public opinion; strategic risk arising from adverse business decisions including competition; transactional risk arising from issues such as internal controls, collections, information systems, reporting, and employee integrity—all associated with service delivery; and compliance risk arising from nonadherence or nonconformance with laws, rules, and ethical practices.[61]
- **Credit enhancement mechanism.** Securitization of infrastructure assets requires adequate support in the form of external credit enhancement to match the ratings and risk expectations of institutional investors.

---

[61]   Office of the Comptroller of the Currency, US Department of the Treasury. *Categories of Risk.*

- **Institutional mechanisms.** Monitoring and oversight mechanisms for the underlying asset pool should be provided by a third party to assure independent reporting to investors. There should also be an appropriate legal and tax framework developed that facilitates asset sale and separation and protects both issuers and investors.
- **Secondary market.** Given the long-term nature of infrastructure assets, a secondary market for securitization must be promoted to provide investors with viable exit options.

Case Studies

In 2018, the governments of Malaysia and Thailand completed a cross-border asset securitization transaction involving the securitization of a portfolio of Malaysian and Thai government-guaranteed loans. The portfolio was valued at approximately $2.2 billion and was structured as an Islamic securitization in accordance with Shariah principles. It was jointly arranged by a syndicate of banks, including Malayan Banking Berhad, Maybank Investment Bank Berhad, and Standard Chartered Bank Malaysia Berhad. The transaction was issued in two tranches, with the senior tranche rated AA- by Fitch Ratings and the junior tranche rated A+. The senior tranche was issued in Malaysian ringgit and Thai baht, while the junior tranche was issued in US dollar. The securitization was structured to meet the requirements of Malaysian and Thai investors to provide them with stable and predictable cash flows. This was the first cross-border asset securitization between Malaysia and Thailand, and was a significant milestone for the development of the asset securitization market in the ASEAN region.

In April 2017, Singapore launched its first residential mortgage-backed securities (RMBS) issue in the region, with a total value of S$1.5 billion ($1.1 billion).[62] This was the largest RMBS issuance in Southeast Asia, and was backed by the mortgage payments from a portfolio of residential mortgages originated by the Housing and Development Board of Singapore. The RMBS were structured and issued by DBS Bank and arranged by the Monetary Authority of Singapore. It was issued in four tranches with maturities of 3, 5, 7, and 9 years. Each tranche had a different weighted average life (WAL), with the 3-year tranche having a WAL of 2.14 years, the 5-year tranche having a WAL of 4.14 years, the 7-year tranche having a WAL of 6.14 years, and the 9-year tranche having a WAL of 8.14 years. The RMBS included a senior tranche, a mezzanine tranche, and a subordinate tranche. The senior tranche accounted for 70%, the mezzanine tranche accounted for 20%, while the subordinate tranche accounted for 10% of the total issuance with a fixed coupon rate of 3%, 4%, and 5% respectively, for the three tranches. The transaction was structured with an expected loss coverage ratio of 95% for the senior tranche and 90% for the mezzanine and subordinate tranches. The RMBS were also issued with a credit enhancement of 10% in the form of overcollateralization, meaning that the total value of the underlying mortgages was 10% higher than the total value of the RMBS. The 10% overcollateralization was provided by the Government of Singapore through a reserve fund that was established to provide additional protection to investors in the event of default. A liquidity facility of 2.5% was provided by DBS Bank and was designed to support the RMBS in the event of a crunch.

Appendix case study 4 (Clifford Capital Infrastructure Take-Out Facility) provides a detailed explanation of how a finance and debt structuring entity was able to successfully put together a portfolio of 30 projects with stable cash flows and take them to the financial markets through the issuance of Notes. A 10% first loss was borne by the issuer. This was Asia's first securitization of project finance and infrastructure loans and was a step forward in recognizing infrastructure as an asset class. It also released debt financing of the banks, thus contributing to additional liquidity and capital adequacy.

---

[62] Conversion rate: $1 = S$1.35.

4.4.4 Convertible Debt Structures

📑 Key Objective

The key objective of convertible debt structures is to improve access to local financing and to build local lending capacity. These structures are employed to tackle issues of lack of track record, technology standards, and comparable benchmarks faced by local financial institutions in financing infrastructure projects. They also provide an opportunity for venture capital and institutional investors to take a stake in start-up or capital-intensive projects with a medium- to long-term gestation period and a positive risk-adjusted return prior to its market capitalization.

🗓 Description of the Financing Model

Convertible debt structures are broadly categorized as convertible loans and convertible grants.

Convertible loans

- can be converted to equity at certain milestones or pre-agreed terms and
- help to lower cost of capital by providing contingent claims to capture equity upside.

Convertible grants

- can be converted into loans at certain milestones and
- provide safety buffer for project developers (beneficiaries of public finance support) should desired outcome not materialize.

Originating from US railway firms that needed an inexpensive way to finance mass expansion of the rail network, convertible debts are currently issued by a large variety of companies, including those with large market capitalization. The US and European markets combined have about 75% of the global convertible debt market.

🏭 Sector and Project Fit

Convertible debts are subordinate classes of debt used to provide credit enhancement for infrastructure projects and are employed to mitigate project risks in the following scenarios:

(i) If a project is delayed or cancelled, the project company can avoid bankruptcy since the loan can be converted to equity.

(ii) During the fundraising stage of a project, issuing convertible debt rather than equity can reduce tax deductions, which lowers the cost of capital.

(iiii) In a low interest rate environment, bond-like characteristics of a convertible debt could benefit the investors by generating excess yield. In addition, the convertible debt would expect to increase in value over time due to the growth potential from an increasingly valuable equity conversion option. This results in returns in excess of the equivalent traditional bonds with no such optionality.

👥 Key Stakeholders

- **Special purpose vehicle.** The entity that issues convertible debt.
- **Capital market investors.** Banks, insurance companies, mutual funds, pension funds, etc., that are the purchasers of convertible debt.
- **Arranger.** Investment banks responsible for structuring the securities, which coordinate with other parties (such as investors, rating agencies, and legal counsel) to execute the transaction successfully.

⚙ Financing Model Framework

The basic difference between convertible loans and convertible grants is shown in Figure 5.

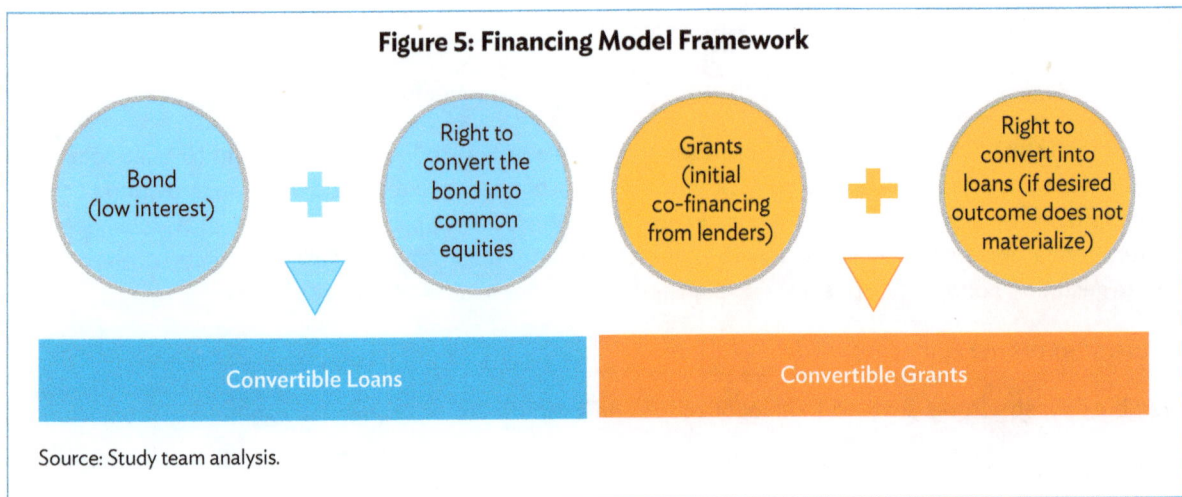

Figure 5: Financing Model Framework

Bond (low interest) + Right to convert the bond into common equities → Convertible Loans

Grants (initial co-financing from lenders) + Right to convert into loans (if desired outcome does not materialize) → Convertible Grants

Source: Study team analysis.

Critical Success Factors

- **Determining the event that triggers the conversion.** Events such as revenue threshold, financing threshold, or business milestone must be agreed upon between entrepreneurs and investors.

- **Determining the conversion rate.** Depending on the project, if the conversion rate is set too low or a discount is not given, investors may not be interested to exercise the option. If the conversion rate is set too high, project owners' equity stake may be over-diluted.

- **Determining what will happen to the investment if conversion event does not occur.** If debt is not converted to equity, it could remain as debt or additional clauses could be included to attract investors.

Case Study

In Indonesia, a large government-backed convertible debt structure was established by PT Pertamina, the state-owned oil and gas company, to help finance infrastructure projects in 2019. The structure involved a 10-year debt instrument with a coupon rate of 6%. The convertible debt could be converted into equity at the option of the holder at any time during the 10-year period. The conversion rate was based on a 20% discount to the market price of the government's preferred equity. The convertible debt structure was designed to provide the government with additional financing options while also providing investors with an attractive return. The size of the issue was Rp12 trillion ($8.3 billion).[63] The structure was designed to provide the government with access to alternative sources of financing for infrastructure projects and was also seen as a way to mitigate the risk of default, as the government was backing the debt. The convertible debt structure was oversubscribed, with more than Rp15 trillion ($10.4 billion) raised in total. The proceeds were utilized for infrastructure projects, such as the construction of roads and bridges, and the development of telecommunications networks. As of March 2021, approximately Rp4 trillion ($2.8 billion) of debt has been converted into equity.

Appendix case study 5 on Geothermal Development Facility provides grants to developers for exploratory drilling, thus offering an incentive for transitioning to a renewable non-fossil fuel energy source and de-risking the developer. If successful, the grant is converted to a loan and the developer repays 80% of the amount received.

---

63   Conversion rate: $1 = Rp14,460.

4.4.5   *Municipal Bonds*

📇 *Key Objective*

The key objective of municipal bonds is to secure funding for public projects (such as schools, roads, utilities, and other community necessities) in a more cost-effective manner than conventional project financing options such as bank loans. Municipalities with strong balance sheet positions and robust project cash flows can leverage this financing method.

🔖 *Description of the Financing Model*

- **A municipal bond** is a debt liability issued by a state or local government, or one of its agencies or authorities (including cities, towns, villages, counties, special districts, and other political subdivisions—collectively referred to as "municipal entities").[64]

- During the **typical lifespan of a bond, known as its maturity**, the issuer is required to repay the bondholders the principal amount plus interest. The payment is usually paid from current tax collections or specific revenue sources.

- **Yields for municipal bonds** vary depending on the tenor and amounts being raised, as well as the currency in which the bonds have been issued.

- Municipal securities have **varying maturities**, ranging from short-term, which can be just a few months to 2 years, to 30 years or more. Longer maturities are determined based on the expected lifespan of public assets.

- A primary feature of most municipal securities is that **interest payments received by investors purchasing the bonds are typically exempt from federal and often state and local income taxes**. Hence, investors would be willing to accept lower interest rates compared to taxable corporate bonds. State and local governments, therefore, enjoy lower costs for borrowing money.

🏛️ *Sector and Project Fit*

Bonds are particularly suitable for funding municipal infrastructure projects. They are typically used for public projects and not for projects directly benefiting the private sector or for partnerships with the private sector to build, design, operate, or maintain an infrastructure asset.[65]

👥 *Key Stakeholders*

- **Investors.** Bond purchasers (pension funds, institutional investors); private/commercial banks; government development banks, municipal development funds, bond banks, etc.; and international development banks/donors (e.g., the International Finance Corporation)

- **Market facilitators.** Credit rating agencies (e.g., Moody's and S&P Global Ratings); financial and other advisors; and project preparation facilities (e.g., C40 Cities Finance Facility)

- **Risk bearers/mitigators.** Insurers, credit enhancement facilities (e.g., United States Agency for International Development)

- **Borrowers.** Municipality, urban utility (e.g., water utility)

⚙️ *Financing Model Framework*

The steps involved in the issuance of the municipal bonds are shown in Figure 6.

---

64   Municipal Securities Rulemaking Board. 2017. *Municipal Securities: Financing the Nation's Infrastructure.* Washington, DC. https://www.cdfa.net/cdfa/cdfaweb.nsf/0/77658F1C2EFBD906882581AD005749E1/$file/MSRB-%20Municipal%20Bond%20 Infrastructure%20Finance%20with%20Comments%20on%20Tax%20Reform.pdf.

65   R. Puentes and P. Sabol. 2015. *Building better infrastructure with better bonds.* Brookings. https://www.brookings.edu/research/building-better-infrastructure-with-better-bonds/.

Figure 6: Financing Model

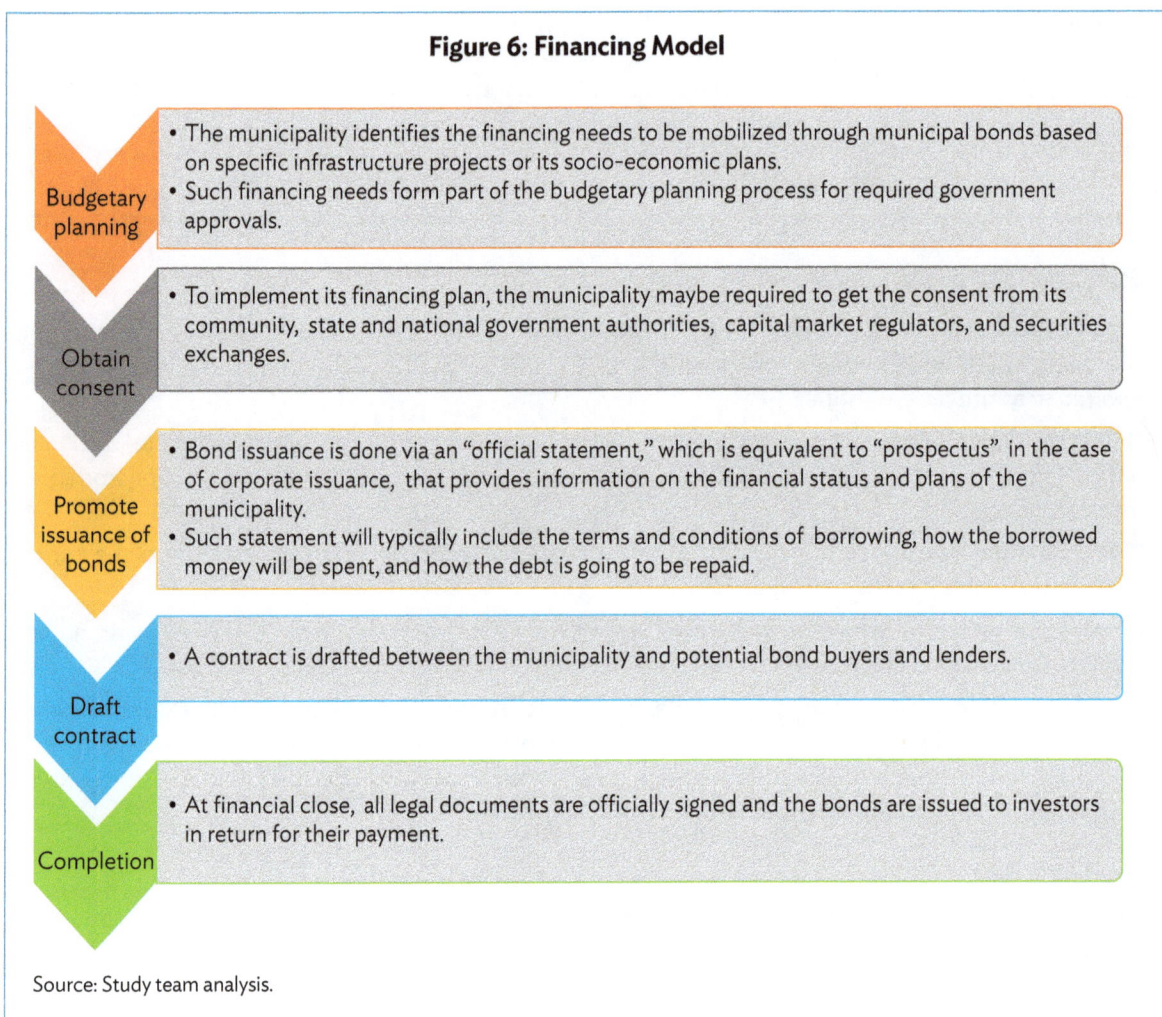

Budgetary planning
- The municipality identifies the financing needs to be mobilized through municipal bonds based on specific infrastructure projects or its socio-economic plans.
- Such financing needs form part of the budgetary planning process for required government approvals.

Obtain consent
- To implement its financing plan, the municipality maybe required to get the consent from its community, state and national government authorities, capital market regulators, and securities exchanges.

Promote issuance of bonds
- Bond issuance is done via an "official statement," which is equivalent to "prospectus" in the case of corporate issuance, that provides information on the financial status and plans of the municipality.
- Such statement will typically include the terms and conditions of borrowing, how the borrowed money will be spent, and how the debt is going to be repaid.

Draft contract
- A contract is drafted between the municipality and potential bond buyers and lenders.

Completion
- At financial close, all legal documents are officially signed and the bonds are issued to investors in return for their payment.

Source: Study team analysis.

👍 Critical Success Factors

- **Favorable financial market conditions.** The number and structure of participants, values and preferences of participants, information technology, transaction costs, and regulation would contribute to a successful implementation of the municipal bond issuance. In addition, an active secondary market would allow buyers an option to sell the bond before maturity.

- **Enabling legal and regulatory frameworks.** Most municipalities have an institutional structure (consisting of laws, regulations, and conventions) that enables them to practice bond financing using municipal bonds.

- **Financial track record of municipal entities.** In order to attract investors, municipal authorities must have robust and audited financials, stable tax and revenue inflows to service dividend payments, strong corporate governance and accountability, and must obtain a credit rating.

- **Establish a robust compliance and management framework for the bond program.** Stringent requirements for public disclosure of financial information are crucial to attract investment from financial intermediaries and credit agencies, as well as to promote investor familiarity and confidence with these instruments. Credit enhancement structures, such as pooled financing arrangements and government guarantees, can be considered to lower borrowing costs.

Case Study

Malaysia has been issuing municipal bonds since the 1980s and has made a number of successful issues. A notable example was the RM2 billion ($530 million)[66] bond issue in 2016, which was structured to meet the needs of both retail and institutional investors. The bond had a 10-year maturity and was structured as a floating rate note linked to 3-month Kuala Lumpur Interbank Offered Rate. The bonds are issued in denominations of RM1,000 and are backed by the full faith and credit of the issuing local government, thus offering investors a secure investment with a fixed rate of return. The bonds usually have a maturity of 10 years and are listed on the Bursa Malaysia stock exchange. Returns from the bonds are generally exempt from income tax. The coupon rate for the 2016 RM 2 billion bond issue was 3.9%. The bonds were oversubscribed and the issue was a success, providing the Malaysian government with much-needed funds to finance its infrastructure projects.

The Pune Municipal Bond is an excellent example (Appendix case study 6) of how the organization, through a series of well-documented actions involving government, regulatory, and rating agencies and commercial banks successfully listed the municipal bonds on the stock exchange. This model was replicated by several other municipalities in India and has become a source of finance by leveraging future cash flows.

4.4.6 Green Bonds and Sustainable Bonds

Key Objective

Green and sustainable bonds are similar to traditional bonds in structure, risk, and returns. The prime difference between green and sustainable bonds lies in their use of proceeds or allocation of funds. Green bonds finance specific new or existing projects with dedicated positive climate and environmental benefits such as renewable energy, energy efficiency, waste water management, green buildings, pollution prevention, sustainable agriculture, fishery and forestry, protection of aquatic and terrestrial ecosystems, clean transportation, and supporting eco-friendly industries and technologies. Though the terms "green bonds" and "climate bonds" are often used coterminously, the latter are a subset of green bonds to raise funds for projects that address climate mitigation or adaptation. Sustainable bonds are not always ring-fenced to be applied toward green solutions and include projects and activities that deliver social benefits. Sustainable bonds financing extends to both green initiatives as well as social outcomes such as education, poverty reduction, public health, etc.

Green bond financing has seen growing interest from global institutional investors such as pension funds, insurance companies, and sovereign wealth funds that seek to invest in climate-smart initiatives to meet investment guidelines and provide positive risk-adjusted returns.

The ASEAN+3 sustainable finance market has significant potential to mobilize private capital to support inclusive and sustainable economic recovery. Local policy makers and regulators, in collaboration with development partners, can play a variety of roles in fostering the growth of sustainable finance. To meet the demand of investors, the region must increase the number of issuers of sustainable bonds and expand the eligible project pipeline. Development partners can play a crucial role in enhancing the technical capacity of potential issuers, financial advisors, and underwriters of sustainable bonds. As the Secretariat of the Asian Bond Markets Initiative, ADB provides technical assistance to establish the ecosystem required for the development of sustainable finance in the ASEAN+3 region.[67] It works closely with potential issuers and underwriters to provide intensive support throughout the sustainable bond issuance process by enhancing their knowledge and capacity to identify eligible projects, assets, and expenditures that meet the requirements of applicable sustainable bond principles and standards. ADB recently published a handbook on green

---

[66] Conversion rate: $1 = RM3.77.

[67] ADB. 2020. *Technical Assistance Report: Creating Ecosystems for Green Local Currency Bonds for Infrastructure Development in ASEAN+3*. Manila. https://www.adb.org/sites/default/files/project-documents/53300/53300-001-tar-en.pdf.

bond issuance, which is available in several ASEAN member languages and explains the process and critical factors to consider when issuing green bonds.[68]

With the right policies and a healthy domestic sustainable finance ecosystem, the process of issuing sustainable bonds could be streamlined, issuance costs could be reduced, and time to market shortened to enable greater pricing certainty. The presence of local green bond verifiers with in-depth knowledge of local contexts, regulations, and market practices could be a key driver for sustainable bond issuance. Local reviewers who operate in the same country, work in the same time zone, and speak the same language as issuers will help reduce issuance costs as their fees are generally lower than those charged by international reviewers. This would make it more accessible and affordable for smaller issuers as they progress on their sustainable finance bond journey. Currently, ADB is collaborating with several local green bond verifiers in the region and assisting them on pilot verifications of green bonds issued under the Climate Bond Standards.

The ASEAN Capital Markets Forum (ACMF) comprises of capital market regulators from ASEAN countries who are tasked with the primary responsibility of promoting greater integration and connectivity of regional capital markets. Recognizing the different levels of development among the ASEAN member states, the ACMF adopts a pragmatic approach to enabling countries to opt-in to join initiatives based on their market readiness. The ACMF has developed distinct guidelines based on internationally accepted principles developed by the International Capital Markets Association. The guidelines include: *ASEAN Green Bonds Standards*; *ASEAN Social Bonds Standards*; *ASEAN Sustainability Bonds Standards*; and *ASEAN Sustainability-linked Standards*.[69] The guidelines are intended to enhance transparency, consistency, and uniformity within ASEAN; contribute to the development of a new asset class; reduce due diligence; and assist investors to make informed investment decisions.

To facilitate greater issuance of sustainable bonds, the availability of standardized bond documentation that enables the issuance of sustainable bonds to professional investors in multiple jurisdictions would significantly streamline the issuance process and promote intraregional bond issuance and investment. One example is the use of the ASEAN+3 Multicurrency Bond Issuance Framework (AMBIF), a policy initiative under the Asian Bond Markets Initiative. Under this framework, an issuer from an AMBIF-participating market can issue local currency (LCY) denominated sustainable bonds in other participating markets using the same bond documentation. As AMBIF targets only professional investors, AMBIF bonds can be issued in a more flexible and timely manner because professional investors do not require the same level of investor protection as retail investors.

While some countries have implemented green bond grant programs, others might not have the financial resources to offer comparable subsidies. Instead, regulators may offer a so-called "green lane" or "sustainable lanes" without financial subsidy. This scheme can also be implemented to streamline the cross-border issuance of financial instruments and facilitate intraregional capital flows. This could shorten time to market and compensate the additional resources required for issuance of sustainable bonds.

💲 *Financing Model*

Green bonds are debt instruments where proceeds are used exclusively to fund qualifying green investments. They are the same as traditional bonds in terms of deal structure and recourse to the issuer. However, they have different requirements for reporting, auditing, and proceed allocations. Usually, green bonds must undergo third-party verification, such as from the Climate Bond Standard Board, to establish that funded projects are generating environmental benefits. The steps required to follow best practices in labeling bonds are shown in Figure 7.

---

[68] ADB. 2021. *Detailed Guidance for Issuing Green Bonds in Developing Countries*. Manila. https://asianbondsonline.adb.org/green-bonds/pdf/green-bonds-factsheet-en.pdf.

[69] ACMF. Sustainable Finance. https://www.theacmf.org/initiatives/sustainable-finance.

Figure 7: Outline of the Bond Labeling Process

Source: Asian Development Bank. https://asianbondsonline.adb.org/green-bonds/index.html.

Some types of green bonds and their debt recourses and proceeds allocations are shown in Table 4.

Table 4: Types of Green Bonds

Type of Green Bonds	Proceeds raised by bond sale	Debt recourse	Example
Green "Use of Proceeds" Bond	Earmarked for green projects	Recourse to the issuer: same credit rating applies as issuer's other bonds	European Investment Bank (EIB) "Climate Awareness Bond"; Barclays Green Bond
Green "Use of Proceeds" Revenue Bond/Asset-Backed Security	Earmarked for and/or refinances green projects	Revenue streams from the issuers through fees, taxes, etc., are collateral for the debt	Hawaii State (backed by fee on electricity bills of the state utilities)
Green Project Bond	Ring-fenced for the specific underlying green project(s)	Recourse is only to the project's assets and balance sheet	Invenergy Wind Farm (backed by Invenergy Campo Palomas Wind Farm)
Green Securitized Bond	Refinance portfolios of green projects or proceeds are earmarked for green projects	Recourse is to a group of projects that have been grouped together (e.g., solar leases or green mortgages)	Tesla Energy (backed by residential solar leases); Obvion (backed by green mortgages)
Covered bond	Earmarked for eligible projects included in the covered pool	Recourse to the issuer and, if the issuer is unable to repay the bond, to the covered pool	Berlin Hyp Green Pfandbrief; Sparebank 1 Boligkreditt green covered bond
Loan	Earmarked for eligible projects or secured on eligible assets	Full recourse to borrower(s) in the case of unsecured loans. Recourse to the collateral in the case of secured loans, but may also feature limited recourse to the borrower(s).	MEP Werke, Ivanhoe Cambridge and Natixis Assurances (DUO), OVG
Other bonds	Earmarked for eligible projects	-	Convertible bonds or Notes, Schuldschein, commercial paper, *sukuk* debentures

Source: The Climate Bonds Initiative, 2019. https://asianbondsonline.adb.org/green-bonds/index.html.

Some types of green bonds and their debt recourses and proceeds allocations are shown in Box 4.

Box 4: Global Green Bond Issues

The first green bond was issued by the European Investment Bank in 2007. Since then, the global green bond issuance has experienced impressive growth. The Climate Bonds Initiative reports that global green bond issuance in 2021 amounted to $507 billion as compared to $167.3 billion in 2018. The United States, the People's Republic of China, and France remained the top three markets for green bonds.[a] In ASEAN, outstanding green bonds reached $333.6 billion at the end of the first quarter of 2022, accounting for nearly 70% of the regional sustainability bond stock. The People's Republic of China, Thailand, and Singapore continue to be the major issuers. Singapore announced that government agencies will issue up to S$35 billion of green bonds by 2030 to finance eco-friendly public sector infrastructure projects which are expected to provide long-term environmental benefits to current and future generations.[b]

In Asia, India has issued $2 billion of sovereign green bonds in 2023 as it seeks cheaper financing to fund renewable energy targets.

[a] T. Tsanova. 2019. Green bond issuance inches up to USD 167bn in 2018 - prelim. *Renewables Now*. https://renewablesnow.com/news/green-bond-issuance-inches-up-to-usd-167bn-in-2018-prelim-640100/.
[b] D. Loh and F. Regalado. 2022. ASEAN governments rush to issue green bonds. *Nikkei Asia*. 4 July. https://asia.nikkei.com/Business/Markets/Bonds/ASEAN-governments-rush-to-issue-green-bonds.
Source: Study team analysis.

Sector and Project Fit

Energy-related (renewable energy and energy efficiency) projects have continued to dominate project categories to be financed by green bond proceeds as seen in Figures 8 and 9.[70] There is potential for a broader sector spread of projects to use green bond financing in transport, water, and waste and recycling sectors.

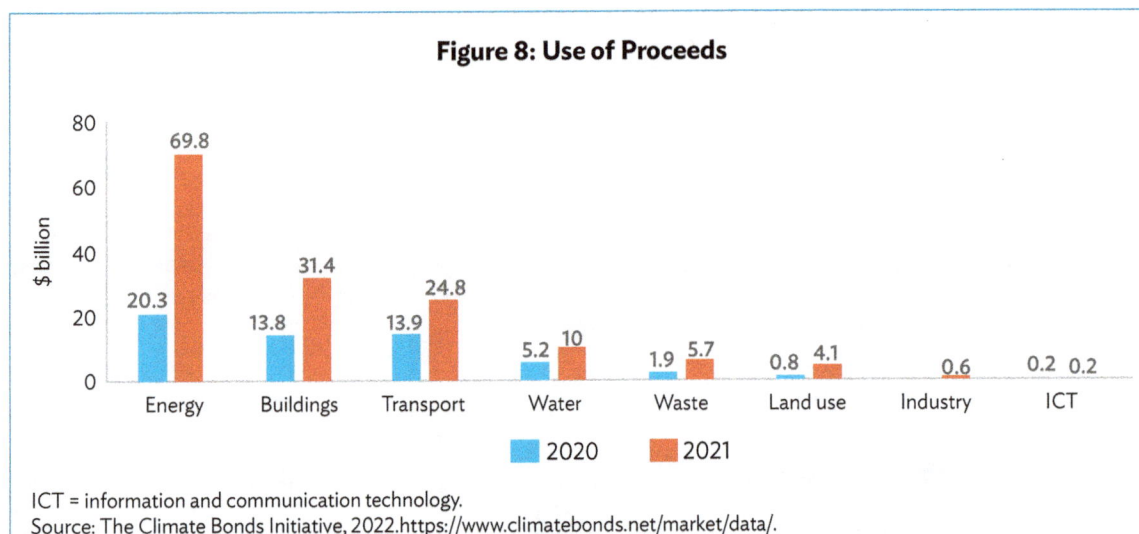

Figure 8: Use of Proceeds

ICT = information and communication technology.
Source: The Climate Bonds Initiative, 2022. https://www.climatebonds.net/market/data/.

Singapore has published a governance framework for sovereign green bond issuances covering areas like the use of proceeds, evaluation and selection of eligible projects, approach to managing the capital raised, as well as post-issuance allocation and reporting of outcomes. In June 2022, credit ratings agency Fitch assessed that Singapore's plans for green bond issuances will be supported by its moves to establish a green taxonomy, which seeks to allow financial providers to align their investments and lending on the basis of environmental impact.[71]

---

[70]   Climate bonds initiative since 2013. https://www.climatebonds.net/market/data/.
[71]   https://asia.nikkei.com/Business/Markets/Bonds/ASEAN-governments-rush-to-issue-green-bonds.

Figure 9: Allocation of Green Bonds Investments in Association of Southeast Asian Nations

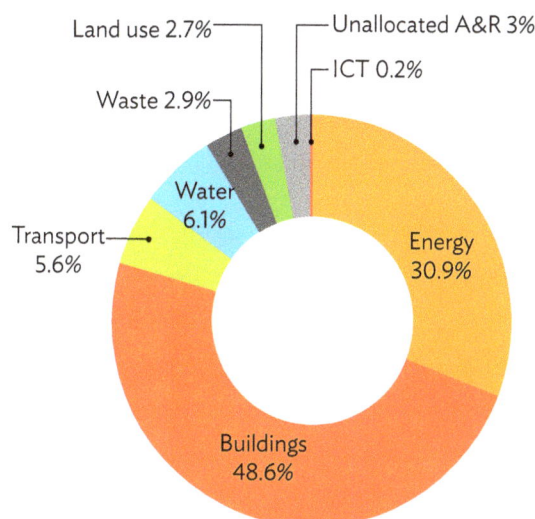

- Land use 2.7%
- Unallocated A&R 3%
- Waste 2.9%
- ICT 0.2%
- Water 6.1%
- Transport 5.6%
- Energy 30.9%
- Buildings 48.6%

A&R = Adaptation and Resilience [projects], ICT = information and communication technology.
Source: Climate Bonds Initiative. *ASEAN Sustainable Finance. State of the Market 2020.*
https://www.climatebonds.net/files/reports/asean-sotm-2020.pdf.

The Green Bond Principles, a set of voluntary guidelines that have been developed by a group of investors, issuers and underwriters, explicitly recognize several broad categories of potential eligible green projects, including but not limited to renewable energy, energy efficiency (including efficient buildings), sustainable waste management, sustainable land use (including sustainable forestry and agriculture), biodiversity conservation, clean transportation, sustainable water management, and climate change adaptation.[72]

Local financial institutions can play an important role in mobilizing private capital and expanding the accessibility and affordability of sustainable financing products for small- and medium-sized businesses. Financial institutions can provide "green loans" or "social loans" to such businesses to support their environmentally and socially responsible investments. Financial institutions can raise funds for this purpose by issuing sustainable bonds and by offering green or social deposit schemes, thereby increasing the availability of sustainable products and making them more accessible to relevant stakeholders (e.g., borrowers, depositors, and/or investors). On the demand side, development partners can act as anchor investors in sustainable bond transactions, especially those involving LCY-denominated bonds. These investors will have more capacity and experience to independently assess the ESG aspects of underlying securities. For example, ADB has invested B3 billion ($98.7 million)[73] in Energy Absolute's first green bond issuance, out of a total issue size of B10 billion.[74] In the corporate sector, Thaifoods Group is the first nonfinancial corporate social bond issuer under the ASEAN Social Bond Standards (Appendix case study 7).

Development partners can also issue LCY-denominated sustainable bonds to finance a pool of eligible projects in member countries. As a result, local institutional investors would have more opportunities to invest in sustainable bonds issued by multilateral institutions. The education bond, which was issued by ADB in February 2021 to fund education-related projects such as technical and vocational training, is one example. Dai-ichi Life Insurance Company, Limited of Japan purchased the entire 10-year bond.

---

[72] Flavia Rosembuj and Sebastiano Bottio. 2016. Mobilizing Private Climate Finance—Green Bonds and Beyond. *EM Compass* Note 25. International Finance Corporation, Washington, DC. https://openknowledge.worldbank.org/bitstream/handle/10986/30351/110881-BRI-EMCompass-Note-25-Green-Bonds-FINAL-12-5-PUBLIC.pdf?sequence=1&isAllowed=y.

[73] Conversion rate: $1 = B32.90.

[74] ADB. 2019. ADB Invests 3 Billion Thai Baht in Energy Absolute's Green Bond for Wind Farm Development. Manila. https://www.adb.org/news/adb-invests-3-billion-thai-baht-energy-absolutes-green-bond-wind-farm-development.

Key Stakeholders

- **Green bonds issuer.** Any company, government agency, or financial institution that develops, registers, and sells a bond; the issuer usually selects a financial institution as an underwriter to administer the issuance of the bond.

- **Green bonds investor.** Individuals, companies, and institutional investors (endowment funds, hedge funds, insurance companies, mutual funds, pension funds, and sovereign wealth funds) purchase green bonds with the expectation of achieving a financial gain.

- **Credit rating agencies and auditors.** Entities that are in charge of confirming adherence to the criteria for green bonds or established credit norms.

- **Regulators.** Entities that are accountable for overseeing capital markets. Known as financial authorities, they review the credentials of underwriters, along with the credit asset securitization and bond custody arrangements. They also supervise the issuance, clearing, and settlement provisions. Regulators may include securities commissions, other regulatory agencies, stock exchanges, and central banks.

- **Credit guarantors and other intermediaries.** In secondary markets, creditor guarantors provide credit guarantees and enhancement products, which alter the underlying bond's risk profile. Various financial intermediaries offer a diverse range of intermediation and credit enhancement services, such as raising investor capital and establishing SPVs.

Financing Model Framework

The typical life cycle for green bond financing is shown in the Figure 10.

Figure 10: Green Bond Financing Framework

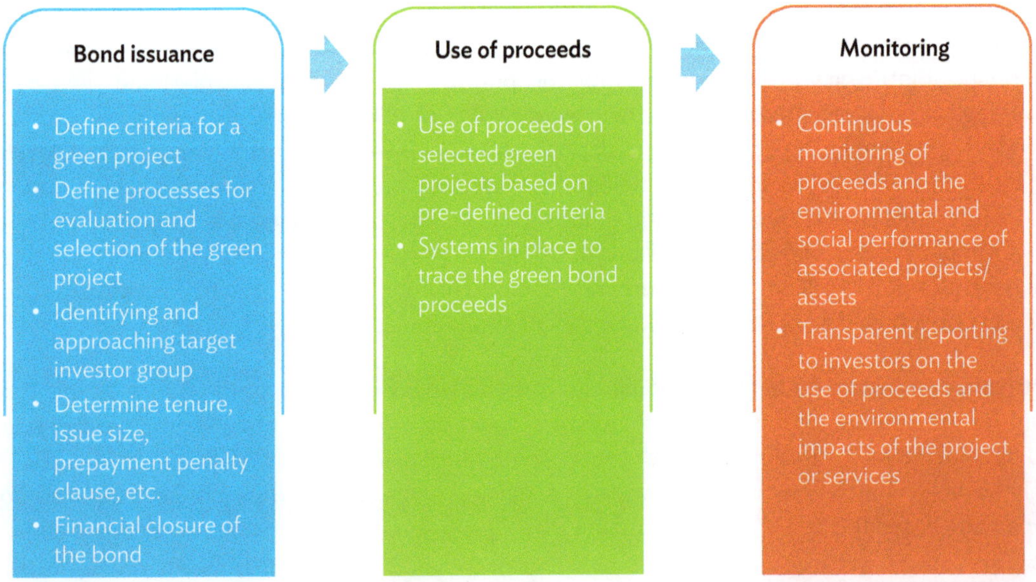

Bond issuance	Use of proceeds	Monitoring
• Define criteria for a green project • Define processes for evaluation and selection of the green project • Identifying and approaching target investor group • Determine tenure, issue size, prepayment penalty clause, etc. • Financial closure of the bond	• Use of proceeds on selected green projects based on pre-defined criteria • Systems in place to trace the green bond proceeds	• Continuous monitoring of proceeds and the environmental and social performance of associated projects/assets • Transparent reporting to investors on the use of proceeds and the environmental impacts of the project or services

Source: Study team analysis.

👍 *Critical Success Factors*

- **Identification of eligible assets.** Finding eligible assets is the starting point and cornerstone of any successful Green Bond issue.[75] The selection of the assets has to be done after establishing internal processes that evaluate its fit within the issuer's wider sustainability strategy, goals, and objectives.

- **Regulated capital market.** For issuing green bonds, it is not mandatory to have a legal requirement, but a regulated capital market is essential. National financial authorities, issuers, and certifying bodies should acknowledge and adopt established international standards like the Green Bond Principles or Climate Bond Standards to ensure transparency and disclosure, and promote integrity in the development of the Green Bond market.[76]

- **Defining any program or an investment as "green."** Although a range of definitions and criteria exists to define what constitutes a green investment or program, it is likely that a prescriptive standard set of definitions of "green" will not meet every investor's need. Hence, issuers need to regularly reflect its commitment to invest in projects with improved environmental performance.

- **Managing additional costs of issuing green bonds.** Additional expenditure for defining green criteria, monitoring and maintaining the proceeds as green, and transparently communicating performance to investors over the lifetime of the bonds may weigh in on the costs of issuing green bonds. Hence, it is imperative to keep the cost in check. There is little upside potential as green bonds provide returns similar to a normal bond.

- **High level of transparency.** A high level of transparency is required for information disclosed on green bond process, criteria, and external reviews. Moreover, green bond investors may also take into consideration the quality of the issuer's overall profile, which carries an inherent reputational risk.

📋 *Case Studies*

Two distinct case studies have been included in the Appendix. Case study 8 on Indonesia Green Sukuk illustrates the features of a Shariah compliant green bond structure while case study 7 on the Thaifood Group provides details of a sustainable bond instrument and the broader environmental and social benefits.

4.4.7 *Government Green Funds and Transition Financing*

📑 *Key Objective*

The key objective of government green funds and transition funds is to attract funding from private players (venture capitalists, corporations, etc.) to support infrastructure investments in renewable energy, transport efficiency, and waste management optimization. One of the major drivers for investments is to enable reduction of greenhouse gas (GHG) emissions by infrastructure projects. The funds involve engaging traditional capital markets in creating and distributing a wide range of financial products and services that deliver both investible returns and environmentally positive outcomes. These funds can be established by government endowments or with a combination of government, multilateral, and financial institution funding support.

ADB estimates that between 2016 and 2030, ASEAN will require $210 billion per year, or 5.7% of members' aggregate annual GDP, to support investments in climate-resilient infrastructure.[77] Clearly, the region's infrastructure financing requirements far exceed regional governments' annual budgets, and private capital must be mobilized to meet these

---

75   International Finance Corporation. *Green Bond Handbook. A Step-by-Step Guide to issuing a Green Bond.* https://www.ifc.org/wps/wcm/connect/f11546a9-b986-4b0d-b1fc-93d798ce86dc/202203-IFC-Green-Bond-Handbook.pdf?MOD=AJPERES&CVID=n.wxr2b.

76   International Capital Markets Association. 2018. *The Green Bond Principles.* https://www.icmagroup.org/sustainable-finance/the-principles-guidelines-and-handbooks/green-bond-principles-gbp/.

77   ADB. 2018. *Promoting Green and Innovative Finance across Southeast Asia.* https://www.adb.org/multimedia/kns/promoting-green-and-innovative-finance-across-southeast-asia-15.html.

needs. To enable the financial viability and bankability of infrastructure projects, mechanisms such as a de-risking facility and credit enhancements are necessary.

⬛ *Description of the Financing Model*

The function of the funds is similar to traditional financial institutions, but there are additional benefits such as providing deeper green finance expertise, direct lending at lower rates than traditional lenders, and financial products to increase the attractiveness of green products to commercial banks and private investors. The establishment of the ASEAN Catalytic Green Finance Facility (ACGF) in April 2019, an initiative of the ASEAN Infrastructure Fund, is one example of how countries can accelerate green infrastructure investments. Development partners such as Agence Française de Développement, the European Investment Bank, the KfW Development Bank, and the Government of the Republic of Korea have already pledged their support to the ACGF. In 2021, four additional partners—the European Union; the Green Climate Fund; Italy's Cassa Depositi e Prestiti; and the Foreign, Commonwealth, and Development Office of the United Kingdom—pledged $665 million toward the ACGF's activities as part of an ASEAN Green Recovery Platform launched at the 26th United Nations Climate Change Conference of the Parties in Glasgow.[78]

The ACGF's mission is to accelerate development of green infrastructure projects in Southeast Asia by better utilizing public funds to create bankable green projects that are able to attract private capital, integrate innovative technologies, and improve management efficiencies. It focuses on projects that promote renewable energy, energy efficiency, green urban transport, water supply and sanitation, waste management, and climate-resilient agriculture. The ACGF includes two lending products with differentiated pricing based on the differing socioeconomic conditions in ASEAN countries.

By the end of 2021, the ACGF was able to attract financing pledges of over $2 billion from nine financing partners, engage four knowledge partners, and support the structuring of 29 projects. The five projects in its formal financing pipeline have a total estimated project cost of $3 billion, and are projected to reduce carbon dioxide emissions by almost 300,000 tons per year.[79] Equally important, technical assistance associated with the ACGF has helped spur a wide array of new innovative concepts, including SDG financing vehicle in Indonesia, a marine financing platform in Cambodia, green and sustainability bonds in Thailand, and a regional blue hub to support project development, among others. The lack of a strong pipeline of projects that are both green and bankable continues to be one of the main barriers to green infrastructure development in Southeast Asia. Technical assistance funds are a fundamental component of ACGF operations and focus, among others, on supporting the development of a pipeline of green and bankable projects across the region, from concept and early-stage design to late-stage structuring.

The typical structure and mechanism of government or government and institutional green funds is exhibited in Figure 11.

---

[78] ADB. ASEAN Green Recovery Platform. https://www.adb.org/sites/default/files/page/555651/asean-green-recovery-platform-flyer.pdf.
[79] ADB. 2022. *Asian Catalytic Green Finance Facility 2021: Financing for a Green Recovery in Southeast Asia*. Manila.
     https://www.adb.org/sites/default/files/institutional-document/784451/asean-catalytic-green-finance-facility-2021.pdf.

Figure 11: Green Fund Mechanism

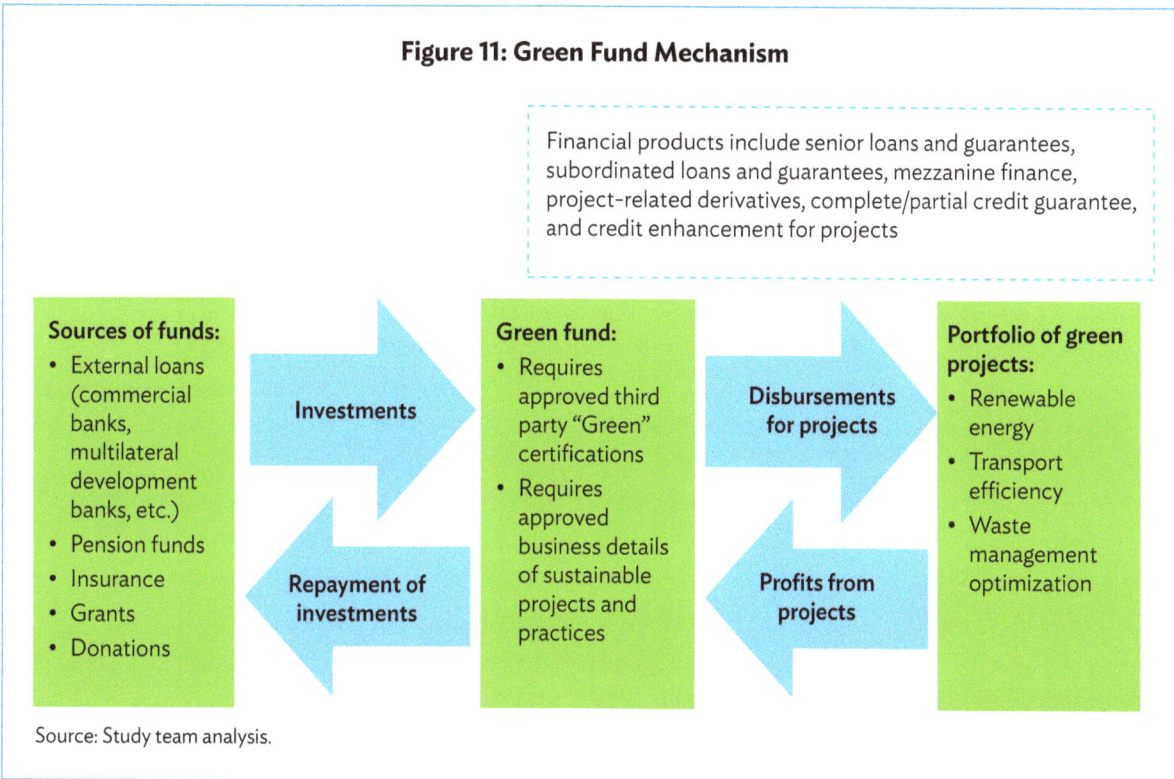

Financial products include senior loans and guarantees, subordinated loans and guarantees, mezzanine finance, project-related derivatives, complete/partial credit guarantee, and credit enhancement for projects

Sources of funds:
- External loans (commercial banks, multilateral development banks, etc.)
- Pension funds
- Insurance
- Grants
- Donations

Investments

Repayment of investments

Green fund:
- Requires approved third party "Green" certifications
- Requires approved business details of sustainable projects and practices

Disbursements for projects

Profits from projects

Portfolio of green projects:
- Renewable energy
- Transport efficiency
- Waste management optimization

Source: Study team analysis.

Box 5: Green Fund Market

As ASEAN+3 member countries transition toward a low-carbon economy consistent with their net zero emission commitments, innovation and sustainability become critical parameters to evaluate project selection and financing. Growth has returned to the "green" sector; while the number of funds have remained relatively constant, invested assets have increased since 2015. Countries that pioneered responsible investments, such as France, and major financial hubs like Switzerland and the United Kingdom, drive the green funds market. The majority of European green funds are equity funds, but the market is gradually diversifying, in particular with the emergence of green bonds fund since 2015. In Sweden, individual investors can choose green funds for part of their retirement savings.

Source: Novethic. 2018. The European Green Funds Market. https://www.novethic.com/sustainable-finance-trends/detail/the-novethic-indicator-on-high-impact-sri-42-5.html.

To achieve these commitments, significant investments must be directed toward key infrastructure sectors, such as low-carbon transport, power generation, waste management, water supply and sanitation, and telecommunications. Limited resources and rising fiscal constraints owing to the COVID-19 pandemic have multiplied the need to target these investments effectively.

Sector and Project Fit

Analysis of fund names shows that asset managers prefer a **combination of environmental and social themes**. However, a few more specific themes are followed by dedicated funds:[80]

---

[80] Novethic. 2017. The European Green Funds Market. https://www.novethic.com/sustainable-finance-trends/detail/the-european-green-funds-market.html.

(i) **Water-themed projects.** Water-themed projects hold more than €8 billion ($9.2 billion)[81] in assets (nearly 40% of the European green funds market) and grew by nearly 10% between 2015 and 2016. Water-themed projects are easily understood by investors and provide fund managers with relatively noncyclical investments and a certain degree of diversification.

(ii) **Renewable energy theme projects.** The renewable energy theme is the most popular theme and renewable energy funds place technologies at the heart of their investment strategies.

Key Stakeholders

- **Investment Committee.** Oversees development of an investment strategy for the fund, sets decision criteria for funding decisions, and reviews portfolio outcomes of funding decisions.
- **Ethics and Audit Committee.** Oversees development and implementation of board policy on ethics and conflict of interest relating to board members, and reviews and makes recommendations to the board with regard to external audit.
- **Risk Management Committee.** Oversees and reviews strategic risks across funds at portfolio and fund-wide levels.
- **Private Sector Advisory Group.** Provides advice on fund engagement with the private sector.
- **Trustee.** Provides advice to the fund on trustee and financial management matters.
- **Investors.** Commercial banks, multilateral development banks, bilateral funding agencies, financial institutions, pension funds, insurance companies, etc.

Financing Model Framework

The key process steps to be adopted for the design and issuance of a green fund financing instrument are shown in Figure 12.

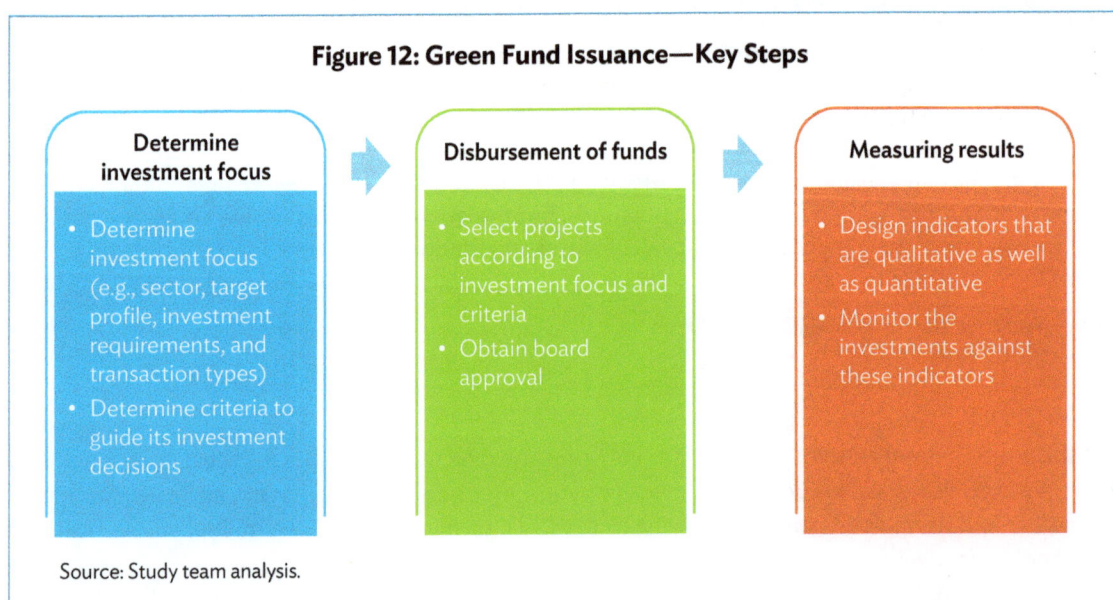

Figure 12: Green Fund Issuance—Key Steps

Determine investment focus
- Determine investment focus (e.g., sector, target profile, investment requirements, and transaction types)
- Determine criteria to guide its investment decisions

Disbursement of funds
- Select projects according to investment focus and criteria
- Obtain board approval

Measuring results
- Design indicators that are qualitative as well as quantitative
- Monitor the investments against these indicators

Source: Study team analysis.

Critical Success Factors

- **Transparent decision-making processes.** Having an independent investment board is important to steer the process, adjust the investment strategy, and ensure sound decision-making.

---

[81] Conversion rate: $1 = €0.87.

- **Experience and knowledge.** The fund manager should be sufficiently experienced and knowledgeable to give credibility and confidence to private sector investors.
- **Long-term vision and commitment.** There needs to be a clearly defined investment strategy, as well as close cooperation between stakeholders, to meet the challenges in establishing and delivering the objectives of the fund.

Case Studies

Four case studies are provided: (i) the ACGF is a multi-partner funded facility that supports ASEAN initiatives such as the Indonesia One Green Facility (Box 6); (ii) Energy Transition Mechanism (Box 7); (iii) Green Municipal Fund (Appendix case study 9), which is a fully government-endowed fund that provides financing for government entities such as municipalities; and (iv) the Rantau Dedap Geothermal Power Project in Indonesia, which showcases the financing of a green infrastructure project (Appendix case study 10).

Box 6: Sustainable Development Goals Indonesia One Green Finance Facility

The ASEAN Catalytic Green Finance Facility project structuring team developed and discussed concepts for national facilities that can help de-risk green projects in Cambodia, Indonesia, the Philippines, and Viet Nam. In Indonesia, SDG Indonesia One, a national facility to finance projects that contribute to the achievement of the Sustainable Development Goals (SDGs), was launched in October 2018 under PT Sarana Multi Infrastruktur, a state-owned company under the Ministry of Finance of Indonesia.

Technical assistance under the ASEAN Catalytic Green Finance Facility supported the creation of the SDG Indonesia One Green Finance Facility (SIO-GFF). The facility aims to combine four principles: (i) support green or SDG-related infrastructure, (ii) provide a de-risking financing mechanism through innovative use of public funds, (iii) leverage commercial funds into projects with a multiplier three times on average, and (iv) help design and structure green projects and innovative finance instruments.

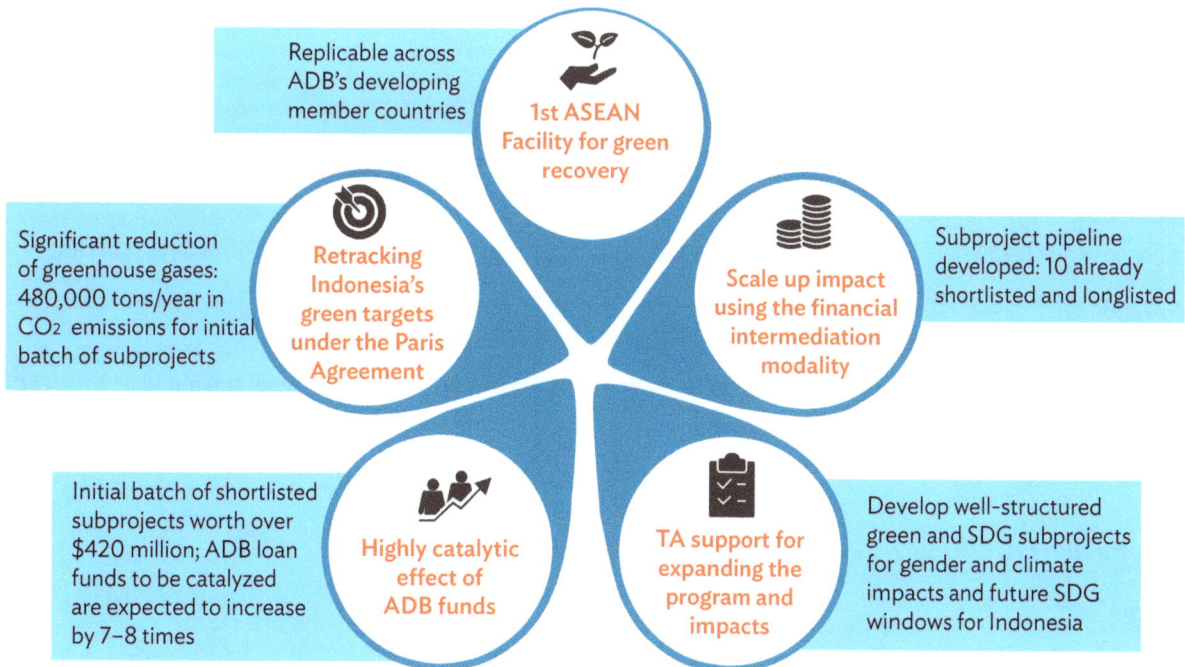

Replicable across ADB's developing member countries

1st ASEAN Facility for green recovery

Significant reduction of greenhouse gases: 480,000 tons/year in CO_2 emissions for initial batch of subprojects

Retracking Indonesia's green targets under the Paris Agreement

Scale up impact using the financial intermediation modality

Subproject pipeline developed: 10 already shortlisted and longlisted

Initial batch of shortlisted subprojects worth over $420 million; ADB loan funds to be catalyzed are expected to increase by 7–8 times

Highly catalytic effect of ADB funds

TA support for expanding the program and impacts

Develop well-structured green and SDG subprojects for gender and climate impacts and future SDG windows for Indonesia

continued on next page

Box 6 *continued*

The SIO-GFF will design and operationalize a model (replicable for other SDGs) using innovative financing tools for project de-risking with clear green and SDG frameworks, and a pipeline of green infrastructure projects blending private and sovereign funds, with at least 450,000 tons of carbon dioxide equivalent per year reduced by SIO-GFF financed projects. The SIO-GFF will also contribute to the country's economic stimulus for a sustainable post-pandemic recovery, generate employment, and ensure an SDG focus in sectors including infrastructure, health, and eco-tourism, which were adversely affected by the pandemic. In February 2022, the Asian Development Bank provided a 20-year intermediation loan of $150 million that is estimated to inject at least $137 million for climate mitigation and adaptation into SIO-GFF's initial pipeline. The initial funds will be used by PT Sarana Multi Infrastruktur to partially finance up to 10 projects worth $423 million, at an average of 35% per subproject.

ADB = Asian Development Bank, ASEAN = Association of South East Asian Nations, CO_2 = carbon dioxide,
SDG = Sustainable Development Goal, TA = technical assistance.
Source: Asian Development Bank 2022. SDG Indonesia One: Green Finance Facility. Manila.
https://www.adb.org/sites/default/files/publication/806411/sdg-indonesia-one.pdf.

Box 7: Energy Transition Mechanism

The Energy Transition Mechanism (ETM) program is a blended-finance initiative that has been created by the Asian Development Bank (ADB) in collaboration with its developing member countries in the Asia and Pacific region. It aims to retire current coal-fired power plants on an accelerated schedule and replace them with clean power capacity. The program will utilize public and private investments from various sources including governments, multilateral banks, private sector investors, philanthropies, and long-term investors. Its is designed to be scalable and collaborative, and investments will be used to establish country-specific ETM funds that will allow for the early retirement of coal power assets and assist in mitigating the negative effects of climate change. ADB signed a Memorandum of Understanding with partners in Indonesia in November 2022 to jointly explore the early retirement of the first coal-fired plant owned by an independent power producer.

ADB also established the Energy Transition Mechanism Partnership Trust Fund in June 2022 as a multi-partner trust fund to mobilize resources for ETM. The fund's primary focus is to support projects that involve one or more of the following activities:

- reducing greenhouse gas emissions from coal-fired power plants through either the early retirement or repurposing of such plants for clean energy purposes;

- increasing clean energy share, which can be achieved by enhancing grid capacity and other related efforts;

- assisting developing member countries in the development and implementation of policies and regulatory measures aimed at accelerating the transition from coal to clean energy; and/or

- supporting the transition to cleaner energy in a manner that is just and equitable for all stakeholders involved.

Source: Study team analysis.

4.4.8 Public–Private Partnerships

Key Objective

Public–private partnership (PPP) structures have been used in most developing and developed countries for infrastructure development. The projects are collaboration ventures between public and private entities and both parties are bound by a contractual agreement stipulating the terms and conditions of engagement and mutual responsibilities. Such partnerships offer an opportunity to the private sector to take part in sectors that were often the preserve of or dominated by public investments. Lack of public capital, inadequate expertise in specific sectors and industries, poor capacity in managing enterprises that require to be operated along commercial lines, and encouraging private sector engagement in infrastructure projects have all contributed to adopting the PPP investment model. Often involving large infrastructure projects that are capital intensive and long term, PPPs impose significant risk and management responsibility on the private partner as returns are linked to performance. Since the private partner is financially exposed, it is at times incentivized with a greater share of the rewards.

Description of the Financing Model

As each PPP venture is unique with its own set of variables (ownership, shareholding, financing terms, management responsibility, sector, industry, requirements of land, equipment, etc.), there are no standardized contracts, apart from general principles of collaboration. The PPP structures are, therefore, bespoke and tailor-made for each venture with each party managing what it does best. A variety of PPP arrangements are in existence and are listed below:

- Management and operations and maintenance contract
- Build–own–transfer
- Build–own–operate–transfer
- Build–own–operate
- Build–transfer–operate
- Rehabilitate–operate–transfer
- Design–build–finance–operate
- Design–construct–manage–finance
- Viability gap funding
- Lease
- Concession

Sector and Project Fit

A majority of the PPP projects have been set up in the energy generation, pipeline development, mining, toll roads, real estate development, waste disposal, telecommunications, and water management. These involve concessions, management and lease contracts, greenfield and brownfield projects, divestitures, and transfer of equity, all of which could have a distinct operating and management format. Payment or revenue earnings for operators can be based on "user pays" (toll roads) or "government pays" (hospitals or prisons), where government is the sole source of revenue. In addition, PPP mechanisms have been successfully employed for social infrastructure projects in education (school and university construction/renovation, public libraries, and child care facilities); health (hospitals and medical centers); housing (affordable and public housing); and recreation (parks, sport facilities, and cultural and community centers).

Key Stakeholders

- Private sector shareholder
- Government or public sector organization
- Lenders
- Contractors and/or external technical partner or operator

Financing Model Framework

Infrastructure PPP projects are often implemented through an SPV and the shareholders may include the developer; engineering, procurement and construction contractors; and other financial investors. A simplified PPP structure is shown in Figure 13.

Critical Success Factors

- **Well-balanced allocation of risks and returns.** A structured PPP project would have a well-balanced allocation of risks and returns between stakeholders in the public and private sector.

- **Detailed feasibility studies.** Detailed feasibility studies are required to determine the project's commercial viability and risk allocation.

- **Recurrent income streams.** The PPP project should have recurrent income streams over long-term concessions.

- **Strong political commitment.** Project development is complex and time-consuming, and may fail without strong political support to implement the project.

- **Expeditious dispute resolution.** Robust legal, institutional, and dispute resolution framework for PPPs will minimize wastage of time and resources.

- **Optimized risk sharing.** A project that is well-structured with proper risk allocation between the government and the private partner is likely to run smoothly.

- **Investor interest.** Potential interest in financing by international and domestic lenders will guarantee long-term success.

- **Access to government subsidies and guarantees.** Asian governments and development agencies may provide viability gap funding and credit guarantees to support major projects.

- **Expertise.** Private sector sponsors with the skill and experience will be able to deliver the project over the entire concession period.

- **Smooth approvals and clearances.** Government takes the lead in securing all licenses and approvals.

- **Ease of access to land.** Land ownership and acquisition process is clear and implementable.

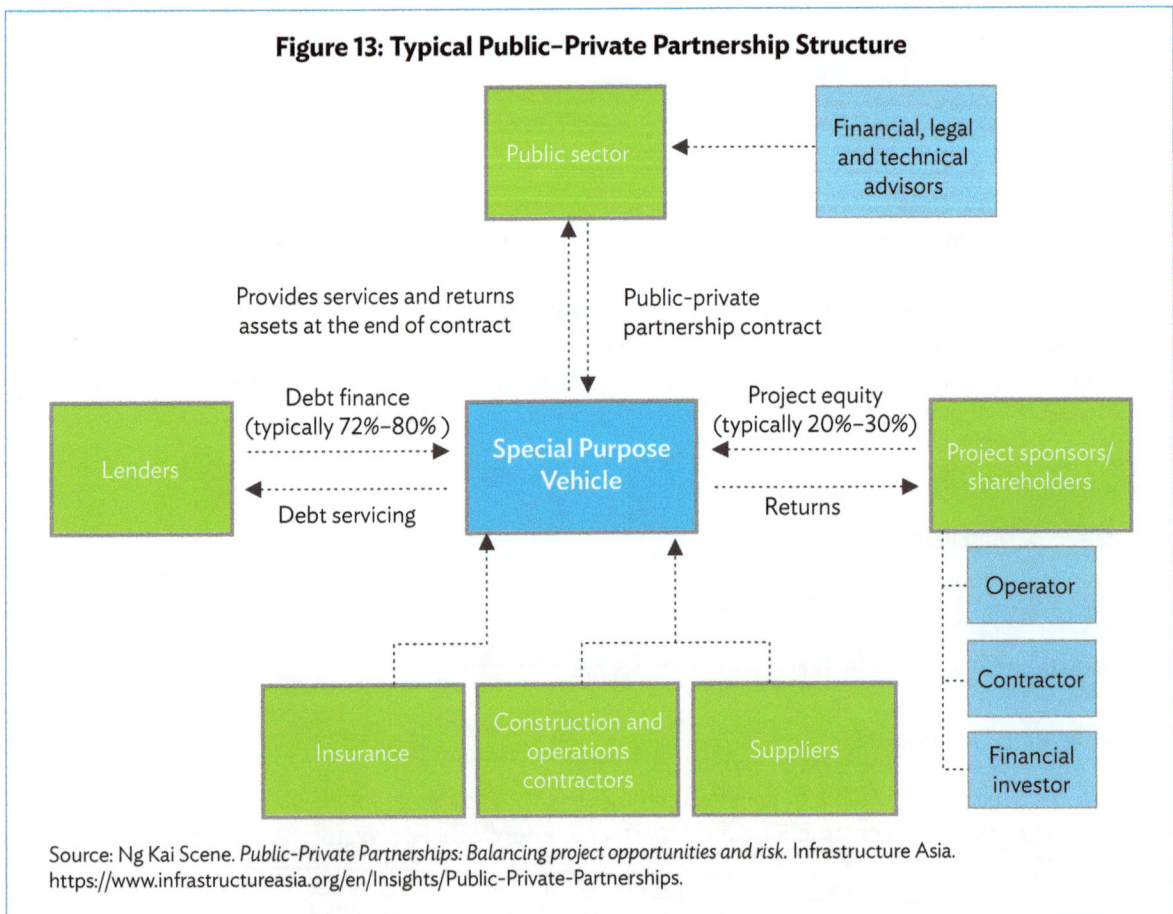

Figure 13: Typical Public–Private Partnership Structure

Source: Ng Kai Scene. *Public-Private Partnerships: Balancing project opportunities and risk.* Infrastructure Asia. https://www.infrastructureasia.org/en/Insights/Public-Private-Partnerships.

Case Studies

The Keppel Marina East Desalination Plant is a PPP between the Singapore's National Water Agency (PUB) and Keppel Infrastructure Holding (KI). The plant was jointly developed and funded by the two parties. The Government of Singapore provided the land, infrastructure, and the necessary regulatory and technical support, while KI provided the necessary private sector expertise, technology, and financial resources to develop and operate the desalination plant. Under the agreement, the PUB takes ownership of the desalination plant and owns the long-term water supply rights. In addition, the PUB is responsible for the cost of providing seawater to the plant, while KI is responsible for the cost of constructing the plant, operating and maintaining the plant, and disposing of the produced water. Both parties have agreed to share the costs of any upgrades and improvements to the desalination plant. This includes capital investments for additional capacity, technological upgrades, as well as operational and maintenance costs. The sharing of costs will be determined by an independent dispute resolution process in the event of a disagreement. The plant is an innovative large scale desalination facility and is the world's first dual-mode desalination facility built with the ability to treat both freshwater and seawater, depending upon weather conditions. It began operations in June 2020 and is operated by a wholly owned subsidiary of KI for a 25-year concession period (2020–2045) under the design–build–own–operate arrangement with PUB.

Malaysia's Putrajaya Smart City PPP Project seeks to develop Putrajaya, Malaysia's administrative capital, into a smart and sustainable city. The project will deliver a range of infrastructure, including public transport; water and sanitation; energy; information and communication technology; and smart city services. The project is expected to create more than 10,000 jobs and generate more than $3.2 billion in investments. It will provide a range of infrastructure, including

- high-speed broadband networks and services;
- smart city applications and platforms, such as smart parking and traffic management systems;
- public transportation systems, such as mass rapid transit and light rail transit;
- sustainable energy sources, such as solar and renewable energy;
- waste and water management systems, such as water recycling and treatment;
- smart buildings, including telemedicine and smart health management systems;
- smart retail and entertainment centers; and
- smart education systems, such as online learning platforms.

The PPP project is led by the Government of Malaysia in collaboration with a consortium of private partners. The consortium consists of three companies—Telekom Malaysia, Axiata Group, and UEM Edgenta—who are responsible for developing and delivering the project, including the design, construction, and operation and maintenance of the smart city infrastructure. The project is expected to be completed in 2024.

The Umbulan Drinking Water project in East Java Province, Indonesia, demonstrates the application of the PPP approach. It is a pro-poor project that was built to provide clean high quality drinking water to the poor people at an affordable tariff (Appendix case study 11).

4.4.9 Climate Risk and Catastrophe Insurance

Key Objectives

The increasing frequency and severity of weather-linked extreme events (floods, droughts, typhoons, cyclones, hurricanes, etc.), and natural hazard events (earthquakes, tsunamis, volcanic eruptions, etc.,) impact the productive capacity of the country and its people. Such an event disproportionately impacts the most vulnerable section of the population through loss of livelihood and assets, pushing them deeper into poverty. Affected communities are forced to adopt desperate coping strategies for food and economic security as they have no means to ensure basic sustenance. Climate risk insurance provides agricultural communities a guaranteed payout in instances where adverse weather damages their crops or leads to lower than estimated yields. Disaster insurance provides payouts based on the level of damage due to specific catastrophic events that are covered in the insurance policy.

Weather-linked insurance products have been successfully implemented in Asia, Africa, and Latin America providing smallholder farmers, fishing communities, and other marginalized groups with a de-risking and economic protection mechanism that reduces their vulnerability to extreme climatic occurrences. The insurance is a disaster risk management tool that compensates affected people if they suffer financial losses as a consequence of a specific peril (floods, inadequate rainfall, drought, etc.) in return for a small premium that is required to be paid for securing the insurance cover. It enables a timely recovery and contributes to sustainable and climate resilient development.

Description of the Financing Model

Climate risk insurance forms part of large government social protection programs and is actively advocated and supported by multilateral development institutions, bilateral funding agencies, as well as nongovernment organizations (NGOs). Insurance companies have increasingly streamlined and fine-tuned their policy structures to adapt to the requirements of their clients by providing simpler policies and quicker payouts. Insurance companies pool the premiums across diverse regions and risks to be able to compensate policy holders in the event of a weather-induced disaster. As the sum of premium paid is very small in comparison to the likely payout in the event of a disaster, it is important to create awareness about the advantages of the insurance product in the targeted vulnerable communities to facilitate adoption of this risk reduction instrument.

In the case of climate risk insurance products such as crop insurance, insurance companies comprehensively map and analyze weather patterns for the specific region taking into account annual precipitation, frequency of floods, droughts, soil yields, type of crops harvested, etc. Based on an actuarial valuation, an insurance plan is developed that assesses risk, potential losses, and pricing issues, and recommends a payout structure.

Most governments in developing countries (such as Cambodia, India, and Bangladesh) have subsidized climate risk insurance premiums to enable smallholder farmers to avail themselves of the risk reduction benefits offered by the insurance guarantee. Over time, government subsidies are phased out, as farmers increasingly recognize the benefit of the insurance instrument and can pay the premium on their own.

Sector and Project Fit

Climate risk and catastrophe risk insurance is primarily extended to agriculture, fisheries, tourism, public utilities, and transportation where it provides reliable and timely financial relief for reconstruction, rehabilitation, and livelihood support, thus providing security in the post-disaster period.

Key Stakeholders

- Governments, state agencies and departments (meteorological, disaster management)
- Smallholder farmers, fishing communities, vulnerable groups
- Small and medium business, tourism and hospitality industry
- Insurance companies
- Agricultural banks and microfinance institutions
- Multilateral banks (ADB, World Bank), bilateral agencies, humanitarian and development agencies (United Nations, World Food Programme), NGOs

Financing Model Framework

The financing model adopted for climate risk insurance involves close collaboration between the government agencies at the village and district levels, insurance companies and their agents, and microfinance and agricultural banks. The government agencies and insurance representatives are primarily responsible for creating awareness of the insurance product, its benefits, and the triggers for payouts. Following the awareness drive, insurance companies solicit the participation of potential members and collect the insurance premium. In case the premium is subsidized, the government provides the subsidy amount to the insurance company. In some cases, the insurance company may use the services of local banks, microfinance agencies, and agricultural banks as delivery channels to complete documentation, collect premium, and make payouts on their behalf. As specific triggers for payouts are already identified, in the event of a climate event, the insurance company or the finance institutions representing them are obliged to compensate the insured parties according to the payment schedule. The government agencies are responsible for monitoring and evaluation as well as grievance handling to ensure that timely payments are made.

The ASEAN+3 region has witnessed rapid economic growth but is extremely vulnerable to the impacts of climate change and extreme weather-induced events. The financial costs of disasters have been constantly increasing and were estimated at $4 billion per annum over the last decade.[82] The ASEAN Agreement on Disaster Management and Emergency Response is a collaborative step to build resilience through communications, resource mobilization, financing, and partnerships. Currently, funding for the ASEAN Coordinating Centre for Humanitarian Assistance on Disaster Management is response-driven and, therefore, requires an endowment fund to make it self-sufficient to respond to disaster and extreme events.

Critical Success Factors

- **Simple product structure and awareness generation for ease of user understanding.** Climate risk insurance should have a simple and clear structure to facilitate an understanding of the product in terms of the triggers for payment and the schedule for compensation. Awareness and sensitization workshops need to be organized to assist a proper understanding of climate insurance features.
- **Close collaboration between stakeholders.** Close collaboration is required among government agencies (meteorological, disaster, and emergency response), insurance companies, and delivery channels (banks, microfinance institutions) to ensure timely and correct payouts if a weather-linked event is triggered or a disaster precipitated. Access to accurate meteorological and other weather data is critical.
- **Proactive approaches and promptness.** Prompt assistance after a climate shock saves more lives and livelihoods and ultimately is more cost-effective.
- **Solutions customized to local conditions.** Risk transfer solutions to protect the poor and vulnerable people from extreme weather events must always be tailored to the local needs and conditions in terms of the climatic risk as well as the economic and social needs of the clients.
- **Integrated climate risk management approach.** Governments should develop an integrated climate risk management approach with risk reduction strategies to build resilience to potential climate shocks through social protection programs related to livelihood support and food assistance. This will help reduce risk, access insurance, increase savings, enable a quicker recovery, and generate greater support for climate risk insurance.
- **Involvement of beneficiaries.** Successful climate risk insurance is based on the inclusive and accountable involvement of beneficiaries and other local stakeholders. A transparent insurance that involves communities in the design and implementation is one that generates trust.

Case Study

In 2021, the Government of Cambodia, with support from ADB, initiated a pilot design and testing of a weather-indexed crop insurance scheme in three provinces under the Climate Resilient Rice Commercialization Sector Development Plan. Under this scheme, indemnity payments are based on a rainfall index that is measured at a local weather station and can also be verified using satellite data. The payments are not based on the consequence of the weather or on actual crop yield. A weather index-linked crop insurance approach was adopted as traditional crop insurance schemes had failed in the past with farmers complaining about the quantum of payouts and insurance entities voicing concerns

---

[82] ASEAN Secretariat. *ASEAN Vision 2025 on Disaster Management*. Jakarta. https://asean.org/wp-content/uploads/2021/01/fa-220416_DM2025_email.pdf.

on costs of implementation. As the insurance is weather-index linked (in this case rainfall), the insurance company does not have to visit the farm to determine premiums or assess the damage as it receives data from the weather stations. If the rainfall at specific stages of the crop (sowing, growing, and harvesting) is either below or above a pre-specified threshold, a payout as per the payment schedule is triggered. This significantly reduces the transaction costs of the insurance company and provides a no-questions-asked payout to the farmer. Two insurance companies, with the support of reinsurance entities, are actively involved in this pilot project. The project is ongoing and would enlist 10,000 farmers as policy holders.

The Southeast Asia Disaster Risk Insurance Facility (SEADRIF) is a multi-country catastrophe risk insurance facility supported by Cambodia, Indonesia, Japan, Lao PDR, Myanmar, the Philippines, Singapore, and Viet Nam, with technical support from the World Bank, to strengthen the financial resilience in the ASEAN region to climate and disaster shocks. The SEADRIF is designed to provide catastrophe risk coverage by making indemnity payments to member countries that suffer losses due to a disaster. It is currently offering its first insurance policy that provides a government with 3-year coverage against floods and other disaster risks. The SEADRIF also provides technical and capacity building assistance to its member countries in order to enable advance and more reliable response and recovery to climate and disaster shocks. The SEADRIF is an example of how disaster risk insurance can be used to protect countries from the financial impacts of disasters by reducing their economic losses.

The SEADRIF and the Caribbean Catastrophe Risk Insurance Facility (Appendix case study 13) serve as good models of regional disaster risk insurance entities that can provide timely relief and assistance in the aftermath of extreme climate-induced and natural hazard events.

4.4.10 Crowdfunding

Key Objectives

Crowdfunding involves raising small amounts of capital from a large number of people to finance a new project, or expand or rehabilitate an existing project. It uses social media platforms to reach out to small investors on the internet to fund micro, small and medium-sized ventures based on a presentation of the project offer. It enables the entrepreneur or project initiator to directly appeal to a large body of potential investors based on the offer details, thus avoiding the use of an intermediary to provide a project analysis. Given the small amounts of investment being sought, investors are often willing to finance these projects either as a donation or as an equity contribution.

Description of the Financing Model

There are many types of crowdfunding (Table 5).

Table 5: Crowdfunding Models

Type	Features
Peer-to-peer lending	Investor lends money and is repaid with interest within a given timeframe
Equity crowdfunding	Sale of shares in the venture
Reward-based	Investor donates to a project and receives nonfinancial rewards
Donation-based	Investor donates to a project with no expectation of returns
Debt-security	Investor invests in a debt security issued by the company
Hybrid models	Combination of more than one crowdfunding type

Source: Study team analysis.

Sector and Project Fit

Crowdfunding has been utilized in a number of sectors ranging from micro, small, and medium-sized enterprises. While crowdfunding is often associated with creative projects or social causes, it can also be used to finance infrastructure projects. Here are some sectors and types of infrastructure projects where crowdfunding can be deployed:

- **Renewable energy** comprises small-scale renewable energy projects, such as solar panels on homes or community solar projects. Crowdfunding platforms can also be used to support the development of larger-scale renewable energy projects, such as wind farms or solar power plants.
- **Transportation** comprises infrastructure projects, such as bike paths, pedestrian bridges, or public transportation initiatives. It can also be used to support the development of new transportation technologies, such as electric vehicles or autonomous vehicles.
- **Water and sanitation** infrastructure projects are mainly implemented in underserved communities and may include projects such as building wells, water filtration systems, or public restrooms.
- **Community facilities** comprising parks, libraries, or community centers can help to create more vibrant and connected communities.
- **Telecommunications** includes development infrastructure such as community broadband networks. This can help to bridge the digital divide and improve access to the internet in underserved areas.

Overall, crowdfunding can be a useful tool for financing a wide range of infrastructure projects, particularly those that are smaller in scale or that may have difficulty accessing traditional sources of financing.

Key Stakeholders

- Enterprise developers, project initiators, entrepreneurs
- Investors
- Internet-based crowdfunding platforms that act as intermediaries for the hosting of projects and as payment gateways

Financing Model and Framework

Crowdfunding unlocks early-stage investment for innovative companies with diverse objectives and social missions and also empowers the "crowd of investors" to actively fund companies they are confident about. In most cases, investors seek to benefit from the growth of the business. This mechanism does not rely on traditional financing channels, such as banks, which may not lend to these companies or ventures based on their lack of collateral, experience profile, new product risk, untested revenue stream, etc. Entrepreneurs and ventures are thus able to mobilize financing for the project without satisfying the more stringent project evaluation undertaken by a bank, a venture capital entity, or an angel investor. It also provides investors the opportunity to invest small amounts in multiple ventures, thereby diversifying their portfolio and maximizing their chances of a good return.

Critical Success Factors

- Provide the unique value proposition, project details, revenue stream, and returns to investor
- Market analysis, realistic financial projections, and information on suppliers and end users
- Usage of funds and experience profile of the project team

Case Study

Music Securite Impact Investment (Appendix case study 14) demonstrates how a small crowdfunding platform with its unique "half donation, half investment" model was able to finance hundreds of small- and medium-scale businesses and infrastructure projects through individual fund structures. It has now grown into a multimillion fund that supports several projects, including reconstruction activities.

4.4.11   Land Value Capture

Key Objectives

Land value capture (LVC) is an innovative funding approach that has been adopted by a few Asian governments as a model to bridge the infrastructure gap. It is a process whereby the public sector transfers the ownership of a piece of land to the private sector in exchange for payment of money or services. It is used to help fund vital public projects and services and is a way to generate revenue without issuing public debt. In order to raise capital for infrastructure development, governments and their agencies

- trigger a rise in land values through a range of actions, including accessibility-improving infrastructure investments or regulatory changes;
- institute a process to retain part of the value-add through public projects; and
- use LVC proceeds to fund ongoing or planned infrastructure investments or to offset any potentially negative impacts of public infrastructure projects.

The LVC approach helps to unlock the value of public land and attract private investment which can be used to fund public services or infrastructure.

Description of the Financing Model

To integrate LVC techniques into urban planning and public infrastructure finance, the first hurdle is to quantify the land value uplift that can occur. A review of 61 studies of mass rapid transit (MRT) in both advanced and developing economies shows that the price premium for properties within a catchment area of an MRT station is 5% for residential properties and 30% for commercial properties; beyond the catchment area, land prices continue to decline the farther away a property is from a MRT station (by 8% and 15% per kilometer [km] of distance from the station for residential and commercial properties, respectively). However, looking only at average effects of mass transit on property values ignores a vast variation across studies of land price effects of proximity to MRT stations; differences in overall design quality, network accessibility, and economic conditions across cities can account for some of the differences in the effect of MRT on land values.[83]

Through a systematic literature review and quantitative analysis using case studies, ADB estimated the potential for value-add around MRT stations around the world, and particularly in Bangkok, Jakarta, and Manila, and its results show:[84]

- On average, land values in Bangkok increase by $23 per square meter with every 10% decrease in distance from the nearest MRT station. A case study of a new MRT station in Bangkok reveals an incremental land value increase of $5.8 billion within a 5-km radius.
- Land value changes in rail-served Dukuh Atas, a planned integrated transport hub in central Jakarta, are greater than for Harmoni, a bus-served transit hub that will not have access to the light rail transit (LRT) line. Between 2015 and 2018, land prices rose by 38.4% in Dukuh Atas, while prices in Harmoni increased by only 14.3%.
- In Manila, growth in value of land parcels within 1 km of MRT-3 stations has been higher than for parcels more than 2 km away from a station. Since the announcement and construction of the rail line, residential parcel value grew by $154 per square meter more, and commercial parcel value grew by $545 per square meter more in near-MRT-3 areas compared to farther-out comparator parcels. This was despite a similar growth trend in parcel prices for all areas prior to announcement of the MRT-3 project in 1995. Conservative estimates of total value uplift attributable to public investment in MRT-3 is close to $3.4 billion—roughly five times the $655 million construction cost of MRT-3.

---

[83]   ADB. 2019. *Sustaining Transit Investment in Asia's Cities. A Beneficiary Funding and Land Value Capture Perspective.* Manila. https://www.adb.org/publications/sustaining-transit-investment-asia-cities.

[84]   Footnote 83.

There are five proven LVC mechanisms that can be used in combination to provide a practical pathway to successful funding of major transit initiatives.

- **Value capture through the mainstream taxation system.** Working within the existing taxation regime, one can identify potential tax increases that result from the expansionary effects of major transit projects. The future increase in tax base can be utilized as a repayment stream over time, and borrowed against to provide up-front funds for infrastructure delivery.

- **Special fees and levies.** These are new and specific levies on benefits and beneficiaries in accordance with estimates of benefit received. Practical worldwide examples include betterment levies for specific subject areas levied on beneficiaries of a major transit upgrade (particularly based on increases in property value due to enhanced connectivity), connection fees where a charge is paid by major property owners for physically integrating their property to a transit station (new or existing) via a new underground or aboveground walkway connection, and re-zoning fees in return for the value increase achieved where allowable floor space is increased substantially (or transitioned to higher-value and better uses).

- **Auction of development rights.** This involves putting development opportunity and value associated with a new transit facility or line to sale, via open auction.

- **A comprehensive transit-oriented development and urban renewal agency with value capture capabilities.** This would typically be a comprehensive urban renewal authority featuring rezoning powers, master-planning capabilities, plus the intention to generate new property value—working with access enhancements and delivery of needed transit infrastructure. The urban renewal authority may also engage in the delivery of housing and public realm enhancements and can partner with private sector developers on a site-by-site basis within their subject areas.

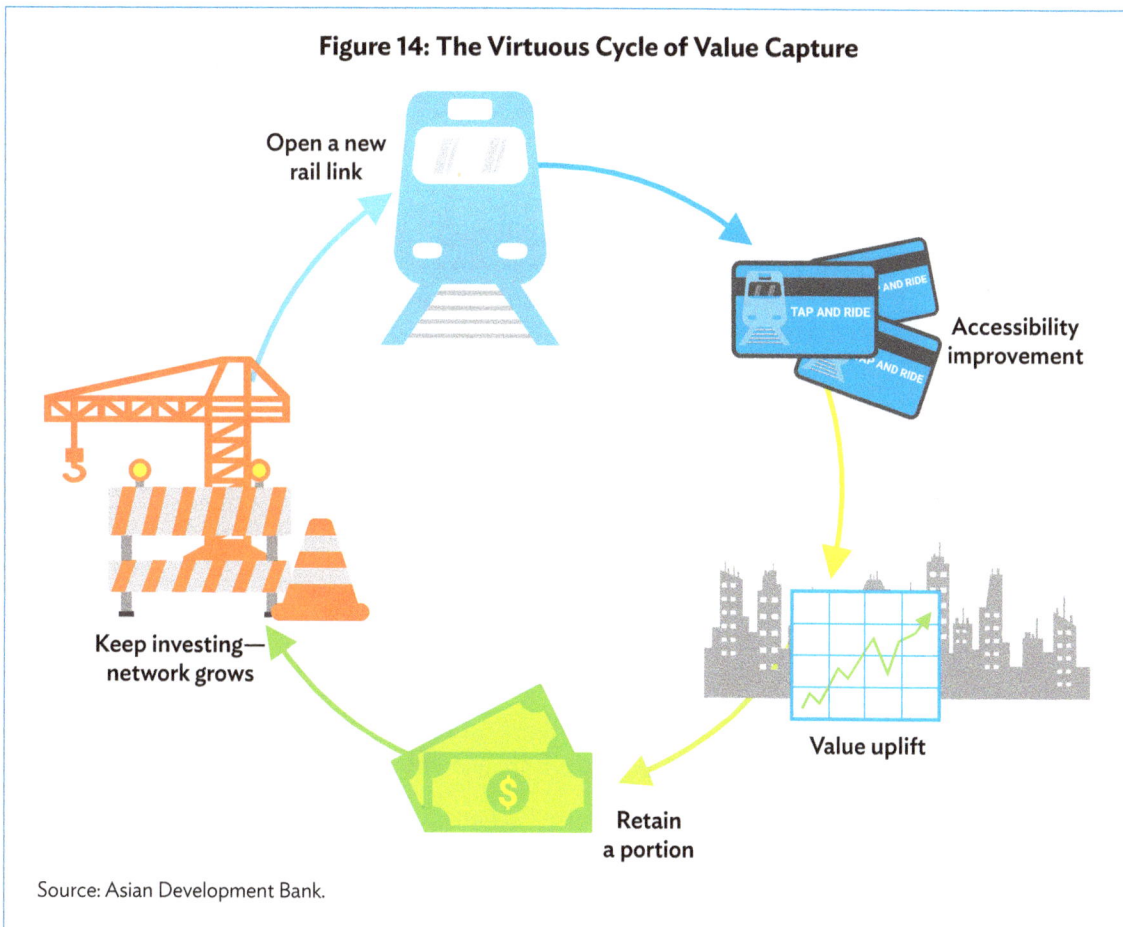

Figure 14: The Virtuous Cycle of Value Capture

Open a new rail link

Accessibility improvement

Value uplift

Retain a portion

Keep investing— network grows

Source: Asian Development Bank.

- **Direct property-rail agency as developer in the "East Asian" style.** This would be a transit operator or agency involved in developing and trading property holdings associated with stations and precinct- or corridor-scale projects on a commercial basis, with the intent to use at least some of the profit from those activities for transit infrastructure and facility funding.

Leading Asian cities such as Singapore and Hong Kong, China tend to use all these mechanisms in tandem for their urban development strategies, rather than relying on just one mechanism.

The LVC strategy can be described as a **virtuous cycle** in which a larger number of much required infrastructure projects can be developed by providing benefits to potential stakeholders and beneficiaries by inviting them to make a manageable contribution to the project that is substantially smaller than the benefits that would accrue to them over a period of time (Figure 14).

Sector and Project Fit

The LVC approach is best suited for projects involving land development, such as housing, commercial, industrial, and public infrastructure projects (transportation, utilities, and public housing). This mechanism can also be beneficial for conservation and land reclamation projects as well as urban planning initiatives. It can be used to fund economic development initiatives that can benefit the community, create jobs, and improve the quality of life. To a limited extent, LVC can also be employed for PPP projects such as public transportation and public infrastructure projects.

Key Stakeholders

- Government entities including municipal and other local bodies that own rights to land
- Public sector undertakings including corporations
- Land and infrastructure developers
- Private sector

Financing Model Framework

The financing model and framework for LVC typically involves a three-step process. The first step is to identify the land parcels that have the potential to generate revenue. Then, the value of the land is estimated and an appropriate tax rate or price point is determined that takes into account the increase in value based on developmental plans. Finally, the revenue generated from LVC is collected and used to fund public infrastructure projects. The framework also includes a comprehensive set of policies and regulations to ensure that the land value is correctly estimated, the land is being used for the public good, and that the revenue generated is used for its intended purpose.

The LVC technique can be adopted to finance public investment to reduce vulnerabilities due to floods and environmental degradation as well as to reclaim land or convert existing unusable land into prime real estate. It unlocks land values and recoups the cost of development from the real estate returns as a result of the public infrastructure development project. It thus attracts capital for projects that would not have been serviced by traditional sources of financing.

A range of tools used to capture gains from land value capture are explained in Table 6.

Table 6: Land Value Capture Tools

Leveraging public real assets	Disposition (sale or lease) of excess/underutilized public assets (land, property) for cash that is re-invested in local infrastructure.
Development charges	Developer receives development rights (or tenure rights in land, or approval of land use changes) in exchange for obligation to compensate in cash (or provide in kind) the cost of certain items of public infrastructure benefiting larger area.

continued on next page

Table 6 *continued*

Sale of development rights	Development rights or certificates of additional density are sold for cash to finance infrastructure improvements.
Land pooling/ readjustment	Land owners or occupants voluntarily contribute part of their land for infrastructure development and for sale to cover some project cost. In return, each land owner receives a serviced plot of smaller area with higher value within the same neighborhood.
Special assessments/ betterment levies	Locally administered tax increments (property taxes, sales taxes, etc.) that generate additional tax revenues for re-investment in local infrastructure.
Tax increment financing	Capturing increases in property/land tax base (after infrastructure upgrades) and using such incremental tax proceeds as collateral and refinancing source for infrastructure loans.

Source: Global Facility for Disaster Reduction and Recovery and World Bank. *Land Value Capture. Investment in Infrastructure.* https://www.gfdrr.org/sites/default/files/publication/Land%20Value%20Capture.pdf.

Critical Success Factors

- **Public support gained through consultative communication.** Securing public support through consultative communication channels is important for the successful implementation of LVC projects. Benefits from the proposed public infrastructure development should be explained and laid out at the very outset. Consultation processes should also be held with landowners and other stakeholders who may be affected by the project to garner their support and alleviate their concerns.

- **Clear and fair rules.** Unambiguous, transparent, and fair rules should be established for the LVC process that can be easily understood and enforceable in law. It is observed that LVC is better accepted by landowners when charges are derived from the increase in land value as a consequence of a public improvement project rather than being charged based on public costs.[85]

- **Local government capacity.** Successful implementation of LVC requires developing greater local government capacity as they have the responsibility for determining the fee, negotiating with landowners and developers, implementing the project, and managing the land asset.

- **Equitable and sustainable development.** Land value increase should be based on equitable and sustainable development that is backed by good spatial planning and enforcement of land use regulations. Land value capture should not result in overdevelopment and congestion, thus causing adverse environmental impacts.

- **Market-driven approach.** Adopt a market-driven approach by defining the scale and timing of the developments based on market demand, location characteristics, and institutional capacity.[86]

- **Transfer commercial risk.** Transfer commercial risk to private developers through PPPs and external partnerships.

Case Study

The city of Ahmedabad in India had an impaired riverfront and was combating several environmental degradation issues as a consequence of the unplanned slum development and related inaccessibility that constrained any redevelopment activity. A $17 million public investment plan resulted in a development project that created a 22 km promenade, slum resettlement, sewage upgrade, and land reclamation. River access was opened to the public by creating a walkable waterfront, 202 hectare (ha) of land was made available for real estate development, and erosion management solutions were adopted to reduce flood risk. The city sold 30 ha of the reclaimed land and 15% of the sale proceeds recovered the cost of the entire public project investment.[87]

---

[85] OECD. 2022. *Global Compendium of Land Value Capture Policies.* https://www.oecd-ilibrary.org/sites/4f9559ee-en/index.html?itemId=/content/publication/4f9559ee-en.

[86] World Bank. 2017. *Railway Reform: Toolkit for Improving Rail Sector Performance.* https://documents1.worldbank.org/curated/en/529921469672181559/pdf/69256-REVISED-ENGLISH-PUBLIC-RR-Toolkit-EN-New-report-date-2017-12-27.pdf.

[87] Global Facility for Disaster Reduction and Recovery and World Bank. *Land Value Capture, Investment in Infrastructure.* https://www.gfdrr.org/sites/default/files/publication/Land%20Value%20Capture.pdf.

A more detailed case study on the Hong Kong, China mass transit system is available in Appendix case study 15.

4.4.12 Other Innovative Financing Mechanisms: Debt-for-Nature Swaps

Key Objectives

A debt-for-nature swap (DFNS) is a financing mechanism that involves discounting or forgiving a part of the debt owed to a creditor country, converting the residual amount into local currency, and investing it into environmental conservation activities or projects (Figure 15). In a post-pandemic world and the current economic recessionary scenario, where increasingly a number of developing countries are stressed to make debt payments, DFNS or debt-for-climate swaps could provide some relief while ensuring that environmental objectives and SDGs are achieved.

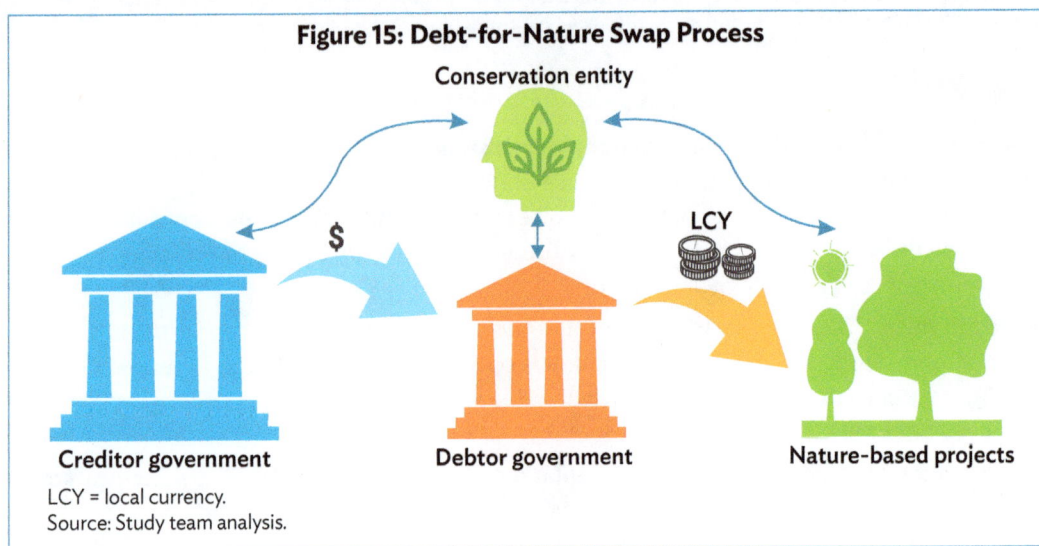

Figure 15: Debt-for-Nature Swap Process

Conservation entity

$

LCY

Creditor government   Debtor government   Nature-based projects

LCY = local currency.
Source: Study team analysis.

Description of the Financial Model

The swap usually involves borrowing economies that are debt-distressed and burdened, finding it difficult to repay foreign loan liabilities. The swap is often initiated by an environment or conservation entity that structures the swap and is involved in detailed negotiations for the loan forgiveness or discounting.

Though the general principles may remain the same, no two DFNS are similar. Typical steps are as follows:

- General guidelines are provided by the debtor country for a DFNS process and it initiates discussions with environmental or conservation organizations to develop a conservation program.

- The conservation organizations validate the availability of funding for the debt purchase and willingness of lenders to consider debt forgiveness or discounting.

- Discussions with the relevant central banks and governments are held to negotiate the specific terms of the swap including the exchange rate from foreign currency to local currency, the redemption rate, and the local investment instrument. The amount of conservation funds generated depends on the redemption rate, which is the percentage of the face value debt that is redeemed in local currency. The redemption rate is sometimes 100% of the face value debt, but it is often less, depending on negotiations among the parties involved. The redemption rate must exceed the purchase price of the debt by a large enough margin to make the transaction worthwhile.[88]

- On acquisition of the debt, the central bank of the indebted country cancels the debt in its books and allocates funds in local currency for the conservation activities.

---

[88] J. P. Resor. *Debt-for-nature swaps: a decade of experience and new directions for the future.* Food and Agriculture Organization. https://www.fao.org/3/w3247e/w3247e06.htm.

Sector and Project Fit

Debt-for-nature swap can be deployed across various sectors or types of projects that contribute to environmental conservation and protection. Some of the sectors and types of projects that can benefit from DNFS are:

- **Biodiversity conservation.** DFNS can be used to fund conservation projects in protected areas, national parks, and other areas with high biodiversity value. These projects may include habitat restoration, species monitoring and management, and community-based conservation initiatives.
- **Forest conservation.** DFNS can support sustainable forest management, reforestation, and forest restoration projects. These projects may also include efforts to combat illegal logging, promote community-based forest management, and reduce deforestation.
- **Climate change mitigation and adaptation.** DFNS can fund projects aimed at reducing greenhouse gas emissions and increasing resilience to the impacts of climate change. These projects may include renewable energy initiatives, energy efficiency programs, and climate-smart agriculture.
- **Coastal and marine conservation.** DFNS can be used to support the conservation and sustainable management of coastal and marine ecosystems, including coral reefs, mangroves, and seagrass beds. These projects may also involve community-based initiatives that promote sustainable fishing practices and reduce marine pollution.
- **Sustainable tourism.** DFNS can fund projects that promote sustainable tourism practices, such as ecotourism, and help conserve natural and cultural heritage sites.

Overall, DFNS can be used to finance a wide range of environmental conservation and protection projects that contribute to sustainable development and poverty reduction in debtor countries.

Key Stakeholders

- Central bank and finance ministry in the indebted country
- Central bank, finance ministry, and environment entities in the lending country
- Independent conservation and environmental authorities

Financing Model Framework

The financing model framework for a DFNS mechanism typically involves four primary components.

(i) **Eligible debt** is the government or commercial debt that will be part of the swap.

(ii) **Conservation projects** are the activities or investments that will be funded through the debt-for-nature swap.

(iii) **Investors** are the entities that will purchase the eligible debt in exchange for the conservation projects.

(iv) **Intermediaries** are the organizations that facilitate the swap and help to ensure that the swap is successful. They may also provide technical and financial assistance to the conservation projects.

Critical Success Factors

- The DFNS mechanism works when nations are at the risk of debt default or are unable to meet some loan obligations due to other financial commitments. This enables debt buyers to purchase the debt at prices that are below face value or discounted and then deploy the funds toward conservation activities.
- Investors do not seek profit but use the discounted mechanism to obtain additional funds for conservation projects. There is no transfer of ownership of the debt or repatriation of capital in foreign exchange.

Case Study

The DFNS is not a new mechanism; it was implemented as far back as 1988 in the Philippines when the World Wildlife Fund purchased an initial $390,000 of the Philippine debt at a discounted cost of $200,000 (51% of the face value). The Central Bank of the Philippines redeemed the debt at the full-face value of the original debt in local currency. The arrangement enabled the Central Bank to retain the money in the country and utilize it for conservation projects. Appendix case study 16 on Seychelles DFNS provides further details on this innovative financing mechanism.

4.4.13 Other Innovative Financing Mechanisms: Carbon Credit Markets

Key Objectives

Carbon credit markets are markets that allow companies to trade and purchase carbon credits, which represent a certain amount of emissions that have been reduced by a particular environmental project. Carbon credit mechanisms are a way to incentivize companies to reduce emissions and invest in cleaner energy sources by issuing tradable credits to organizations that are able to reduce their emissions to certain levels or invest in renewable energy sources. Companies that are unable to reduce their own emissions can use these credits to purchase offsets which are projects that help capture carbon dioxide from the atmosphere, thus allowing the company to comply with regulations. The money should be used to finance climate action elsewhere to remove the same amount of carbon from the air. Carbon offsets can be generated either through avoidance (renewable energy) or through removal (sequestration projects like reforestation).

Description of the Financial Model

Carbon market mechanisms can typically be classified as compliance and voluntary markets. Compliance market mechanisms are used by companies and governments that are required by law to provide an account for their carbon emissions. These are regulated by national, regional, and international carbon reduction administrators and are mainly relevant for large emitters, such as power generators, oil, iron, steel, cement, glass, and paper manufacturing and processing plants. Carbon pricing is regulated by an Emission Trading System (ETS) or by levying a carbon tax. The ETS is employed on a "cap-and-trade" principle where regulators set a limit or cap on the total amount of emissions allowed in a given period. Companies that emit less than their cap are then able to sell their "credits" to companies that exceed their cap, thus creating a financial incentive for businesses to reduce their emissions. The Clean Development Mechanism (CDM) is a flexible mechanism established under the Kyoto Protocol of the United Nations Framework Convention on Climate Change is a good example of an international compliance marketplace. The main objective of the CDM is to assist developed countries in meeting their emission reduction targets by promoting sustainable development in developing countries. The mechanism allows for the implementation of projects that reduce emissions in developing countries and earn Certified Emission Reduction credits, which can then be traded on the international market and used by developed countries to offset their emissions. The CDM also provides an opportunity for countries to share technology and transfer funds, while generating additional benefits such as job creation, improved health, increased energy access, and increased economic activity.

Carbon tax is a compliance market mechanism and is levied on the production, distribution, sale, or use of fossil fuel based on the amount of carbon dioxide they emit. Countries that levy a carbon tax include Canada, France, and Ireland. The tax is intended to reduce emissions and to encourage the use of renewable energy sources.

Voluntary carbon markets provide opportunities to both buyers and sellers of carbon credits. A project can register its emission reduction or removal activity by establishing the baseline scenario of emissions. Carbon credits are verified and issued on the basis of the emission reduction achieved and these can then be purchased by entities to either comply with international and domestic policies or be in line with their corporate ESG standards on GHG mitigation. The voluntary credit market mechanisms are either independent carbon crediting standards (such as the Verra Carbon

Registry, Gold Standard, and American Carbon Registry) that are independently managed by third-party organizations or domestic crediting mechanisms that are administered by a government-designated authority.

The basic unit traded for both carbon credits and offsets is same—one tradable carbon credit equals one ton of carbon dioxide or the equivalent (tCO_2e) amount of different GHG reduced, sequestered, or avoided. Carbon credits are an integral part of the global effort to reduce GHG emissions and combat climate change. Credits are usually issued by national or international governmental institutions. The value of carbon credits depends on the market and the specific project. Generally, carbon credits are priced based on the cost of reducing or offsetting the emissions from a particular activity. Carbon credits can range from a few cents to several dollars per credit, depending on the project and the market. The price of carbon credits also fluctuates over time, as the demand for credits increases or decreases. Carbon credits are also often bundled with other environmental services, such as renewable energy credits and water credits, to create a more marketable product.

Carbon credits can be bought and sold on the open market through various carbon credit exchanges and brokers. The most common exchanges include the Chicago Climate Exchange, the European Union Emissions Trading System, the California Carbon Trading Market, and the Canadian Carbon Offset System. Carbon credits can also be bought and sold through trading exchanges and brokerages, such as Carbon TradeXchange, Carbon Credit Exchange, AirCarbon Exchange, Xpansiv and Karbone. These exchanges and brokers provide access to a wide range of carbon credit projects, allowing buyers and sellers to find the right credits for their needs.

Though almost all ASEAN+3 countries have participated in carbon credit mechanism such as the CDM, the establishment of a structured carbon market is still in the offing. The ASEAN+3 nations have a high potential to generate carbon credits which gives the advantage of reducing their emissions and earning money for developmental activities. Most countries are in the process of reviewing their regulatory framework and working toward establishing a common market mechanism. Thailand and Viet Nam have plans to establish domestic emissions trading markets.

Key Stakeholders

- International and domestic government entities
- Project developers
- Existing GHG emitting manufacturing and processing facilities
- Carbon exchanges and brokers
- Carbon verification and certification entities

Financing Model Framework

The financing model framework for carbon markets involves the following:

- **Carbon credit market structure.** Carbon credit markets operate through a cap-and-trade system, where a regulator sets an overall limit (the "cap") on the amount of carbon that can be emitted, and allocates allowances (the "trade") to emitters. The allowances can be traded among emitters, and emitters that exceed their allowances must purchase additional credits from other emitter-traders in the market.

- **Financial modeling.** Financial models are used to analyze the cost and benefit of trading carbon credits. These models take into account factors such as the availability and price of credits, the emissions reduction targets, and the projected costs and benefits of emissions reduction.

- **Pricing mechanisms.** Carbon credit markets use several pricing mechanisms to set a fair price for carbon credits. These include auction markets, fixed rate markets, exchange markets, and over-the-counter markets.

- **Risk management.** Risk management tools are used to protect emitters from potential losses due to changes in the market for carbon credits. This includes hedging, insurance, and derivatives.

- **Regulatory framework.** Carbon credit markets are regulated by government agencies in order to ensure compliance with environmental laws

Critical Success Factors

- **Establishing a robust regulatory framework.** The success of carbon credit markets depends on the establishment of a well-defined regulatory framework. This includes setting clear targets, regulations, and enforcement mechanisms for reducing greenhouse gas emissions.

- **Ensuring transparency.** Transparency is essential for creating an efficient and effective carbon credit market. This includes creating a transparent and accessible data platform, providing accurate and timely information, and creating a system to track and monitor trading activities.

- **Establishing effective pricing mechanisms.** Properly designed pricing mechanisms are necessary to ensure fair pricing for carbon credits and a competitive market for trading.

- **Developing effective risk management tools.** Risk management tools are necessary to protect emitters from potential losses due to changes in the market for carbon credits. This includes hedging, insurance, and derivatives.

- **Encouraging innovation.** Carbon credit markets must continually evolve and adapt to new technologies, trends, and regulations. This requires innovation and creativity in order to stay ahead of the competition.

Case Studies

- Indonesia has adopted a hybrid cap-and-trade pilot scheme for the electricity generation sector (coal-fired power plants only). The scheme will not be a classic cap-and-trade system as it will not limit the total emissions of the plants. It will set different benchmarks for different categories of coal-fired power plants and will be intensity-based as the intention of the government at this stage is to reduce the GHG emissions per unit of output. Permits will be given to coal-fired plants, at no cost, to cover some of their emissions.

- In September 2022, Thailand established its first carbon credit exchange, FTIX. The exchange will be operated by the Federation of Thai Industries and its supporting platform will allow firms and government agencies to buy and sell carbon credits and track emissions on an online dashboard.

- In 2019, Singapore introduced a carbon tax through the Carbon Pricing Act that mandated any industrial facility that emits direct GHGs equal to or above 2,000 tCO_2e annually to be registered as a reportable facility and to submit an Emissions Report annually. The Singapore Exchange (SGX), DBS Bank, Standard Chartered, and Temasek established Climate Impact X (CIX), a global voluntary exchange and marketplace for quality carbon credits. The CIX aims to scale up the voluntary carbon market by connecting partners using satellite monitoring, machine learning, and blockchain to enhance transparency, integrity, and quality of carbon credits. The tax is used to fund green technology and renewable energy projects.

- In December 2022, Bursa Malaysia launched the Bursa Carbon Exchange (BCX), which is Malaysia's first voluntary carbon market. The goal of the BCX is to allow companies to trade voluntary carbon credits from environmentally-friendly projects and solutions, which can offset their carbon emissions and help them reach their climate targets. The introduction of the BCX is in line with Malaysia's target of achieving net zero greenhouse gas emissions by 2050 and also supports the transition toward a green economy for corporate Malaysia. The BCX provides an inclusive ecosystem for carbon trading, allowing more market participants to engage with clients looking for environmental, social, and governance solutions as well as those that are *Shariah* compliant.

V SUMMARY ACTIONS AND CONCLUSIONS

5.1 Recommendations

In order to successfully implement innovative financing mechanisms to bridge the infrastructure gap, ASEAN+3 governments can play a pivotal role by addressing the following key enablers:

(i) Improve regulatory frameworks and create a private sector centric investment-enabling environment. There needs to be a focus on developing strong and stable legal and regulatory frameworks to give a robust foundation that ensures transparency in all transactions, together with independent verification, certification, and ratings to provide confidence to potential investors.

(ii) Promote credit enhancement and de-risking tools. Through credit enhancement, the lender is provided with reassurance that the borrower will honor its repayment through additional collateral, insurance, or a third-party guarantee.

(iii) Explore the possibility and potential to secure an investment grade rating for the project as it provides investors the necessary confidence and assurance that the project satisfies due diligence requirements, has manageable levels of debt, good earnings potential, and a low risk of default. It confirms that the project information complies with rating agency standards and, where applicable, listing regulations. Several institutional investors have an obligation and mandate to invest only in investment grade assets.

(iv) Conduct innovative finance pilots in different sectors to demonstrate potential. This would help to ensure a proper management process of preparation and implementation of projects in line with set rules. Create and enhance relevant processes and procedures and standardize them based on lessons learned, identify weaknesses, and specify necessary amendments to the legal regulations regarding implementation.

(v) Build capacity and create awareness of innovative finance approaches across ASEAN. This could be undertaken through regional events, as well as training courses for policy makers and seminars for private sector potential stakeholders on the range of models available, case studies of successes and lessons learned, and situations where each model may be successful.

(vi) Set up project development units or "infrastructure accelerators" that will be tasked to

    (a) identify potential projects and investment opportunities;

    (b) conduct pre-feasibility studies and project appraisal through third-party market and technical assessment agencies to identify bottlenecks, risks, and financing requirements;

    (c) establish financial viability and due diligence through an independent contractor;

    (d) matchmake and identify potential investors based on their investment criteria;

    (e) work closely with private and institutional investors to understand their investment objectives, risk appetite, and reward expectation;

    (f) foster involvement with potential investors at the design and planning stage;

    (g) liaise with policy makers on regulatory issues and act as an intermediary in all negotiations;

    (h) develop a pipeline of bankable and investment-ready infrastructure projects for potential investors that have factored in all matters relating to risk management, funding model, performance measurement, and stakeholder engagement;

    (i) oversee outreach, publicity, and knowledge management to generate greater awareness and interest in positive development outcomes; and

(j)   provide project development funding to translate concepts into projects; this may include pilots, viability gap funding to harness commercial finance in PPPs, and other de-risking mechanisms.

(vii)   Tap large philanthropic organizations with a strong global footprint and local organizations with avowed ESG objectives.

(viii) Tap multilateral development and funding institutions to access concessional finance, grants, aid, etc., to be used to unlock private capital at scale.

(ix)   Create an enabling environment for PPPs by enacting laws, streamlining procurement and bidding processes; using standardized toolkits for feasibilities, contracts and reporting; introducing dispute resolution mechanisms; strengthening capacity; establishing a robust monitoring and evaluation process; and introducing conditional de-risking mechanisms.

(x)   Leverage private capital as well as the sectoral and technical expertise of the private sector by partnering with them to effectively and efficiently maximize utilization of the infrastructure.

(xi)   Implement effective project management measures to ensure that projects are completed in time, within budgets, and are in compliance with established legal, financial, and environmental norms.

(xii)   Prioritize disaster risk management as an integral component of developing sustainable infrastructure by mainstreaming resilience into planning, policymaking, project execution, and maintenance.

(xiii) Ensure transparency and continuity of policy to build and maintain investor confidence and establish fair dispute resolution and compensation mechanisms.

(xiv)   Explore and undertake new approaches beyond traditional PPP by providing project-linked contributions such as concessional lease land, tax holiday, moratoriums on fees, performance-linked incentives, buy-back of product, etc.

(xv)   Improve the effectiveness and efficiency of how infrastructure investment is utilized. "Up to 38 percent of global infrastructure investment is not spent effectively because of bottlenecks, lack of innovation, and market failures. Fact-based project selection, streamlined delivery, and the optimization of operations and maintenance of existing infrastructure can close this gap, reducing spending by more than $1 trillion a year for the same amount of infrastructure delivered."[89]

(xvi)   Build smart sustainable infrastructure that is cost effective, less polluting, and resilient to climate variability impacts. The benefits of investing in sustainable infrastructure far outweigh the incremental costs with high benefit–cost ratios as it is built to withstand, respond, and recover from climatic and other natural extreme events. Mainstreaming of resilience aspects at the project development stage should be a prerequisite in all infrastructure design and planning activities. This will lead to improved service reliability, increased asset life, and incremental value chain benefits.

5.2 Critical Success Factors

In the current inflationary and volatile financial environment bordering on recession, where return on stock market investments have not yielded good results, investors are seeking new opportunities that offer a steady return and are backed by governments or sovereign guarantees. In addition, investors are seeking to diversify their portfolio and participate in infrastructure projects, despite the longer gestation period, provided it has a long-term revenue generation potential. The critical success factors for developing an innovative financing structure are listed below.

- The key design features of successful innovative financing mechanisms with the potential to mobilize substantial funds are that **they have to be attractive to investors based on the potential returns** that they can offer. Without this critical feature that is adequately protected by financial risk-reduction measures, investors will continue to invest in financial products that consistently promise cash flows.

---

[89]   Footnote 4.

- Capital markets are circumspect and cautious about untested, unproven, bespoke, or exotic financing mechanisms. They **prefer tried-and-true standardized solutions** that are not complex, have low transaction costs, and are substantiated by successful outcomes. Innovative financing solutions that are underpinned by traditional financing instruments find greater acceptance as investors are familiar with the base mechanisms.

- Innovative finance solutions **must have scale** to interest large institutional investors such as pension funds and insurance companies that look to maximize investments in specific sectors, reduce transaction costs, and seek long-term returns.

- The solutions **must be replicable** as successful experiences can be duplicated leading to reduction in cost and time. Investors are interested to invest in repeat projects, as they are familiar with the modality, structure, and outcome.

- Significant savings can be achieved by **applying best practices** developed by leading countries. Research based on 400 global case studies suggests that governments can save up to 38% on infrastructure spending by focusing on three areas: improving project selection, streamlining delivery, and optimizing the use of existing assets.[90] These actions do not require radical change.

- The value that the **digital economy brings should be leveraged**. A financial institution can now access reliable customer data through its payment channels, thereby providing it with detailed information to assess credit worthiness, spending pattern, and risk tolerance. This information is vital for financial intermediaries and insurance underwriting to design financing approaches that match customer profiles.

- Designing an innovative financing structure requires a **fundamental change in mindset** that signals a clear shift from grant and aid-dependent funding model to a sustainable commercial model with an "on-the-ground capacity to deliver with the discipline and rigor that the capital markets require."[91]

5.3 Conclusions

International capital will cross borders into emerging or developing economies only if it is complemented or matched by equitable or substantial local capital investment that can provide confidence. In recent times, infrastructure investments have become more attractive as they provide a more stable return since infrastructure debt defaults have been low and investors are increasingly seeking alternate asset classes. The current environment coupled with innovative financing mechanisms aimed at de-risking and incentivizing infrastructure investment offers attractive opportunities for both the private and institutional sectors to widen their portfolio to include infrastructure investments.

The innovative financing market is now beyond the nascent stage but is still evolving to meet the multiple development challenges that confront both developed and developing nations. Some of the innovative financing models, such as guarantees, bonds, and PPPs, have already proved successful in catalyzing private capital and have been scaled and replicated in ASEAN across sectors. Other models such as performance-based contracting that are ripe for scaling have been implemented in smaller projects but will require clear mandates on targets and results in each case. The newer concepts of Advance Market Commitment, impact bonds, and resilience-based innovative financing require further detailing and acceptance before they can attract private capital and make a significant contribution toward positive development outcomes.

For the successful development of innovative finance, effective action and collaboration of all stakeholders in the infrastructure project life cycle is critical. More importantly, ASEAN countries will need to reform and improve their policy and institutional mechanisms by improving regulatory frameworks, developing innovative financing policy frameworks, promoting credit enhancement and de-risking tools, and building capacity to consider and implement

---

[90] Footnote 4.
[91] Saadia Madsbjerg and Lorenzo Bernascon. 2017. *What Does it Take to Mobilize Billions of Dollars to Promote the Well-Being of Humanity?* The Rockefeller Foundation. https://www.rockefellerfoundation.org/blog/take-mobilize-billions-dollars-promote-well-humanity/.

innovative finance options, thus creating an enabling environment for infrastructure investments. Agile systems and business models supported by digital platforms will contribute to increased efficiency, productivity, and transparency. This should promote increased private sector participation at scale in large capital-intensive projects that have a significant economic, environmental, and social impact and ensure sustainable development. It is envisaged that as blended finance models begin to scale along with green bonds, access to capital will not be a constraint.

Public funds need to leverage their investment by mobilizing finance from the private and institutional sectors in multiples far beyond the current average of 1:3. They should aim for early double-digit ratios, if not doubling fund sourcing. This will be the tipping point where public, private, and institutional capital can provide adequate resources to reduce the infrastructure investment gap and work toward their commitments in accomplishing their sustainable development goals.

APPENDIX: CASE STUDIES

1: Blended Finance

Name of Project	Africa Agriculture and Trade Investment Fund
Project Location	Africa
Sector	Agriculture
Objective	To uplift Africa's agriculture potential for the benefit of the poor people
Year	2011

Model Description

The Africa Agriculture Trade and Investment Fund (AATIF) is a public–private partnership open to investments from institutional investors, professional investors, and other well-informed private sector investors organized under the Luxembourg Specialized Investment Funds (SIF) law. To incentivize private investment in the fund, a mezzanine layer capitalized by KfW and Deutsche Bank, and a first-loss layer capitalized by Germany's Federal Ministry for Economic Cooperation and Development (BMZ) are utilized.

- **Fund manager:** Deutsche Bank
- **Fund mandate:** Fund that invests across the entire agricultural value chain in Africa through direct and indirect investments in financial institutions and other intermediaries that on-lend to smallholder farmers.
- **Total fund size:** $172 million

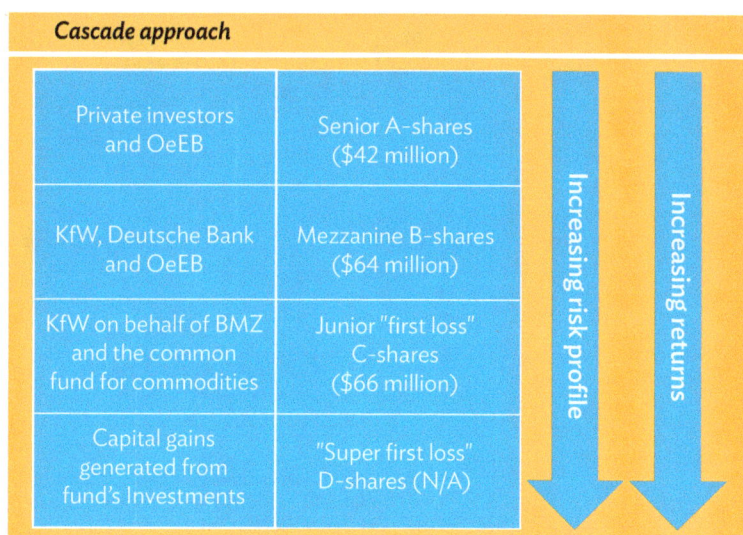

Figure A1: Different Tranches of Shares Issued

Cascade approach

Private investors and OeEB	Senior A-shares ($42 million)
KfW, Deutsche Bank and OeEB	Mezzanine B-shares ($64 million)
KfW on behalf of BMZ and the common fund for commodities	Junior "first loss" C-shares ($66 million)
Capital gains generated from fund's Investments	"Super first loss" D-shares (N/A)

Increasing risk profile   Increasing returns

BMZ = Ministry for Economic Cooperation and Development (Germany), OeEB = Development Bank of Austria.
Source: Study team analysis.

As shown in Figure A1, different tranches were created to match risk profiles of various investors:

- A-tranche: Invested in by private investors and Development Bank of Austria (OeEB)
- B-tranche: Invested in by Deutsche Bank, the Austrian Development Finance Institution (DFI), OeEB, and KfW
- C-tranche: Invested in by BMZ through KfW; provides public "first loss" capital, serving as catalytic risk buffer to attract investment in senior tranches
- D-tranche: Protects A, B, and C shareholders; made of capital gains generated by the fund's equity investments, and provides "super first loss" capital

Alongside the fund, a related technical assistance facility extends grant-based aid to projects to ensure the development potential of AATIF investments is realized. The facility has offered grant funding for various capacity building efforts such as research, employee training, and the establishment of environmental and social management systems. Additionally, the facility plans to allocate funds to support feasibility studies and other project preparation activities (Figure A2).

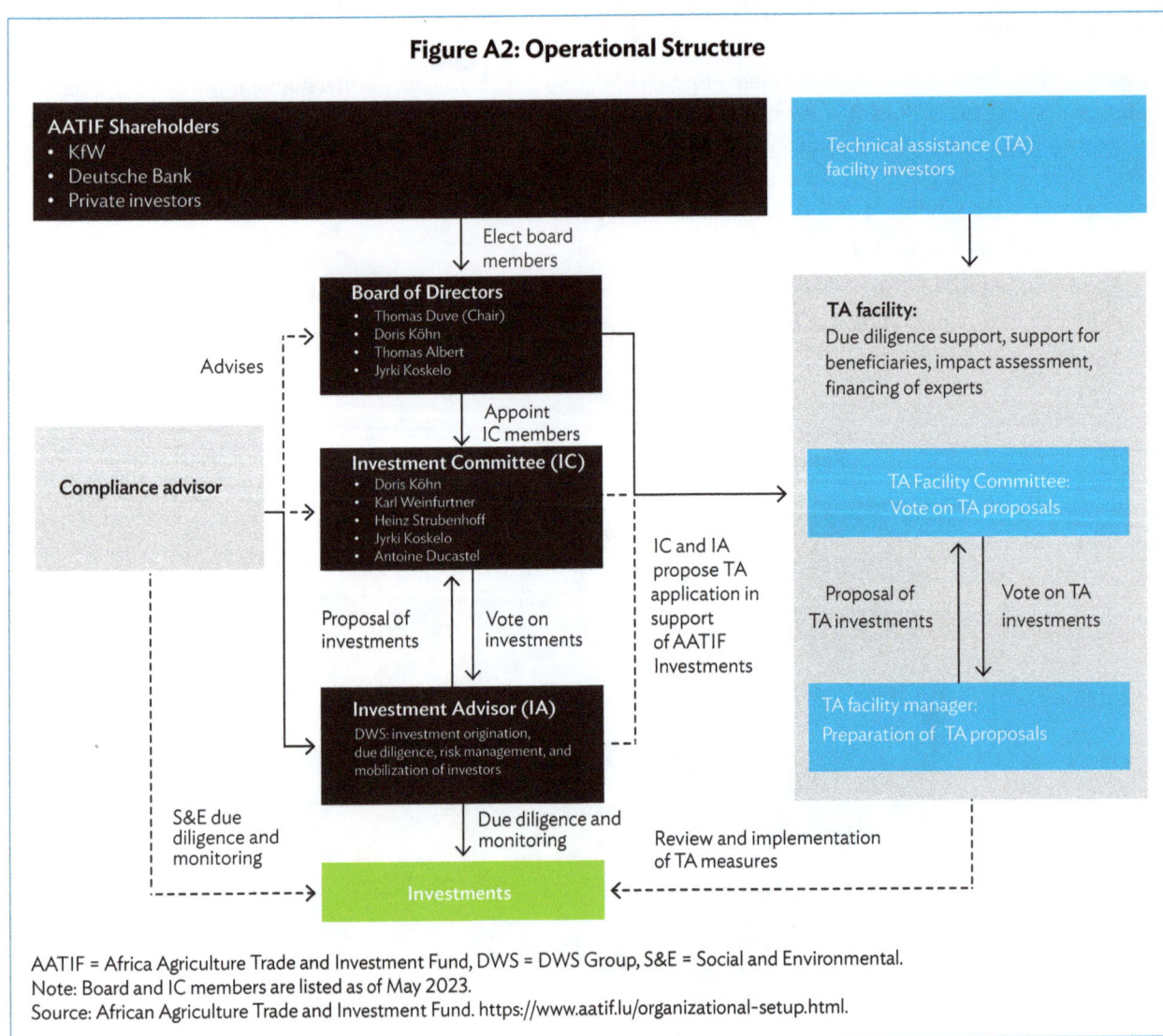

Figure A2: Operational Structure

AATIF = Africa Agriculture Trade and Investment Fund, DWS = DWS Group, S&E = Social and Environmental.
Note: Board and IC members are listed as of May 2023.
Source: African Agriculture Trade and Investment Fund. https://www.aatif.lu/organizational-setup.html.

The eligibility criteria for securing AATIF financing are as follows:

- Principal balance of the AATIF loan is higher than $5 million.
- Equity to total assets ratio post the AATIF investment is greater than ~30%.
- Investee has completed the planning process and is operational.
- Investee has an experienced management team.
- Investee is either already profitable (minimum "Earnings Before Interest, Taxes, Depreciation, and Amortization" positive) or has a strong sponsor/guarantor or the backing of a shareholder.

Specifically, AATIF pursues three primary types of investments, as detailed in Table A1.

Table A1: Financing Products for Eligible Investees

	Intermediary Investment Companies	**Direct Investment Companies**	**Financial Institutions**
Description	Agribusinesses that disburse subloans and/or in-kind loans to their suppliers or producers or finance processing plants beneficial to local economy	Cooperatives, outgrower schemes, commercial farms or processing companies across the value chain	Financing institutions who disburse subloans to clients to finance agriculture projects (e.g., working capital, long-term financing for capital expenditures)
Instrument	Senior Debt Mezzanine Equity Guarantees Risk Sharing	Senior Debt Mezzanine Equity Guarantees	Senior Debt Guarantees Risk Sharing
Size	$5million–$30 million	$5 million–$15 million	$5 million–$30 million
Tenor	Up to 12 years (average is 5–8 years)	Up to 12 years (average is 5–8 years)	Up to 10 years (average is 3–5 years)

Source: African Agriculture Trade and Investment Fund. https://www.aatif.lu/eligible-investments.html.

Implementation Timeline

2011	• The AATIF was established in August 2011 with $51,926 of Class B shares and $58.4 million of Class C shares • Concluded a direct investment of $10 million into Chobe Agrivision Company
2012 onwards	• Several multimillion dollar issues of Class A, B, and C shares to provide loans and set up financing facilities for agriculture value chain entities • Financing provided to private companies and banks to boost agricultural production, smallholder support, export market development, and research and development
2020–2022	• 2020: The AATIF and International Finance Corporation, a member of the World Bank Group, announced a €13 million investment to help Société Africaine d'Ingrédients build an onion dehydration plant in Senegal that will create hundreds of jobs and boost the country's agricultural exports. • 2022: First tranche of €15 million senior loan disbursed to ECOWAS Bank for investment and development, aimed at increasing outreach and lending to the agricultural value chain within least developing countries in West Africa.

Stakeholders Involved

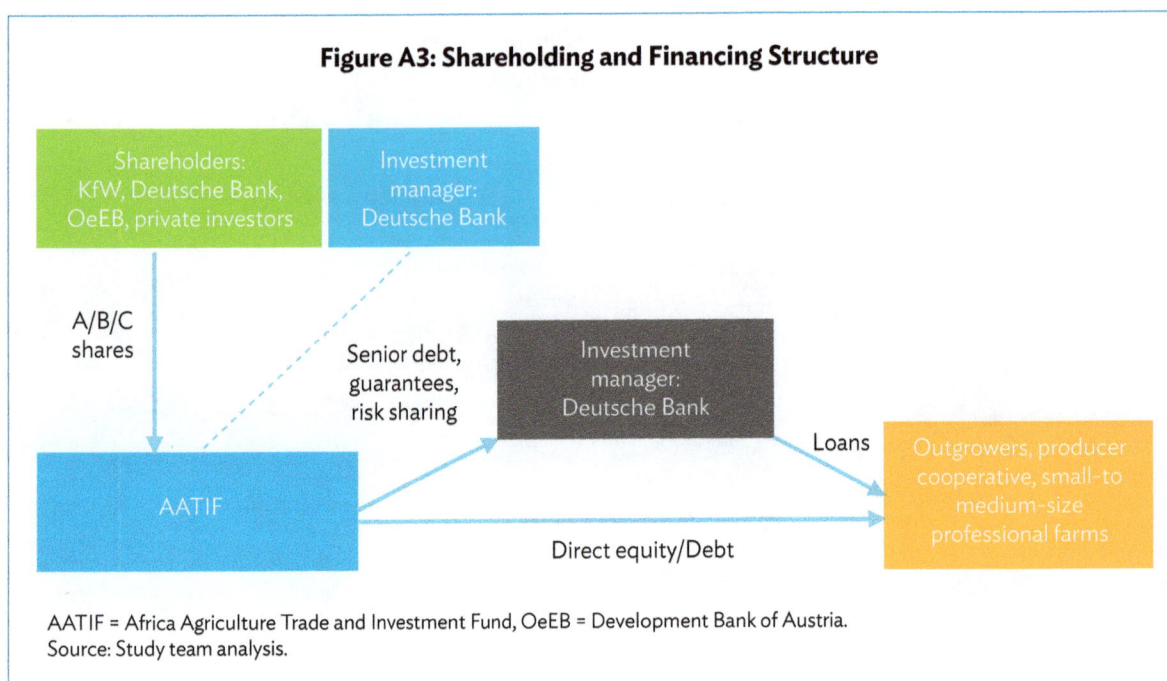

Figure A3: Shareholding and Financing Structure

AATIF = Africa Agriculture Trade and Investment Fund, OeEB = Development Bank of Austria.
Source: Study team analysis.

Benefits and Impact

- The successful blending of public and private finance allows public funds to attract private sector investors who otherwise would not consider investing in certain ventures, like the agricultural sector in Africa due to its risk profile. Utilizing government funding from Germany as C shares allowed AATIF to attract private sector investors into the A shares. By doing so, AATIF can obtain additional sources of private financing to support areas that currently lack appropriate financial services and bridge financing gaps by providing market-based financing to agricultural companies and financial intermediaries.

- Environmentally sustainable investments that can enhance food security, create employment, and boost local incomes are prioritized by AATIF. To ensure that prospective investments meet or can achieve baseline environmental, social, and governance (ESG) standards, including the provision of safe working conditions for employees and sound management of natural resources, the board of directors enforces these goals.

- Investments supported by AATIF typically promote sustainable business growth and improve the economic and social welfare of farmers and company employees. To measure and evaluate the effectiveness of all investments, AATIF regularly monitors indicators such as an increase in agricultural production and productivity levels, creation of additional employment opportunities, outreach to smallholder farmers, and an increase in farm and overall household income.[1]

> The Africa Agriculture and Trade Investment Fund highlights many useful lessons for others considering blended finance, including the need to match fund structure to investors' risk appetite, increased investment opportunities associated with a flexible investment mandate, high economic developmental impact, the need for effective communication among stakeholders, and the benefits of streamlined governance and decision-making processes within the fund.

---

[1] Convergence. 2015. *Africa Agriculture and Trade Investment Fund Case Study*. https://www.convergence.finance/resource/africa-agriculture-and-trade-investment-fund-(aatif)-case-study/view.

2: Blended Finance

Name of Project	Advance Market Commitment to Develop Pneumococcal Vaccines
Project Location	Global
Sector	Health
Objective	Reduce morbidity and mortality from pneumococcal disease
Year	2007 to date

Model Description

Advance Market Commitment (AMC) is an innovative funding mechanism that was launched in 2007 to incentivize vaccine makers by accelerating the development, availability, and production of affordable vaccines for low-income countries by providing a legally binding forward commitment to buy vaccines at per predetermined terms. It received a commitment of $1.5 billion from five countries and the Bill and Melinda Gates Foundation. The fund was utilized to purchase nearly 2 billion doses of pneumococcal conjugate vaccines (PCV). Two contracted pharmaceutical manufacturers, GlaxoSmithKline and Pfizer, agreed to sell the vaccines to low-income countries at a value not exceeding $3.50 per dose for the next 10 years thus creating a market for life-saving vaccines for children in the poorest countries. A third manufacturer (Serum Institute of India) was contracted in 2019 to develop a new PCV. The AMC mechanism is best used for social development outcomes as manufacturers are provided funds to invest in research and development and to expand manufacturing capacity, especially where the cost of developing a new product is too high to be worthwhile for the private sector to invest without a significant advance buy-back guarantee in place (Figure A4).

All funds have now been disbursed (August 2022) and the total contracted supply through 2029 amounts to 1.75 billion doses.

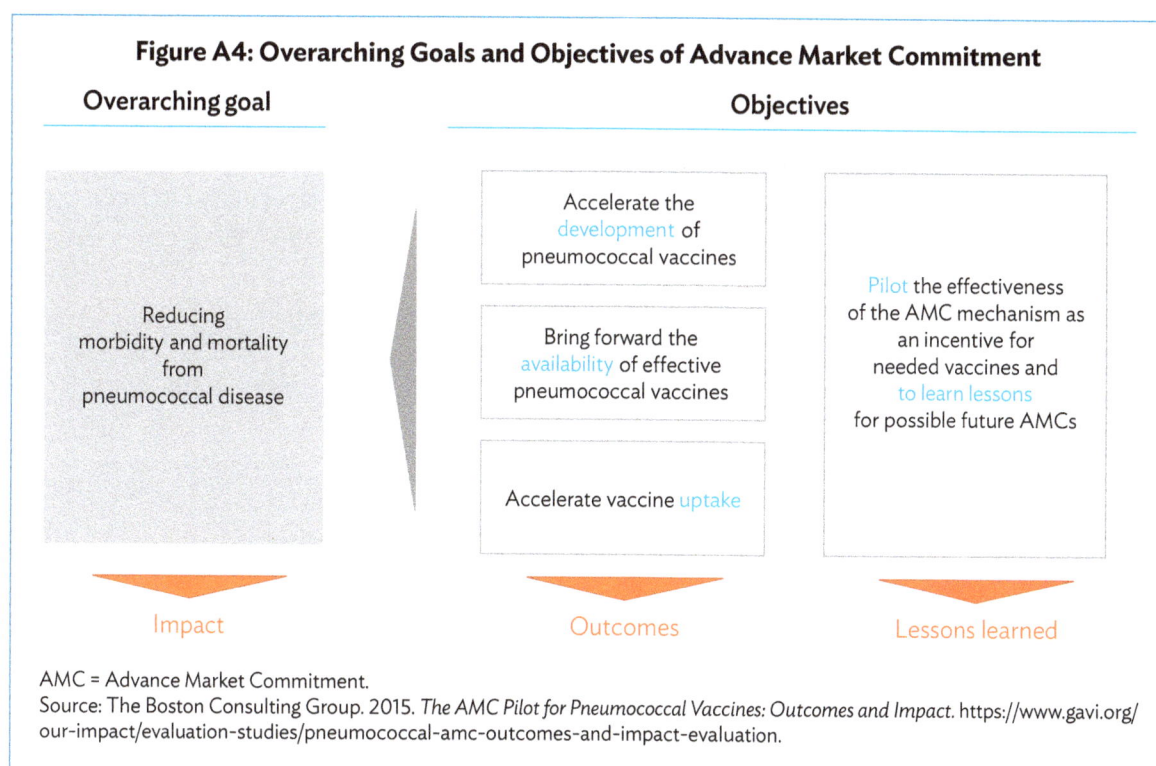

Figure A4: Overarching Goals and Objectives of Advance Market Commitment

AMC = Advance Market Commitment.
Source: The Boston Consulting Group. 2015. *The AMC Pilot for Pneumococcal Vaccines: Outcomes and Impact.* https://www.gavi.org/our-impact/evaluation-studies/pneumococcal-amc-outcomes-and-impact-evaluation.

Implementation Timeline

2005	• Centre for Global Development published a report on AMCs
2006	• G8 countries launch a consultative process for a pilot
2007	• Pilot launched funded by the Bill and Melinda Gates Foundation
2009	• Advance Market Commitment is operational
2010	• First long-term manufacturing commitments made
2012	• 58 million vaccines procured; 10 million children vaccinated (cumulative)*
2014	• 100 million vaccines procured; 46 million children vaccinated (cumulative)*
2016	• 164 million vaccines procured; 108 million children vaccinated (cumulative)*
2018	• 149 million vaccines procured; 179 million children vaccinated (cumulative)*
2019	• 161 million vaccines procured; 217 million children vaccinated (cumulative)*
2020	• 139 million vaccines procured

* All figures from *AMC for Pneumococcal Vaccines Annual Report 1 January – 31 December 2020*

Stakeholders Involved

- Public donors: Canada, Italy, Norway, Russian Federation, and United Kingdom
- Private philanthropic donor: Bill and Melinda Gates Foundation
- Operational, administrative, and financial support: Global Alliance for Vaccines and Immunization
- Procurement management: United Nations International Children's Fund (UNICEF)
- Collection and disbursement of funds: World Bank
- Vaccine manufacturing: GlaxoSmithKline, Pfizer, and Serum Institute of India

Benefits and Impact

- The continuous scaling up of the program with the inclusion of as many as 63 countries, with enhanced procurement, and vaccinations has accelerated immunization coverage and is estimated to result in over 700,000 prevented deaths by 2020. It improved health standards and developed a market for PCVs in low-income countries that can be sustained even after the conclusion of the AMC.
- By making PCVs more affordable to procure and administer, the AMC contributed to increased vaccine supply, availability, and uptake in developing countries.
- Participating suppliers have expanded their manufacturing capacity and with successive supply commitments, manufacturers are able to offer reduced prices (initially down from $3.50 to $2.90 and now to $2.00 after the introduction of a third manufacturer).
- The AMC pilot provided proof of concept and validation of the innovative financing mechanism as it achieved its development objectives, received interest from more donors including countries and the private sector, and attracted additional manufacturers that expressed interest in joining the initiative.
- The initiative led to a successful association with the biopharmaceutical industry providing them with an investment opportunity based on their core technical capabilities while ensuring commercial viability. The AMC pilot created trust and provided a foundation that can be leveraged to contribute to infrastructure development in sectors other than health.

Advance Market Commitment is an effective innovative financing mechanism when private suppliers of goods and services are involved in catering to a need that requires a very high capital outlay to enhance delivery to meet an ever-increasing demand. The high fixed cost investment, risks associated with accessing markets, and cost-effective priced solutions all combine to deter private companies from making the additional infrastructure investment. The AMC created incentives for vaccine research and its production for use in low-income developing countries with donor fund commitments that guaranteed uptake and price of the vaccine, thus mitigating investment risk and achieving social development. The success of the financing mechanism will enable countries of the Association of Southeast Asian Nations to mobilize resources to expand infrastructure facilities in a post-COVID-19 pandemic world.

3: Asset Recycling

Name of Project	National Highways Authority of India (NHAI) Operational Toll Road Concession Pilot Bundle
Project Location	India
Sector	Road
Objective	Finance construction of a large cross-country road program "Bharatmala"—a centrally sponsored and funded road and highways program of the Government of India
Year	2018

Model Description

- **Identifying public assets for monetization.** The first bundle of road projects for asset recycling consisted of nine state-owned highways in Andhra Pradesh, Gujarat, and Odisha. The aggregate length of nine projects was 680 kilometers (km), and all of the projects had been in commercial operation for at least 2 years.
- **Asset monetization through long-term lease concession.** The NHAI tendered this first bundle under the toll–operate–transfer (TOT) scheme. Key features of the 30-year concession included
  » upfront lease payments to NHAI in exchange for the operation and maintenance based on specified key performance indicators of nine highways;
  » the concessionaire taking demand risk, subject to a "rolling concession period structure" where the concession period may be lengthened or reduced depending on actual road user volume (traffic); and
  » capacity augmentation, if any, undertaken by NHAI.
- **Reinvestment of proceeds.** The upfront lease payments were recycled as capital for other infrastructure projects, primarily construction of new highways.
- **De-risking of investment.** The TOT scheme provided a de-risked platform for private players to acquire operations and maintenance rights of existing toll roads, thereby reducing NHAI's involvement in projects after construction.

Implementation Timeline

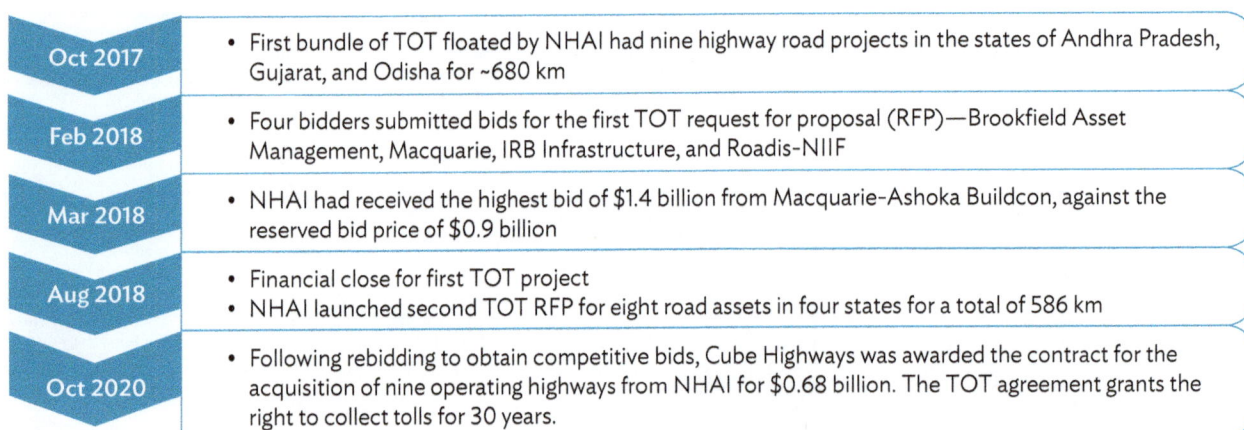

Oct 2017	• First bundle of TOT floated by NHAI had nine highway road projects in the states of Andhra Pradesh, Gujarat, and Odisha for ~680 km
Feb 2018	• Four bidders submitted bids for the first TOT request for proposal (RFP)—Brookfield Asset Management, Macquarie, IRB Infrastructure, and Roadis-NIIF
Mar 2018	• NHAI had received the highest bid of $1.4 billion from Macquarie-Ashoka Buildcon, against the reserved bid price of $0.9 billion
Aug 2018	• Financial close for first TOT project • NHAI launched second TOT RFP for eight road assets in four states for a total of 586 km
Oct 2020	• Following rebidding to obtain competitive bids, Cube Highways was awarded the contract for the acquisition of nine operating highways from NHAI for $0.68 billion. The TOT agreement grants the right to collect tolls for 30 years.

Target

- The NHAI aims to lease 75 operational road projects, spanning 4,376 km, through the TOT scheme.
- The NHAI estimated that it could raise as much as $3.5 billion from the monetization of the highway assets.

Stakeholders Involved

Figure A5: National Highways Authority of India Stakeholder Role and Responsibilities

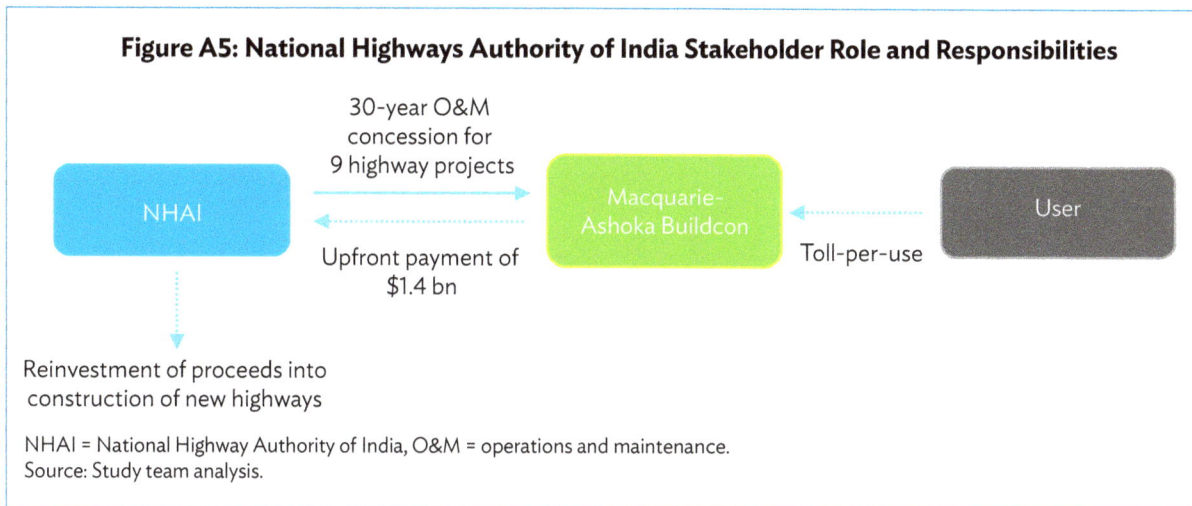

NHAI → 30-year O&M concession for 9 highway projects → Macquarie-Ashoka Buildcon ← Toll-per-use ← User

Macquarie-Ashoka Buildcon → Upfront payment of $1.4 bn → NHAI

NHAI → Reinvestment of proceeds into construction of new highways

NHAI = National Highway Authority of India, O&M = operations and maintenance.
Source: Study team analysis.

Benefits and Impact

- Bid offer of $1.4 billion was about 50% higher than NHAI's estimate of $0.9 billion. By conducting roadshows globally and obtaining international ratings from credit rating agencies such as Moody's and S&P Global Ratings, NHAI has been successful in fostering investor confidence.

- The TOT scheme enables up-front payment of lease to fund other infrastructure projects, which enables capital to be recycled to finance other infrastructure, builds, and upgrade.

- The scheme encourages private sector participation to broaden the funding base and reduces reliance on debt. The project attracted institutional investors including Pension and Insurance Funds and Sovereign Wealth Funds.

- The model provides several advantages, including streamlined operations and maintenance, prevention of toll revenue theft, and the ability to use future toll revenues to enhance new road infrastructure.

- The model harnesses private sector innovation and efficiency. The private sector will operate the assets for a 30-year concession period. The concessionaire is required to implement advanced electronic tolling procedures, as well as state-of-the-art safety measures to guarantee that highway users have a seamless and secure experience on these highways.

The experience of the National Highway Authority of India demonstrates that it is possible to draw in global investors and "patient" capital providers, such as sovereign wealth, pension, and insurance funds, seeking to invest low-cost funds in steady cash-generating public assets as long as the opportunity is well-structured in terms of scale, potential, and risk management. This was India's first asset recycling initiative and sets an example for future monetization of public projects in other sectors such as power, telecommunications, and oil and gas.

Source: R. K. Singh. 2018. View: How NHAI's asset recycling plan is a step forward in the right direction. *The Economic Times.* 7 March. https://economictimes.indiatimes.com/industry/transportation/view-how-nhais-asset-recycling-plan-is-a-step-forward-in-the-right-direction/articleshow/63208325.cms?utm_source=contentofinterest&utm_medium=text&utm_campaign=cppst.

4: Asset Securitization

Name of Project	Clifford Capital Infrastructure Take-Out Facility
Project Location	Singapore
Sector	Across eight industry sectors
Objective	To address Asia Pacific's infrastructure financing gap by mobilizing a new pool of institutional capital
Year	2018

Model Description

The Infrastructure Take-Out Facility (TOF) was designed and structured by Clifford Capital Pte. Ltd. (Clifford Capital) with a view to mobilizing institutional capital for infrastructure debt in the Asia and Pacific region and the Middle East by facilitating the transfer of exposure in long-term project and infrastructure loans from banks to institutional investors.[2] The diversified portfolio of 37 project finance and infrastructure loans, spread across 8 industry subsectors and 16 countries in the rapidly-expanding Asia-Pacific and Middle East regions, was initially financed by an issue size of $458 million (Figure A6). The portfolio comprised of 30 projects that have reliable and predictable long-term cash flows, including offtake agreements with well-established and creditworthy counterparties, such as major global corporations, government-linked sponsors, and state-owned enterprises (Figure A7). The debt service cash flows from the underlying loans are mainly denominated in US dollars, aligning them with the debt service cash flows of the Notes.

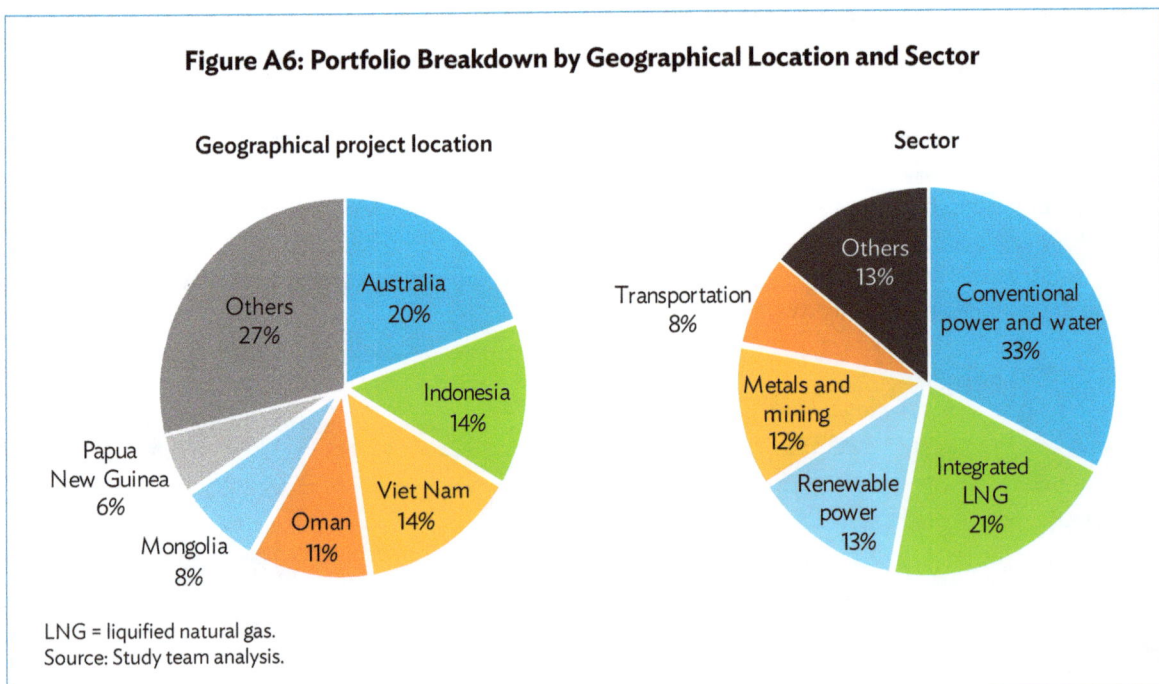

Figure A6: Portfolio Breakdown by Geographical Location and Sector

Geographical project location

Others 27%
Australia 20%
Indonesia 14%
Viet Nam 14%
Oman 11%
Mongolia 8%
Papua New Guinea 6%

Sector

Conventional power and water 33%
Integrated LNG 21%
Renewable power 13%
Metals and mining 12%
Transportation 8%
Others 13%

LNG = liquified natural gas.
Source: Study team analysis.

---

2   Clifford Capital. 2018. https://www.cliffordcap.sg/resources/ck/files/20180725%20Press%20Release%20-%20TOF.pdf.

Figure A7: Portfolio Breakdown by Asset Type

24.4% of assets were in advanced stages of construction, and benefit from sovereign or parent guarantees

75.6% of assets relate to operational projects with stable and predictable cash flows

Source: Study team analysis.

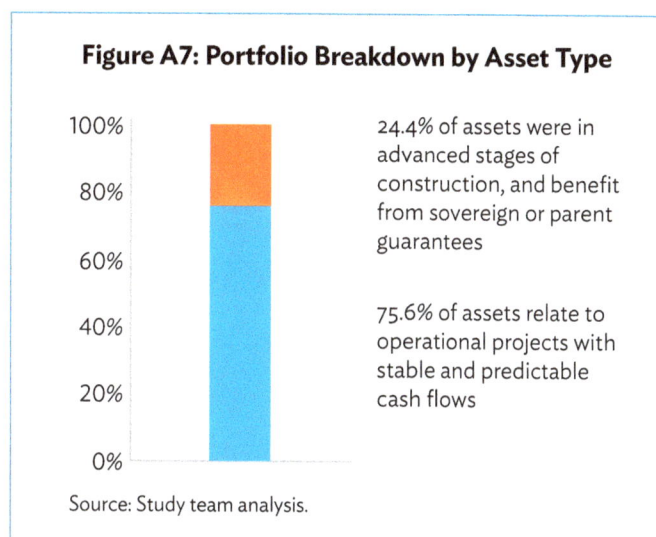

- **Overview of the issuance.** Bayfront Infrastructure Capital Pte. Ltd., which is sponsored by Clifford Capital, issued four classes of Notes. Three classes of investment-grade rated Notes (Classes A, B, and C) were offered to institutional investors and listed on the Singapore Exchange (SGX). The Notes were rated as Aaa, Aa3, and Baa3 respectively by Moody's. Clifford Capital will take a subordinated 10% first-loss piece of the capital structure, which it will hold to maturity.

- **New entity.** Following the success and viability of the Infrastructure TOF concept with the issuance of Asia's first securitization of project finance and infrastructure loans, Clifford Capital entered into a strategic partnership in 2019. It established Bayfront Infrastructure Management (BIM), a vehicle 70% owned by Clifford Capital Holdings and 30% by the Asian Infrastructure Investment Bank. BIM is expected to be capitalized at $1.98 billion, comprising $180 million in equity and $1.8 billion in debt issuance capacity.

- **New asset class.** Acknowledging the substantial disparity and gap in Asia's infrastructure financing requirements and the growing necessity to mitigate and adapt to climate change-related infrastructure challenges, the stakeholders recognize the need for more investments to sustain the high rate of economic growth. BIM aims to address this need by raising a fresh pool of institutional capital through the issuance of infrastructure asset-backed securities (IABS) and providing investors with access to a diversified portfolio of project and infrastructure loans across various geographies and sectors.

- **Infrastructure asset-backed securities features.** IABS are structured Notes backed by diversified portfolios of high quality, senior ranking project, and infrastructure loans that offer investors (i) structural protections, including "first loss" risk retention by the issuer; (ii) regular monitoring by the collateral manager of performance metrics, including over-collateralization and interest coverage ratios, and cash diversion in the event of a breach; and (iii) dedicated portfolio management by the collateral manager with specialized domain knowledge, as well as the ability for the collateral manager to substitute assets in the portfolio on a limited basis during credit events and loan prepayment events.

- **Bayfront Infrastructure Management operations.** The business activities of BIM involve (i) acquisition, warehousing, and management of a portfolio of project and infrastructure loans; (ii) sponsoring, structuring, and managing all future distributions of these loans to institutional investors; and (iii) investing in the equity tranche or vertical slice of every sponsored IABS issuance.

Figure A8: The Take-Out Facility Value Proposition

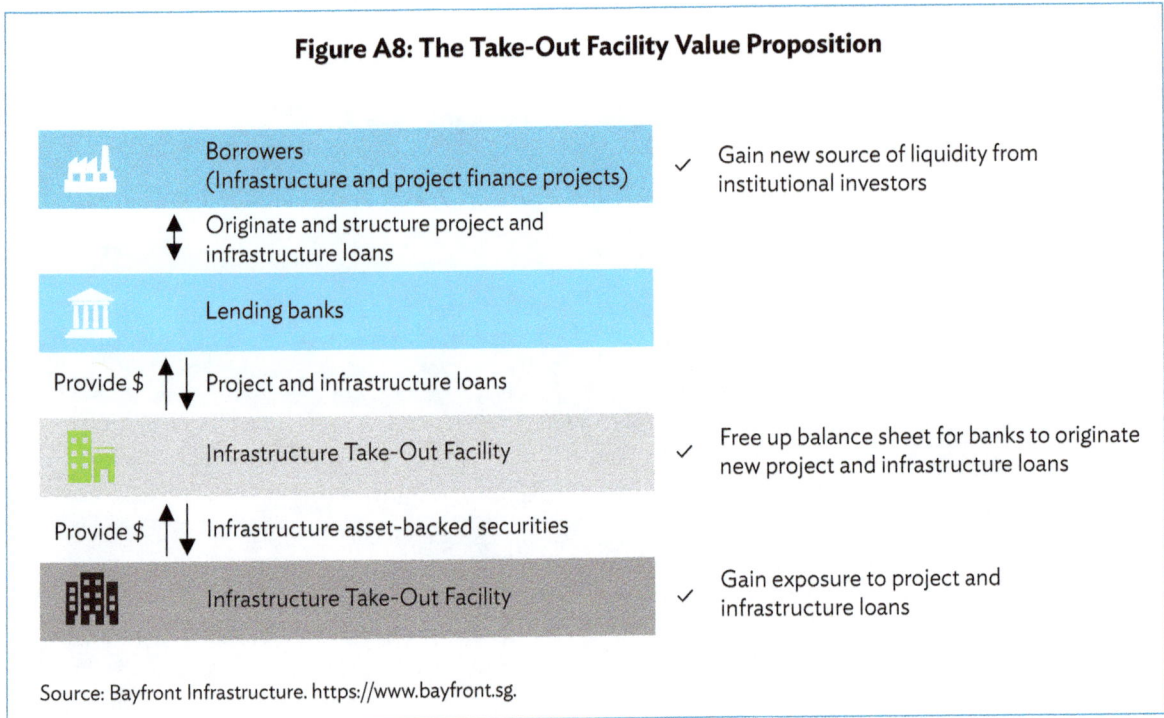

Borrowers
(Infrastructure and project finance projects)

✓ Gain new source of liquidity from institutional investors

Originate and structure project and infrastructure loans

Lending banks

Provide $ | Project and infrastructure loans

Infrastructure Take-Out Facility

✓ Free up balance sheet for banks to originate new project and infrastructure loans

Provide $ | Infrastructure asset-backed securities

Infrastructure Take-Out Facility

✓ Gain exposure to project and infrastructure loans

Source: Bayfront Infrastructure. https://www.bayfront.sg.

Implementation Timeline

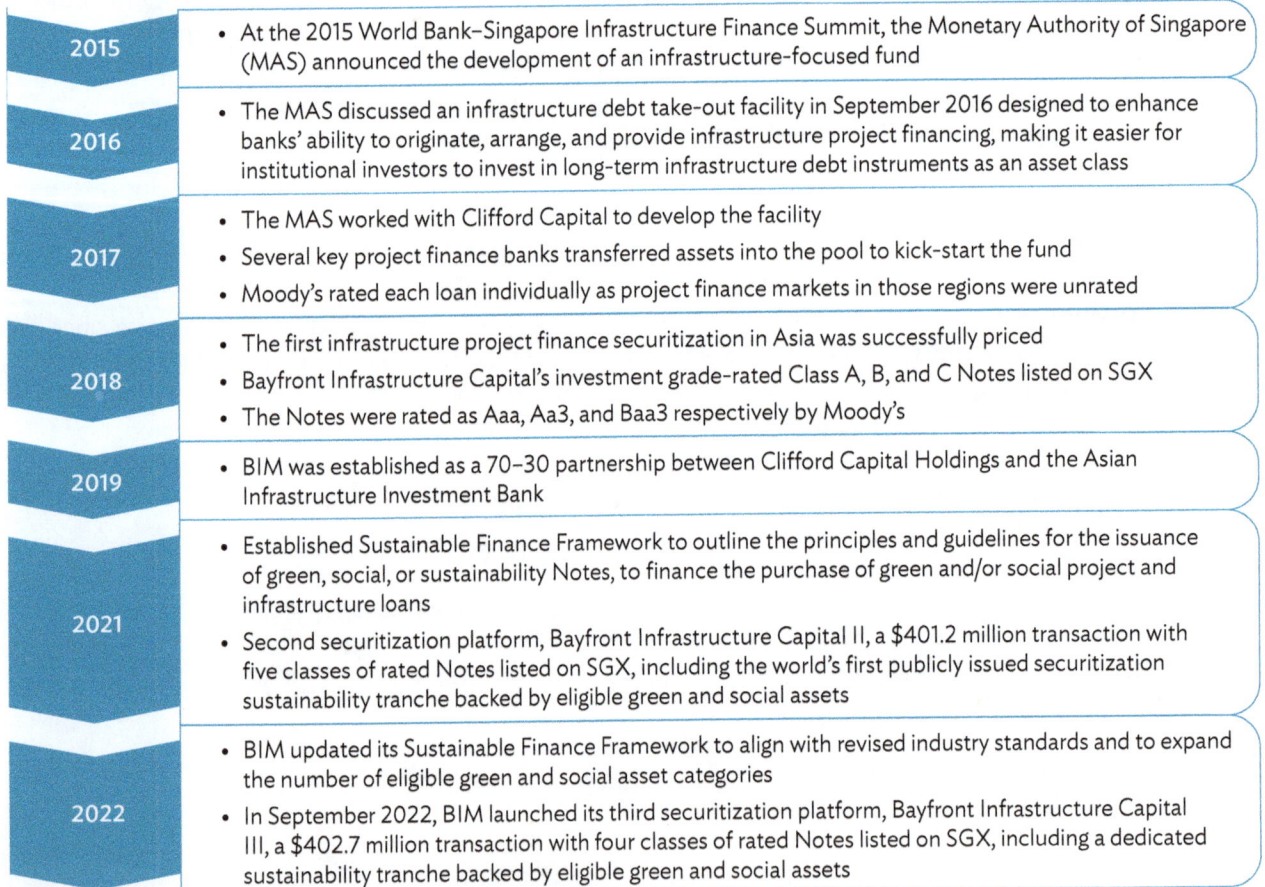

Year	Details
2015	• At the 2015 World Bank–Singapore Infrastructure Finance Summit, the Monetary Authority of Singapore (MAS) announced the development of an infrastructure-focused fund
2016	• The MAS discussed an infrastructure debt take-out facility in September 2016 designed to enhance banks' ability to originate, arrange, and provide infrastructure project financing, making it easier for institutional investors to invest in long-term infrastructure debt instruments as an asset class
2017	• The MAS worked with Clifford Capital to develop the facility • Several key project finance banks transferred assets into the pool to kick-start the fund • Moody's rated each loan individually as project finance markets in those regions were unrated
2018	• The first infrastructure project finance securitization in Asia was successfully priced • Bayfront Infrastructure Capital's investment grade-rated Class A, B, and C Notes listed on SGX • The Notes were rated as Aaa, Aa3, and Baa3 respectively by Moody's
2019	• BIM was established as a 70–30 partnership between Clifford Capital Holdings and the Asian Infrastructure Investment Bank
2021	• Established Sustainable Finance Framework to outline the principles and guidelines for the issuance of green, social, or sustainability Notes, to finance the purchase of green and/or social project and infrastructure loans • Second securitization platform, Bayfront Infrastructure Capital II, a $401.2 million transaction with five classes of rated Notes listed on SGX, including the world's first publicly issued securitization sustainability tranche backed by eligible green and social assets
2022	• BIM updated its Sustainable Finance Framework to align with revised industry standards and to expand the number of eligible green and social asset categories • In September 2022, BIM launched its third securitization platform, Bayfront Infrastructure Capital III, a $402.7 million transaction with four classes of rated Notes listed on SGX, including a dedicated sustainability tranche backed by eligible green and social assets

Stakeholders Involved

Figure A9: Take-Out Facility Shareholders

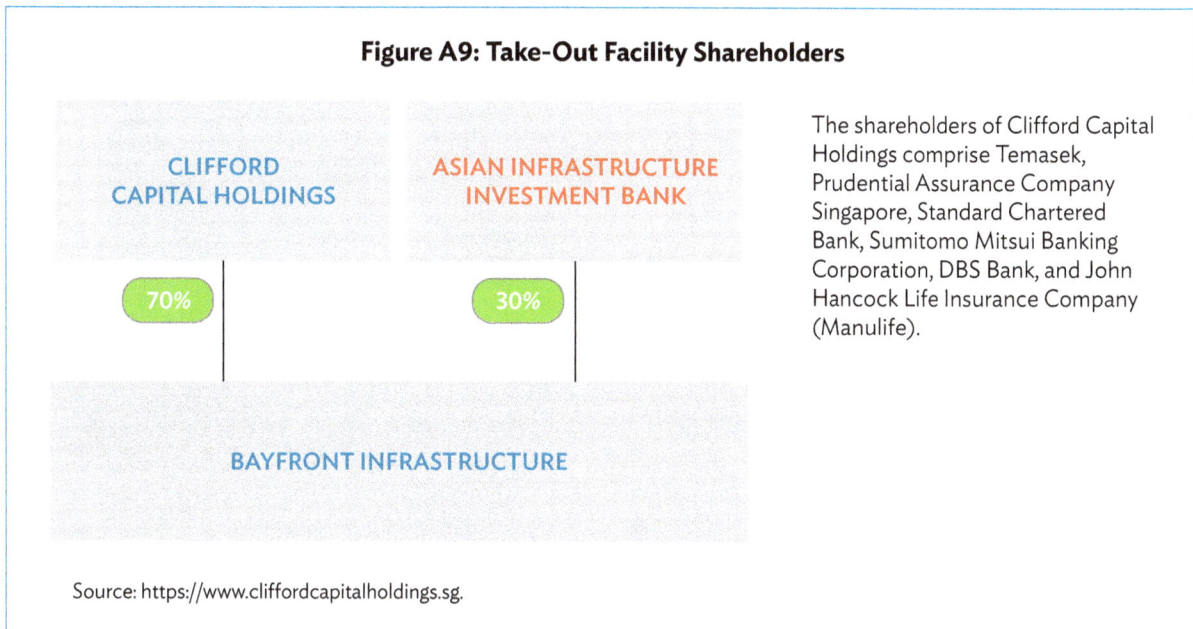

CLIFFORD CAPITAL HOLDINGS — 70%

ASIAN INFRASTRUCTURE INVESTMENT BANK — 30%

BAYFRONT INFRASTRUCTURE

The shareholders of Clifford Capital Holdings comprise Temasek, Prudential Assurance Company Singapore, Standard Chartered Bank, Sumitomo Mitsui Banking Corporation, DBS Bank, and John Hancock Life Insurance Company (Manulife).

Source: https://www.cliffordcapitalholdings.sg.

Benefits and Impact

- Unlock additional capital for Asia's infrastructure financing needs by facilitating capital recycling for banks and provide certainty to banks that the loans would be taken out.
- Create a new asset class for institutional investors who were not actively engaged in the project and infrastructure finance space.
- Create alignment of interests with investors with BIM acting as sponsor, manager, and subordinated Note investor.
- Determine the ideal market timing to initiate a distribution transaction and retain the loans in case unfavorable market conditions arise.

The infrastructure asset-backed securities asset class enables institutional investors to obtain exposures to diversified portfolios of infrastructure loans in bond format denominations, allowing them to leverage on Bayfront's extensive network of bank partnerships to obtain an investment that offers greater liquidity compared to investing in individual loans, along with the benefit of a full range of credit enhancements and portfolio management strategies. This transaction has demonstrated how infrastructure can be developed as a mainstream, investible asset class to help crowd-in institutional capital for the region's fast growing infrastructure funding needs.

5: Convertible Debt and/or Grant Structure

Name of Project	Geothermal Development Facility
Project Location	Latin America
Sector	Energy
Objective	To mitigate geothermal resource risk during exploration drilling process
Year	2016

Model Description

The aim of the Geothermal Development Facility (GDF) is to incentivize public and private investment in geothermal power projects in Latin America. As the first multidonor climate initiative of its kind in the region, GDF is expected to enhance the access of geothermal developers to equity and other funding sources while serving as a catalyst in making geothermal energy a strategic choice in power-expansion planning for participating countries.

Grants will be offered to developers by the GDF through a two-stage application process that is competitive, transparent, and rigorous. The process involves submitting a pre-application expression of interest (EOI) and a full call for proposal (CFP) application for each grant type, namely surface studies or drilling activity (Figure A10).

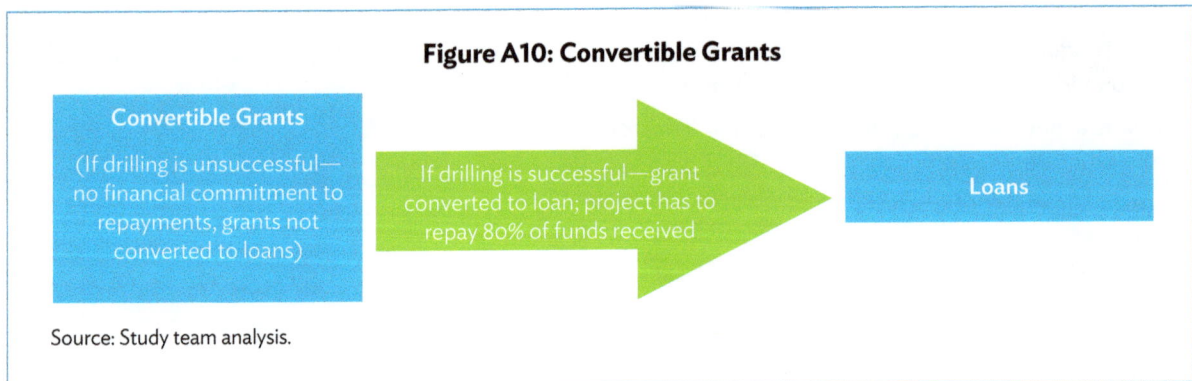

Figure A10: Convertible Grants

Convertible Grants

(If drilling is unsuccessful— no financial commitment to repayments, grants not converted to loans)

If drilling is successful—grant converted to loan; project has to repay 80% of funds received

Loans

Source: Study team analysis.

Grant Description

- **Initial resource:** $75 million
- **Additional top up:** $1 billion
- **Duration of the Facility:** 10 years
- **Fund Manager:** IDA Fund Management, LLC. (IDA is a consortium of Interlink Capital Strategies with Dewhurst Group, LLC.)

It covers the entire value chain of exploratory drilling and allows funding facilities to recover public funds when there are successful drills (Figure A11).

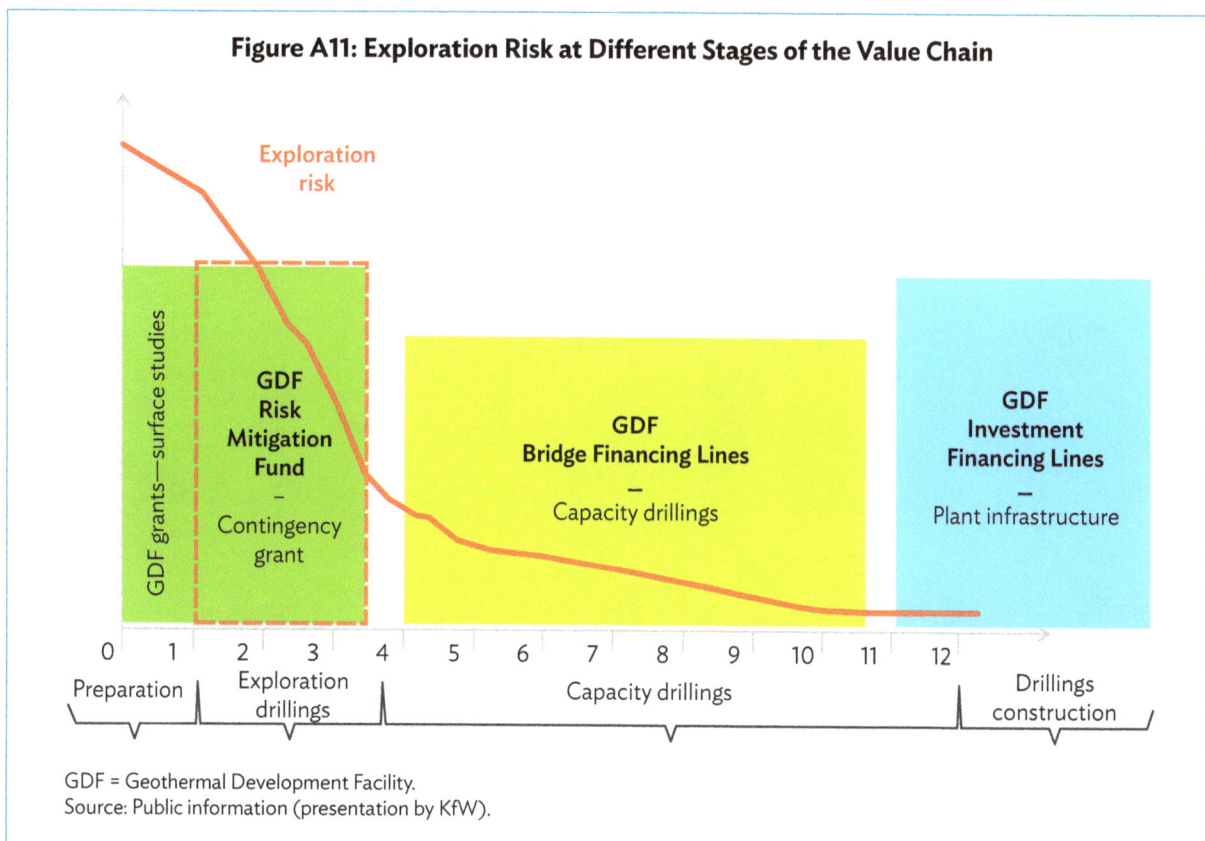

Figure A11: Exploration Risk at Different Stages of the Value Chain

GDF = Geothermal Development Facility.
Source: Public information (presentation by KfW).

Implementation Timeline

Dec 2014	• Conception: The German Federal Minister for Economic Cooperation and Development and the EU Commissioner for Climate Action and Energy, together with high level representatives from KfW, CAF, CABEI, WB, ESMAP, IDB, AfD, EIB, JICA, NDF, BGR, and GIZ GmBH jointly launched the GDF
Apr 2016	• Initiation: KfW introduces the GDF at the World Bank–ESMAP GGDP Roundtable in Reykjavik, Iceland*
Oct 2016	• Introductory pre-application information workshop at the GEA** Geothermal Energy Expo in Sacramento, California
Jan 2017	• First call for EOI
May 2017	• The CFP is opened for applicants who initially enrolled in the EOI. Eight projects are selected for the CFP from 25 EOI applications.
Dec 2017	• The second round of the GDF opens with call of EOI
Jun 2018	• The second CFP is opened for applicants who initially enrolled in the second call of EOI. Of the 16 initial applications for the EOI, 11 were chosen to apply to the CFP stage.
Dec 2018	• Third call for EOI

AfD = Agence Française de Développement, BGR = Federal Institute for Geosciences and Natural Resources (Germany), CABEI = Central American Bank for Economic Integration, CAF = Development Bank of Latin America, CFP = call for proposals, EIB = European Investment Bank, EOI = expression of interest, ESMAP = Energy Sector Management Assistance Program, GEA = Geothermal Energy Association, GGDP = Global Geothermal Development Plan, GIZ GmBH = German Agency for International Cooperation GmbH, IDB = Inter-American Development Bank, JICA = Japan International Cooperation Agency, NDF = Nordic Development Fund, and WB = World Bank.
* https://esmap.org/node/55630.
** GEA merged with Geothermal Rising in 2018 and is no longer a separate entity.

Stakeholders Involved

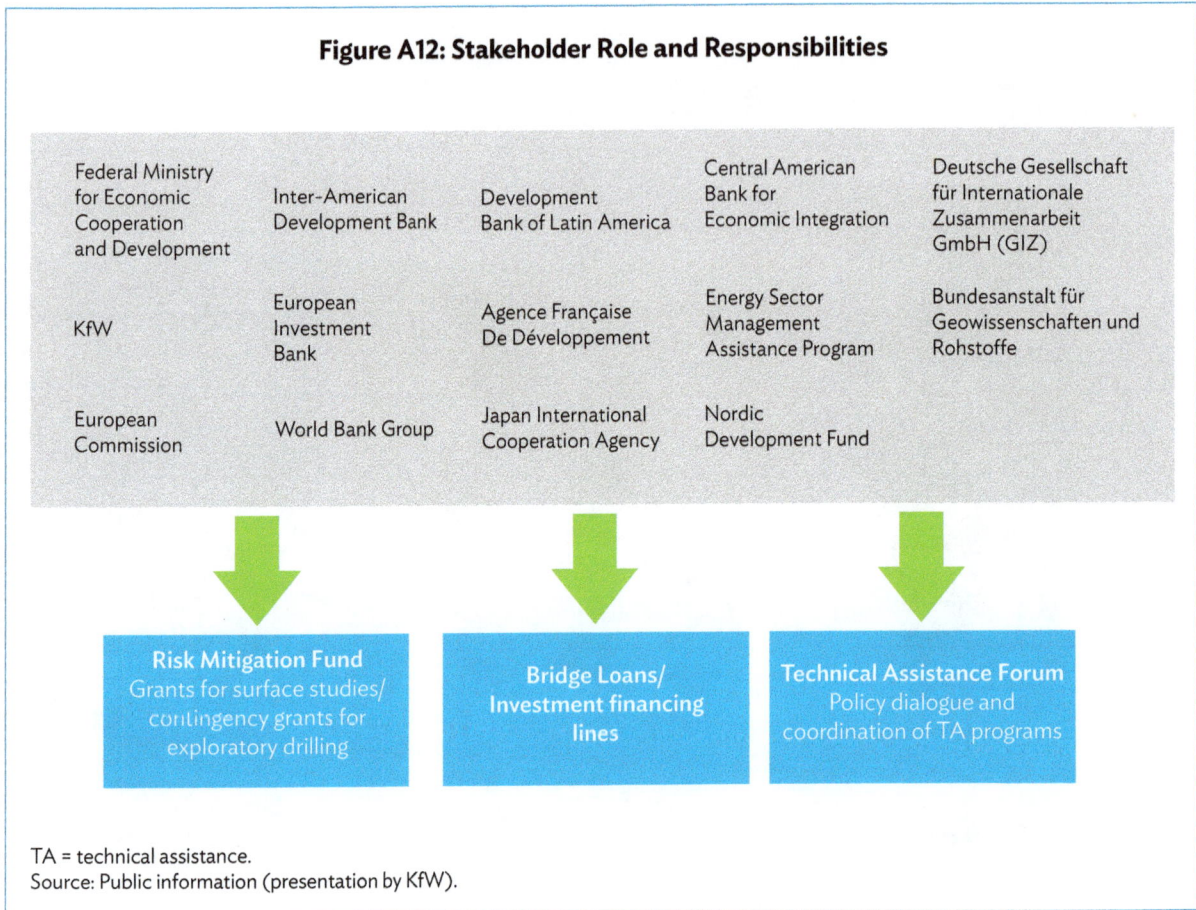

Figure A12: Stakeholder Role and Responsibilities

Federal Ministry for Economic Cooperation and Development	Inter-American Development Bank	Development Bank of Latin America	Central American Bank for Economic Integration	Deutsche Gesellschaft für Internationale Zusammenarbeit GmbH (GIZ)
KfW	European Investment Bank	Agence Française De Développement	Energy Sector Management Assistance Program	Bundesanstalt für Geowissenschaften und Rohstoffe
European Commission	World Bank Group	Japan International Cooperation Agency	Nordic Development Fund	

Risk Mitigation Fund
Grants for surface studies/ contingency grants for exploratory drilling

Bridge Loans/ Investment financing lines

Technical Assistance Forum
Policy dialogue and coordination of TA programs

TA = technical assistance.
Source: Public information (presentation by KfW).

Benefits and Impact

- Grants awarded by the GDF help to catalyze future investments into geothermal development in Latin America. The total anticipated amount of geothermal power generation capacity to be supported through the first and second call under the GDF scheme is expected to reach 520 megawatts.

- Convertible grant agreement has set requirements for the follow-up monitoring and reporting of activities, as well as specifications on the distribution of grant funds. This check and balance ensure that required project milestones are reached and funds are managed appropriately.

- Successful applicants for the convertible grant will be required to certify that they will meet all relevant local rules for health, safety, and labor standards.

> *The Geothermal Development Facility was awarded the first Geothermal Congress for Latin America and the Caribbean prize for best financing program in geothermal energy within Latin America. It expects to surpass its original goal of seeding 350 megawatts of geothermal power in the region. Due to its success and the continued interest in renewable baseload and geothermal energy, it will continue discussions to increase its funding beyond the initial amount seeded by KfW and the European Union.*
>
> Source: Geothermal Development Facility. https://gdflac.com/gdf-latin-america-geolac-award-winner/.

6: Municipal Bonds

Name of Project	Pune Municipal Bonds Program
Project Location	India
Sector	Water
Objective	Finance the project to supply safe and equitable water to all citizens 24 x 7 for the next 30 years
Year	2017

Model Description

In June 2017, the Pune Municipal Corporation (PMC) launched the first and largest listed municipal bonds program in India to finance its ambitious 24×7 water supply project. It attracted more than 20 institutional investors when the first tranche of the $317 million bond was listed at BSE (formerly Bombay Stock Exchange). The tranche was oversubscribed by more than six times.

- **Loan amount:** $28 million—first tranche
- **Coupon rate:** 7.59%
- **Maturity:** 10 years
- **Interest payment:** The frequency of interest payment for these bonds is semi-annual (20 June and 20 December of every year).
- **Principal repayment:** Bullet repayment
- **Interest subsidy:** Government of India decided not to grant municipal bonds tax-free status but it incentivized the municipal corporations to issue bonds to its investors at attractive coupon rates by giving a compensation of 2% interest subsidy on the total size of the bond issue.
- **Additional incentive:** Government of India further incentivized the issue by providing PMC with $3.64 million as a special aid grant to encourage other municipal bodies to opt for municipal bonds.
- **Credit rating:**
  - » The PMC was rated as "IND AA+/Stable Outlook" by India Ratings and "CARE AA+/Stable" for the bond issue by CARE Ratings.
  - » The ratings assigned to PMC as a bond issuer provide investors with a highly favorable evaluation and guarantee the quality of their investment as one of the top performers in its category.
  - » The key drivers for these issue ratings were the structured payment mechanism put in place for the timely servicing of both interest and principal, creation of a sinking fund account, safety preconditions on further borrowings by PMC in case of nonadherence to debt servicing requirements, and high reliance on PMC's own revenue sources.[3]

---

[3]   K. Kumar et al. 2018. *Pune's Pathbreaking Success in the Municipal Bond Market: A Case Study*. Pune. https://smartnet.niua.org/content/9e8f2de1-69af-4888-a41e-60b750311188.

Implementation Timeline

Pre-Aug 2016	• Adoption of National Municipal Accounting Manual and balance sheet preparation • Preparation of detailed report for "24x7 Water Supply Project"; the cost of the project is estimated to be $395 million
Dec 2016	• India Ratings and Research (Ind-Ra) upgraded PMC's long-term issuer rating to "IND AA+" with a "stable" outlook
Jun 2017	• Approval from Standing Committee and General Body of PMC to raise bonds for the project
Jun 2017	• Approval from Government of Maharashtra to issue municipal bonds at BSE
Jun 2017	• Pune Municipal Corporation underwent an exercise of dual ratings for its bond issue—Ind-Ra assigned a final rating of "IND AA+" with a "stable" outlook, while CARE Ratings assigned "CARE AA+" with "stable" outlook
Jun 2017	• Pune Municipal Corporation launched India's largest municipal bonds program; first tranche of $28 million at the BSE
Target	• Bond program is expected to raise approximately $317 million in 5 years

Stakeholders Involved

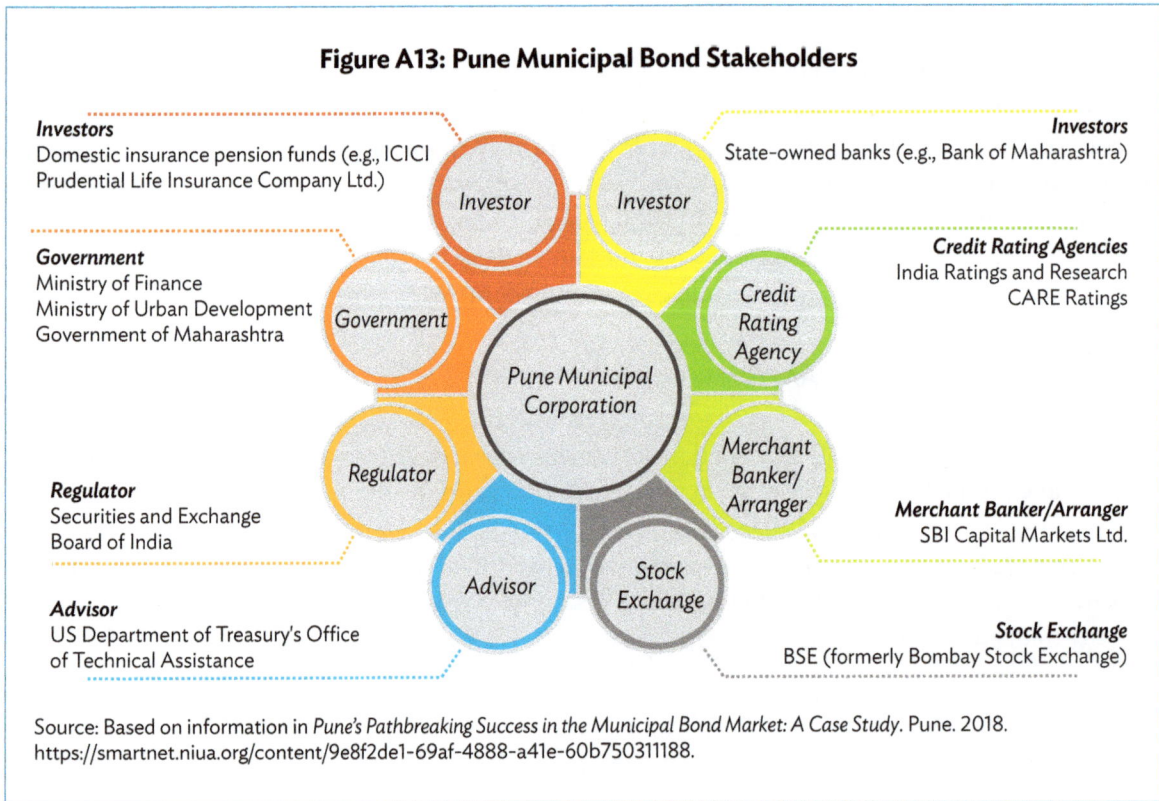

Figure A13: Pune Municipal Bond Stakeholders

Investors
Domestic insurance pension funds (e.g., ICICI Prudential Life Insurance Company Ltd.)

Government
Ministry of Finance
Ministry of Urban Development
Government of Maharashtra

Regulator
Securities and Exchange Board of India

Advisor
US Department of Treasury's Office of Technical Assistance

Investors
State-owned banks (e.g., Bank of Maharashtra)

Credit Rating Agencies
India Ratings and Research
CARE Ratings

Merchant Banker/Arranger
SBI Capital Markets Ltd.

Stock Exchange
BSE (formerly Bombay Stock Exchange)

Source: Based on information in *Pune's Pathbreaking Success in the Municipal Bond Market: A Case Study*. Pune. 2018.
https://smartnet.niua.org/content/9e8f2de1-69af-4888-a41e-60b750311188.

Benefits and Impact

- The PMC was able to leverage future cash flows from a specific infrastructure project to finance capital expenditure and attract new long-term investors and resources into the project.
- The decision to issue municipal bonds is an important step toward reducing the excessive dependence of urban local bodies (ULBs) on grants from the central and state governments and intergovernmental organizations.
- This will also push ULBs to implement stringent reporting and disclosure standards, which would mean greater transparency and accountability toward its citizens.
- The exercise of credit-rating prompts ULBs across India to become more prudent and disciplined in the management of their financial resources.

Pune was the first city in India to issue municipal bonds since the publication of Issue and Listing of Debt Securities by Municipalities Regulations, 2015 by Securities and Exchange Board of India. The successful development of the municipal bond market in India will go a long way toward introducing innovation and creativity in public finance.

7: Sustainable Bonds

Name of Project	Thaifoods Group
Project Location	Thailand
Sector	Food industry
Objective	Provide credit facilities to value chain partners and subsidiaries
Year	2021–2022

Model Description

Thaifoods Group (TFG) is an integrated food production company specializing in chicken and pork products and animal feed with operations in Thailand and Viet Nam. It is the first nonfinancial corporate social bond issuer under the Association of Southeast Asian Nations (ASEAN) Social Bond Standards.[4]

Totaling $30.5 million and with a maturity of 5 years, TFG's social bond was issued in 2020 under the ASEAN+3 Multicurrency Bond Issuance Framework, which facilitates cross-border issuance of debt securities in participating markets. The Credit Guarantee and Investment Facility, a trust fund of the Asian Development Bank, guaranteed 100% of the bond, which was sold to leading Thai institutional investors. The TFG will use the proceeds from the bond to lend money to subsidiaries for the purpose of financing and refinancing projects and assets associated with job creation and economic advancement in local communities. Following its inaugural issuance, the TFG issued two additional social bonds in July 2022, making it the only Thai company to have issued social bonds in Thailand.

As the first nonfinancial corporate social bond issuer in the region, the TFG faced several challenges:

(i) It was difficult to compile a list of eligible expenditures that complied with ASEAN Social Bond Standards and the Social Bond Principles. The finance division was instrumental in coordinating the efforts of the various departments of TFG to ensure that the eligible projects listed in the framework make a quantifiable contribution to positive environmental and social outcomes.

(ii) It was challenging to put together the sustainable finance framework, which explains to investors the company's sustainability policy and how it is being applied throughout its operations. To report on the impact of its social projects, the TFG also needed to set up procedures for tracking the relevant data. Close coordination between the company's various divisions, from senior management to factory managers, was necessary for this process.

(iii) The TFG learned that choosing an external reviewer who is familiar with the local social context can help speed up the external review process. Unlike developed countries, a third of Thailand's workforce is employed in the low-income agricultural sector, and heavily reliant on government loans or other assistance to cope with falling farm prices.[5] The majority of Thailand's bottom 40% lives in poverty (earning about $1,000 per year), with many of them comprising urban workers and rural farming families. This is in stark contrast to farmers in more developed countries who mostly earn significantly higher annual incomes. As social needs vary from country to country, choosing the right external reviewer is critical from the perspective of social bond issuers.

The TFG has provided annual sustainability reports since 2017 and introduced several environment-friendly and sustainable measures and initiated social initiatives in its operations that are detailed in Figure A14.

---

[4]   ADB. 2021. *First Social Bond Issued by Nonfinancial Corporate Issuer Under ASEAN Social Bond Standards*. News Release. 17 November. https://www.adb.org/news/first-social-bond-issued-nonfinancial-corporate-issuer-under-asean-social-bond-standards.

[5]   Judy Yang et al. 2020. Taking the Pulse of Poverty and Inequality in Thailand. World Bank Group. Washington, DC. https://www.worldbank.org/en/country/thailand/publication/taking-the-pulse-of-poverty-and-inequality-in-thailand.

Figure A14: Alignment of Eligible Green and Social Projects, Assets, and Expenditures with Sustainable Development Goals

Project Category	Examples of Eligible Projects, Assets, and Expenditures	Environmental/ Social Benefits	SDG Alignment and Contribution
GREEN			
Renewable energy	- Floating solar power facilities - Solar PV systems on factory roofs - Solar PV systems on existing carparks - Solar PV systems on ground	- Reduce overall energy consumption and lower GHG emissions	7 AFFORDABLE AND CLEAN ENERGY; 13 CLIMATE ACTION
Sustainable water and wastewater management	- Wastewater treatment system - Reuse of treated water	- Improve wastewater management - Reuse of resources for effciency	6 CLEAN WATER AND SANITATION; 12 RESPONSIBLE CONSUMPTION AND PRODUCTION
Pollution prevention and control	- Manure management for swine facilities - Ozone system for odor control at feed mill	- Reuse of resources for effciency	9 INDUSTRY, INNOVATION AND INFRASTRUCTURE; 11 SUSTAINABLE CITIES AND COMMUNITIES
Circular economy adapted products, production processes, and technologies	- Meat and bone factory	- Reuse of resources for effciency	12 RESPONSIBLE CONSUMPTION AND PRODUCTION
SOCIAL			
Access to essential services	- Improve distribution of fresh and healthy food to local communities - Donate quality chicken meat to local communities	- Good health and well-being	2 ZERO HUNGER
Employment generation	- Increase employment within local communities, including women - Employment with higher standards and fair compensation packages compared to normal jobs in local communities - Prioritize recruitment of local employees for new retail shops and provide equal employment opportunities for women	- Achieve full and productive employment - Provide support to local communites	1 NO POVERTY; 5 GENDER EQUALITY
Food security and sustainable food	- Support for local farmers via purchasing commitments and improved food security	- Provide access to safe and afforable food - Good health and well-being	2 ZERO HUNGER; 12 RESPONSIBLE CONSUMPTION AND PRODUCTION; 17 PARTNERSHIPS FOR THE GOALS

GHG = greenhouse gas, PV = photovoltaic.
Source: TFG Sustainable Finance Framework.

Implementation Timeline

2016–2019	• Thaifoods Group issues bonds in Thailand's capital market mostly offering to high-net-worth investors
2019	• Thaifoods Group develops a Sustainable Finance Framework
2020	• In January 2020, TFG issued B2.0 billion worth of bonds guaranteed by the Credit Guarantee and Investment Facility, a trust fund of the Asian Development Bank
2022	• July 2022, TFG issues two additional social bonds

Stakeholders Involved

- Thaifood Group
- Asian Development Bank: ADB provided technical assistance through the ASEAN+3 Asian Bond Markets Initiative (ABMI) to help develop sustainable local currency bond markets in ASEAN, and the People's Republic of China, Japan, and the Republic of Korea (collectively referred to as ASEAN+3). The technical assistance for the TFG bond was developed in accordance with the ABMI's 2019–2022 Medium-Term Road Map, which was endorsed at the 22nd ASEAN+3 Finance Ministers' and Central Bank Governors' Meeting in 2019.
- Value chain partners and subsidiary entities

Benefits and Impact

- The sustainable bond enabled the TFG to raise capital for new and existing projects that deliver environmental benefits and a more sustainable economy.
- The bonds provided much-needed capital for sustainability-related projects thus supporting the TFG's transition to a cleaner future, reduced carbon footprint, and the fulfilment of its social objectives by providing educational and livelihood opportunities.
- Issuance of the bond requires companies to comply with a set of disclosure requirements which help to communicate the sustainability narrative. This promotes transparency and provides investors with relevant information on the social and environmental initiatives of the company and with a means of aligning their asset allocation with sustainability objectives.
- This, therefore, contributes to national climate adaptation, food security, public health, renewable energy, etc.

> *The issuance of the sustainability bond has greatly enhanced the reputation of ThaiFood Group, improved investor portfolio diversification, and, more importantly, provided comparable financial returns with the addition of environmental and social benefits.*

8: Green Bonds

Name of Project	Indonesia Green Sukuk Initiative
Project Location	Indonesia
Sectors	Renewable energy, resilience to climate change, sustainable transport, waste to energy and waste management, sustainable agriculture, sustainable natural resource management, green tourism, and clean energy
Objective	Support Indonesia's commitment in greenhouse gas emissions reduction based on Islamic Law principles
Year	2018

Model Description

In 2018, the Government of Indonesia, through the Ministry of Finance, issued the very first sovereign green *sukuk* (Islamic debt securities) in United States (US) dollars to support its goal of greenhouse gas (GHG) emissions

Figure A15: Eligible Sectors under the Green Bond and Green Sukuk Framework

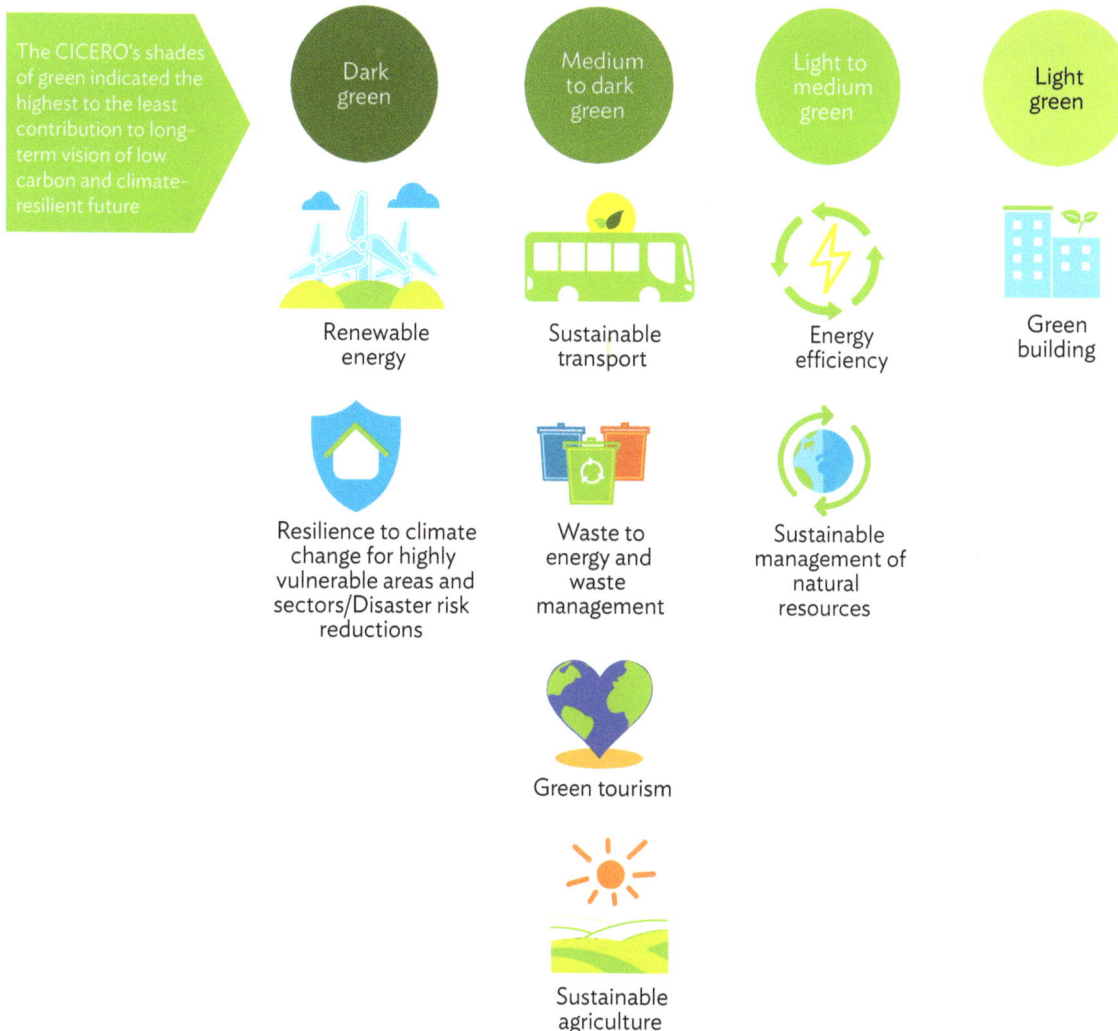

The CICERO's shades of green indicated the highest to the least contribution to long-term vision of low carbon and climate-resilient future

Dark green — Renewable energy

Medium to dark green — Sustainable transport

Light to medium green — Energy efficiency

Light green — Green building

Resilience to climate change for highly vulnerable areas and sectors/Disaster risk reductions

Waste to energy and waste management

Sustainable management of natural resources

Green tourism

Sustainable agriculture

CICERO = Centre for International Climate Research.
Source: Ministry of Finance, Government of Indonesia, Indonesia's Green Bond and Sukuk Initiative.

reduction. The green *sukuk* is a Shariah-compliant bond, where 100% of the proceeds of $1.25 billion is exclusively committed to financing or refinancing green projects that contribute to climate change adaptation and mitigation, as well as biodiversity conservation. The issuance fulfills the Green Bond and Green Sukuk Framework developed by the Government of Indonesia that plans to finance and refinance eligible green projects. The framework is reviewed by the Centre for International Climate Research (CICERO), which is an international independent reviewer. The framework is awarded medium green shading which allows for the possibility of light, medium, and dark green project types as illustrated below (Figure A15).

Table A2: Indonesia's Green Sukuk 2018 Issuance

Obligor	Government of Indonesia, represented by the Ministry of Finance
Issuer	Perusahaan Penerbit SBSN Indonesia III
Issuer Rating	Baa3 Moody's (Positive)/BBB S&P (Stable)/BBB Fitch (Stable)
Format Status	144A / RegS registered, senior unsecured
Maturity	1 March 2023 (5 years)
Tranche	Senior, $1.25 billion
Yield	3.75% p.a. (30/360)
Listings	Singapore Stock Exchange and NASDAQ Dubai

S&P = S&P Global Ratings, p.a. = per annum.
Source: Study team analysis.

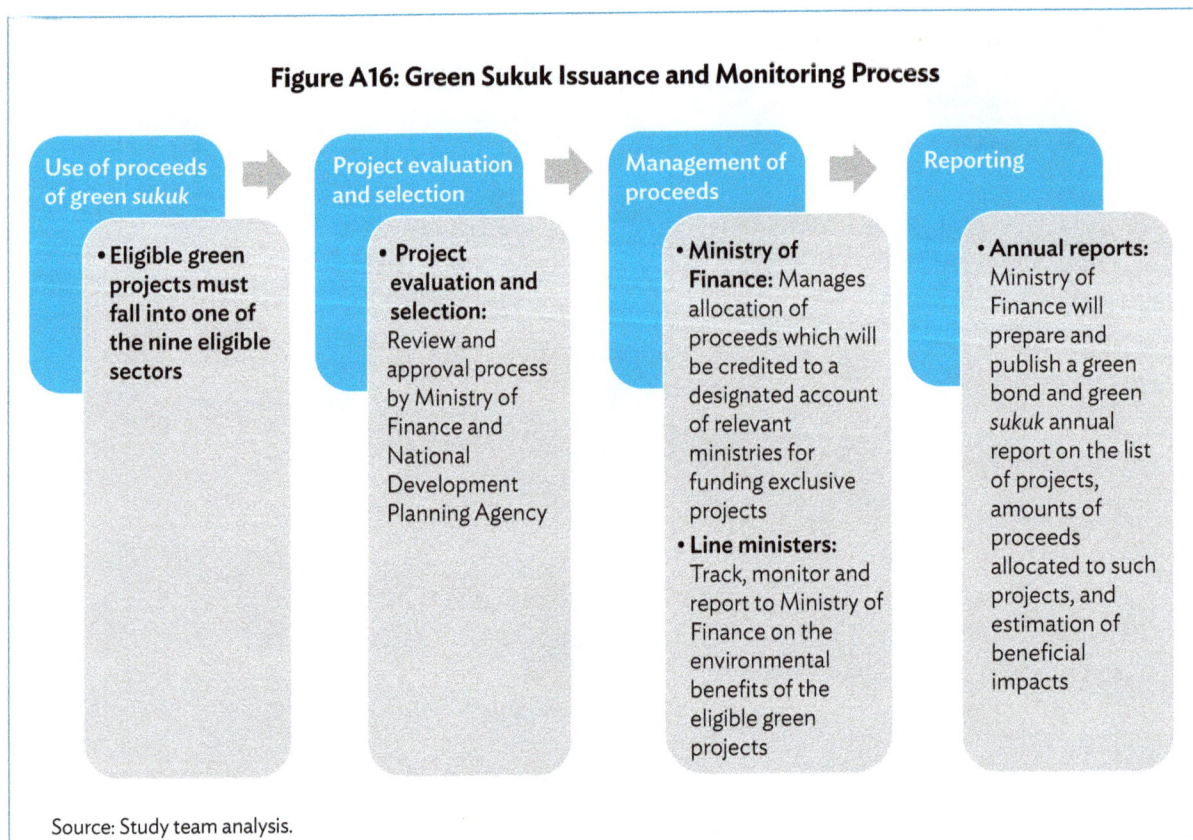

Figure A16: Green Sukuk Issuance and Monitoring Process

Use of proceeds of green *sukuk* → **Project evaluation and selection** → **Management of proceeds** → **Reporting**

- **Eligible green projects must fall into one of the nine eligible sectors**

- **Project evaluation and selection:** Review and approval process by Ministry of Finance and National Development Planning Agency

- **Ministry of Finance:** Manages allocation of proceeds which will be credited to a designated account of relevant ministries for funding exclusive projects
- **Line ministers:** Track, monitor and report to Ministry of Finance on the environmental benefits of the eligible green projects

- **Annual reports:** Ministry of Finance will prepare and publish a green bond and green *sukuk* annual report on the list of projects, amounts of proceeds allocated to such projects, and estimation of beneficial impacts

Source: Study team analysis.

Implementation Timeline

2015	• The Ministry of Finance, supported by the United Nations Development Programme, has been implementing climate budget tagging in order to track climate-related expenditures in the national budget. The tagging process allows the government to get a more accurate idea of the gap in financing required to meet climate change targets.
2016	• Indonesia ratified the Paris Agreement, including submitting an ambitious nationally determined contribution with an unconditional reduction target of 29% against business as usual scenario by 2030, compared with 2010 baseline.
2017	• S&P Global Ratings upgraded Indonesia's credit rating to investment grade.
Jan 2018	• Indonesia appointed banks for a US dollar–*sukuk* offering that could include the first offshore green bond from an Asian sovereign. • Series of fixed income investor meetings in Asia, Europe, and the Middle East conducted.
Mar 2018	• On 1 March 2018, Indonesia launched the world's first sovereign green *sukuk*. The issuance was oversubscribed, reflecting the attractiveness of the green bond/*sukuk* to both investors and issuers.
May 2021	• Issued a three-tranche $3 billion Sukuk Wakala comprising a $1.25 billion 5-year tranche maturing in June 2026; a $1 billion 10-year tranche maturing in June 2031; and a $750 million 30-year (Green) Trust Certificate tranche due in June 2051.
May 2022	• Raised 3.25 billion by selling US dollar denominated Islamic bonds with 5- and 10-year tenures in the country's biggest *sukuk* issuance. The 5-year Notes carry a coupon of 4.4% and the 10-year Notes carry coupon of 4.7%.

Effective coordination and communication between the Ministry of Finance, National Development Planning Agency, Ministries of Environment, and line ministries is essential for the successful planning, execution, and evaluation of the bond issuance.

Stakeholders Involved

- **Obligor.** Government of Indonesia, represented by the Ministry of Finance
- **Issuer.** Perusahaan Penerbit SBSN Indonesia III
- **External reviewer.** Centre for International Climate Research
- **Joint lead managers.** Abu Dhabi Islamic Bank PJSC, Citigroup (B&D), CIMB, Dubai Islamic Bank PJSC, and HSBC (Green Structuring Advisor)
- **Co-Managers.** PT Bahana Sekuritas, PT Danareksa Sekuritas, and PT Trimegah Sekuritas Indonesia Tbk

Benefits and Impact

- The initial issuance attracted investors around the globe (32% Islamic market, 25% Asia, 15% European Union, 18% US, and 10% Indonesia).[6]
- By issuing the bond, Indonesia can diversify its financial assets, while also ensuring that its national priorities, Paris Agreement commitments, and Sustainable Development Goals are met.
- The eligible projects under the green use of proceeds will provide meaningful environmental contributions in terms of improved access and affordability of renewable energy, improved energy efficiency, and improved air quality due to decreased transport-related air emissions, which leads to a transition toward a low-carbon economy.

---

[6] United Nations Development Programme. *Indonesia's Green Bond and Sukuk Initiative.* UNDP Indonesia. https://www.ndcs.undp.org/content/dam/LECB/docs/pubs-reports/undp-ndcsp-green-sukuk-share.pdf?download.

- The use of the climate budget tagging tool by the Government of Indonesia before issuing the bonds led to an increase in the annual budget for climate-related activities between 2016 and 2017. This tool helps monitor the implementation of programs and activities by various line ministries as part of the strategic plan for mitigating and adapting to climate change.

- The market response and the use of proceeds have led to investor confidence. The subsequent *sukuk* issuance are testimony to its success as it has widened the appeal of the *sukuk* beyond its traditional market. While Indonesia remains the only sovereign *sukuk* issuer, Malaysia has pioneered corporate green *sukuk* with about six such issuances in the market by Chinese-backed entities such as Tadau Energy, Quantam Solar, and Cypark Resources. Cagamas Berhad (the National Mortgage Finance Corporation of Malaysia); Majid Al Futtaim, a leading shopping mall and real estate developer across the Middle East; and the Islamic Development Bank also successfully placed maiden green *sukuk* issuances in 2020.

> *Indonesia has recognized the negative effects of climate change and the urgency to mitigate and counteract its impact on the climate system. The country has been proactively improving its internal capabilities and establishing appropriate institutional systems and tools to guarantee transparency and full disclosure in managing and utilizing the proceeds of the bond issuance, as well as to ensure credible impact reporting. These measures will enable Indonesia to implement innovative financing mechanisms to support its green and resilient economy agenda in the future.*

9: Government Green Fund

Name of Project	Green Municipal Fund (GMF)
Project Location	Canada
Sector	Brownfields, energy, transportation, waste, and water
Objective	To support municipalities across the country in their sustainable community development goals, improving the quality of air, water, and land, as well as reducing greenhouse gas (GHG) emissions
Year	2000 to date

Model Description

The Federation of Canadian Municipalities established the Green Municipal Fund (GMF) in 2000 with an initial investment of $550 million from the Government of Canada. Today, the program has grown into a $1.6 billion endowment, which offers competitive interest rate loans to municipalities and invests wisely while following a sound risk management strategy. Over the past 4 years, GMF has implemented a well-planned four-part strategy which includes inspiring innovative practices, connecting sustainability leaders, building local capacity, and financially supporting municipal initiatives.

By providing financial and capacity-building support, GMF helps municipalities secure funding from other public and private sources, and design and implement tailored sustainability initiatives that address the specific needs of their communities. Leveraging its $1.65 billion endowment, GMF focuses on five priority sectors: energy, waste, transportation, land use, and water. By unlocking scalable solutions, accelerating market transformation, and paving the way toward net-zero emissions in these sectors, GMF plays a key role in the transition toward a low-carbon future. Its investments in sustainable initiatives also generate multiple economic benefits at both the local and national levels. They stimulate local economic activity and contribute to municipal prosperity, while creating a path toward a more sustainable future for all Canadians.

Implementation Timeline

2000	• Green Municipal Fund was set up in 2000, with the Government of Canada setting aside $550 million for the Federation of Canadian Municipalities
2002–2011	• The City of Winnipeg's Millenium Project received funds from GMF to perform feasibility studies to reduce energy use and GHGs; the Manitoba Capital Region received funds from GMF to project environmental, fiscal, and socioeconomic growth for 40 years
2012–2014	• The Winnipeg's Community-Wide Climate Change Action Plan was funded by GMF to develop an integrated community-wide strategy to reduce GHG emissions
2015–2016	• The Federation of Canadian Municipalities approved grants worth $5 million for plans, feasibility studies, and pilot projects. They also aim to approve $30 million in loans for capital projects in energy, transportation, waste, and water sectors and a minimum of $20 million in loans for capital projects in brownfield sectors.
2017–2022	• Endowment increased to $1.6 billion. In 2020–2021, approved $116.4 million in loans and $53.1 million in grants—the largest amount approved in a single year. It transferred $155.7 million to establish the Low Carbon Cities Canada network, a partnership with six organizations in seven big cities.

Stakeholders Involved

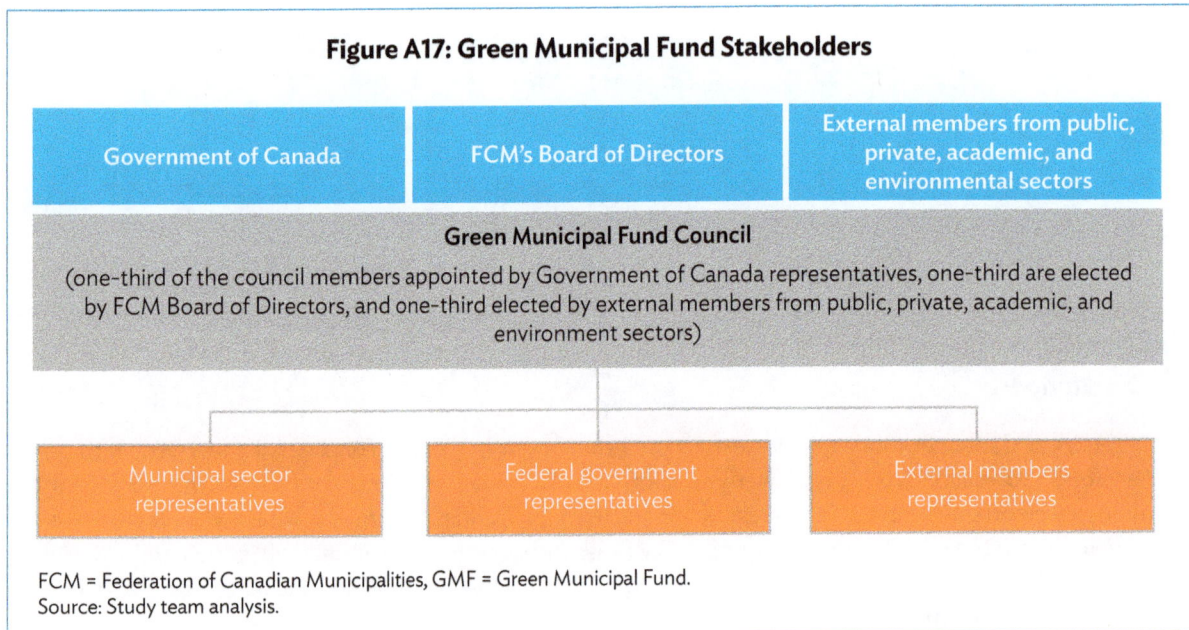

Figure A17: Green Municipal Fund Stakeholders

| Government of Canada | FCM's Board of Directors | External members from public, private, academic, and environmental sectors |

Green Municipal Fund Council
(one-third of the council members appointed by Government of Canada representatives, one-third are elected by FCM Board of Directors, and one-third elected by external members from public, private, academic, and environment sectors)

| Municipal sector representatives | Federal government representatives | External members representatives |

FCM = Federation of Canadian Municipalities, GMF = Green Municipal Fund.
Source: Study team analysis.

Benefits and Impact

- Low interest loans and grants supplement capital projects up to 80% (average loan maximum: $5 million and grants maximum: 15% of loan).
- For private entities and municipally-owned corporations, low effective loan rate is provided after credit risk assessment; loan rates are 1.5% below Government of Canada rate.
- Multiple loan disbursements at clients' selected milestones are possible.
- Funding is stackable against federal and provincial funding programs.
- A triple-bottom-line approach aims at building resilient communities that are environmentally, economically, and socially impactful.
- Broader eligibility based on environmental outcomes implies that more types of initiatives are eligible per sector, and applicants have the flexibility and creativity in developing their specific project.
- Environmental results have been achieved—brownfield sites brought back into productive use, reduced energy consumption, reduced fossil fuel consumption and emissions, waste diversion from landfill, and water treatment.[7]

The endowment of $1.6 billion has enabled Green Municipal Fund to approve a total of 1,931 sustainability projects worth $1.28 billion, avoid 2.82 million tons of greenhouse gases, achieve savings of 860,210 gigajoules of energy per year, and treat 248 million cubic meters of water every year. These initiatives are estimated to have attracted additional investment worth $3+ billion, and have triggered a host of economic, social, and environmental benefits.

---

[7]   *2021–2022 Green Municipal Fund annual report.* https://annualreport.greenmunicipalfund.ca.

10: Green Transition Financing

Name of Project	Rantau Dedap Geothermal Power Project
Project Location	Indonesia
Sector	Renewable energy generation
Objectives	• Environmentally sustainable growth • Inclusive economic growth • Strengthening the international competitiveness of Japanese industries • Generating reliable clean energy power supply
Year	2018 to date

Model Description

In March 2018, Japan Bank for International Cooperation (JBIC), a governmental financial institution of Japan, signed a loan agreement for project finance amounting up to approximately $188 million (JBIC portion) with PT Supreme Energy Rantau Dedap (SERD), an Indonesian company invested in by Marubeni Corporation, Tohoku Electric Power Co., Inc., INPEX Corporation, and other Indonesian sponsors. The loans are co-financed by three Japanese private banks and Asian Development Bank, bringing the total co-financing amount to approximately $539 million. Nippon Export and Investment Insurance, which is also a governmental financial institution of Japan, provides insurance for the portion co-financed by the Japanese private banks.

Project finance is a financing mechanism in which repayments for a loan are made solely from the cash flows generated by the project, thus minimizing the impact on the sponsors' balance sheet. The scheme limits the risks of project participants and makes the project more bankable by ensuring balanced risk allocation and management.

This unique project enables SERD to construct, own, and operate a geothermal power plant with a capacity of 98.4 megawatts in South Sumatra, Indonesia. The electricity generated by the plant is sold to PT PLN (Persero), a state-owned power utility in Indonesia, for a period of 30 years under a power purchase agreement.

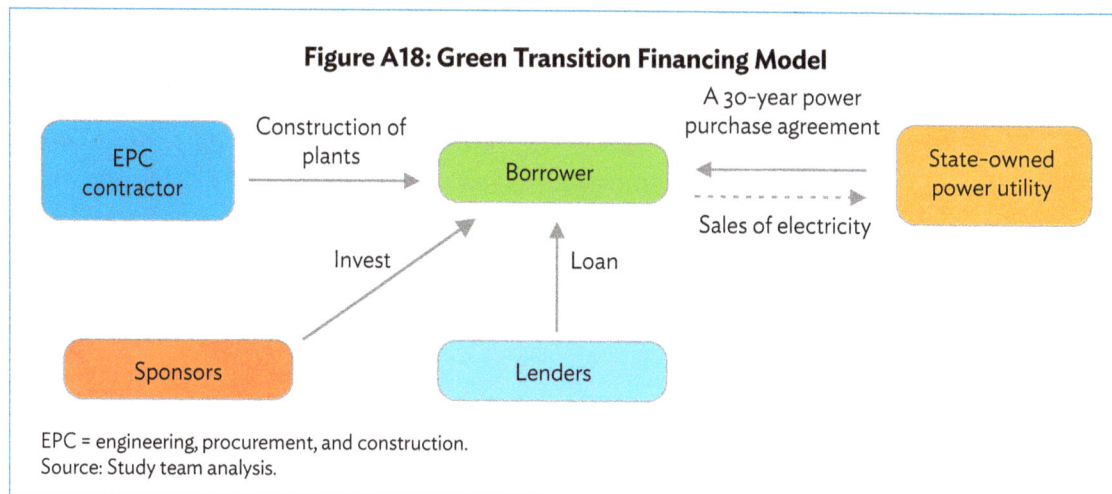

Figure A18: Green Transition Financing Model

EPC = engineering, procurement, and construction.
Source: Study team analysis.

The project is in line with the "Export Strategy for Infrastructure System" of the Government of Japan, which aims to encourage the expansion of infrastructure system orders. This includes the design, construction, operation, and management of infrastructure, as well as an increase in investments in local businesses. The Government of Japan unveiled its "overseas deployment strategy for the power sector" in October 2017. This strategy prioritizes the support of Japanese utility companies in their efforts to emphasize overseas power generation business, with the help of financial instruments provided by the JBIC. Furthermore, Japan announced a new commitment, "Action for Cool Earth 2.0 (ACE2.0)1", at Conference of Parties 21 and pledged to provide approximately ¥1.3 trillion of public and private climate finance to developing countries in 2020 to support efforts to reduce greenhouse gas emissions and mitigate the negative impacts of climate change.

Implementation Timeline

2010	• PT Supreme Energy Rantau Dedap (SERD) was awarded the Rantau Dedap concession
2012	• Signed power purchase agreement between SERD and PT PLN (Persero)
2015	• Completed drilling of six exploratory wells
2018	• Reached financial close
2021	• Achieved commercial operation date

Stakeholders Involved

- **Borrower.** SERD
- **Sponsors.** Marubeni Corporation, Tohoku Electric Power Co., Ltd., and others
- **Lenders.** JBIC, ADB, and Japanese private banks
- **Sellers.** PT PLN (Persero), a state-owned power utility contracted to sell electricity with SERD

Benefits and Impact

- This project contributes to the objectives of Indonesia's National Energy Plan and to the 2015 commitment to the Paris Agreement under the United Nations Framework Convention on Climate Change. It helps Indonesia get closer to achieving its goal of reducing carbon dioxide emissions by 29% within 2030.
- Successful implementation of the project and deployment of concessional co-financing can lead to (i) increased geothermal power generation in Indonesia, (ii) more private sector investment in the geothermal sector, and (iii) increased electrification rate in Indonesia.
- The JBIC provides support for this overseas infrastructure project in which Japanese companies are involved not only as investors but also as operators and maintainers of the power plant. By utilizing advanced technologies, these companies contribute to maintaining and enhancing the global competitiveness of Japanese industries over a long period of time.
- The project has resulted in all-round economic and infrastructure development. Improved access has substantially reduced travel time from nearby villages (Tunggul Bute and Rantau Dedap) to the subdistrict. It has also created prospects for new local businesses and provided livelihood opportunities through the employment of 382 local persons who comprise over 38% of the total workforce.

> *The project delivers on its twin objectives of climate change mitigation and access to project capital for large-scale infrastructure development through the introduction of financial risk reduction mechanisms to attract private sector investment. It aligns with the strategic policy objectives of the Government of Japan by supporting Japanese companies and ensures beneficial outcomes for all stakeholders. More importantly, it provides clean energy to meet the surging demand for electricity, thus contributing to economic development while meeting national environmental commitments.*

11: Public–Private Partnership

Name of Project	Umbulan Water Project
Project Location	East Java, Indonesia
Sector	Water
Objective	High quality drinking water distribution
Year	2021 to date

Model Description

The *Sistem Penyediaan Air Minum, Umbulan* (SPAM, Umbulan) which translates to "Drinking Water Supply System, Umbulan" was conceived as early as the 1980s to provide clean water distribution, better sanitation systems, and efficient utilization of high-quality water resources in East Java. Situated in a province where only 75% of the population had access to a water supply system, the project was not only essential for improving the quality of life in the province but also reducing national averages related to poverty and inequality. Despite a protracted procurement process from 1988 to 1999, during which three bidders were short-listed, financial closures were never successfully obtained. The absence of capital subsidies or government guarantees to increase financial feasibility was recognized as a missing component only around 1997.[8]

Efforts to revive the project were initiated in 2010 with the Government of Indonesia recognizing the need for fiscal facilities to increase the financial feasibility of basic infrastructure projects through a private–public partnership (PPP) mechanism. It acknowledged the importance of private sector involvement in providing technical expertise, innovation, sustainable operation, and capital investment. The government introduced fiscal incentives such as a viability gap fund (VGF) to increase financial feasibility while maintaining low end-user tariffs. Another fiscal instrument, credit enhancement, was also introduced through the Indonesia Infrastructure Guarantee Fund to alleviate political risk. These schemes became feasible after the government issued a Presidential Regulation in 2015, as well as three Minister-of-Finance regulations and two Minister-of-Finance decrees.

The government recognized the importance of the project and decided to take steps to ensure its financial feasibility so as to showcase the success of PPPs. A credible feasibility study was conducted with the assistance of PT Sarana Multi Infrastruktur to create an appropriate financial scheme that would make the project bankable. As local governments and a private consortium could only finance 60% of the project's value, PT Sarana Multi Infrastruktur assisted the East Java Provincial Government through their project development facility to facilitate the project transactions. In December 2016, the project achieved financial closure. The project is registered as a National Strategic Project and Priority Project.

The project aims to provide 93 km of transmission pipe and serve 1.3 million people, at an estimated cost of $143 million. The Ministry of Finance, Government of Indonesia provided $57 million through a VGF scheme to ensure that the water would be accessible to the community at an affordable tariff. The local public water supply company, *Perusahaan Daerah Air Minum* (PDAM), currently sells clean water at the price of $0.25 per cubic meter but cannot meet the demand. Private suppliers sell clean water at the price of $2.7 per cubic meter or nearly 11 times PDAM's price. The new price proposal after completion of the Umbulan project is $0.5 or about 20% of current private supply's price. This new project to service the uncovered poor will distribute bulk water that will surpass World Health Organization standard drinking water quality.

---

8   Asia Pacific Economic Cooperation. 2014. *Infrastructure Public-Private Partnership Case Studies of APEC Member Economies.* http://mddb.apec.org/Documents/2014/MM/FMM/14_fmm_019.pdf.

The regional government of East Java established a special purpose vehicle, PT Meta Adhya Tirta Umbulan, to enter into a PPP with a consortium consisting two partners—a private gas company, PT Medco Gas Indonesia, and a private construction company, PT Bangun Cipta Contractor. After submitting a successful bid, the two partners received a 25-year concession that includes the right to design, build, operate, and maintain the facilities and the water distribution network. Commissioned in March 2021, SPAM Umbulan provides 24 x 7 water accessibility at nearly 4,000 liters per second to 260,000 piped water connections across two cities and three districts of East Java Province.

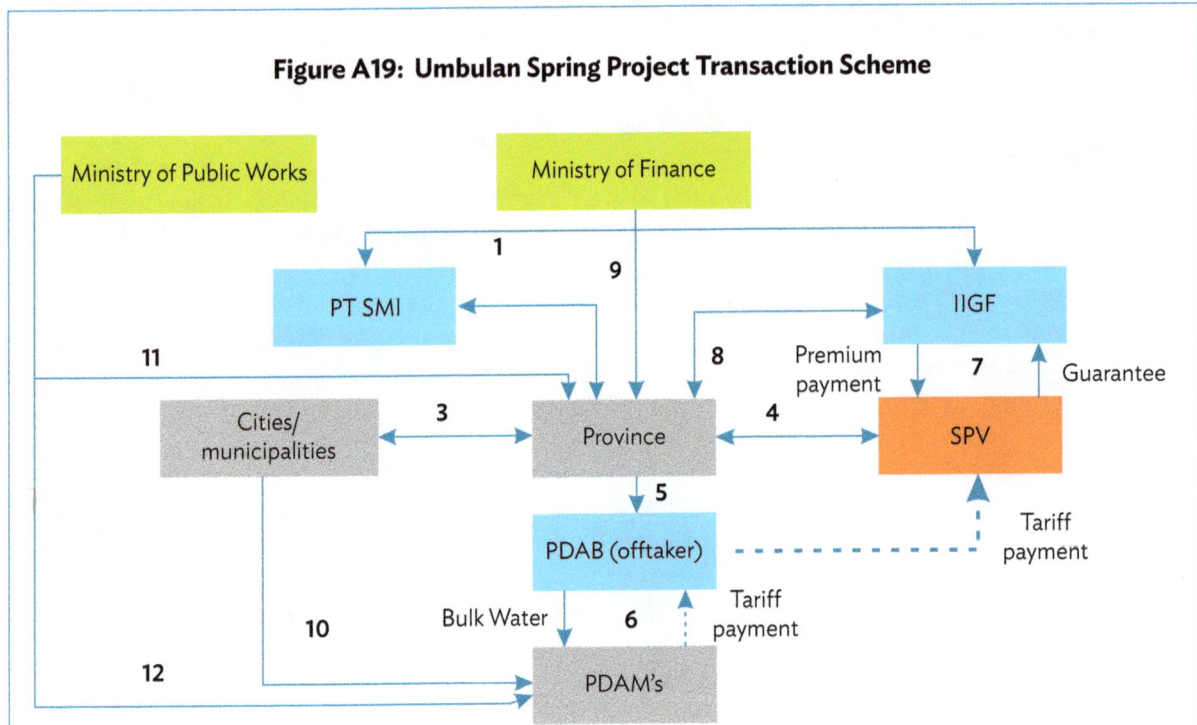

Figure A19: Umbulan Spring Project Transaction Scheme

IIGF = Indonesia Infrastructure Guarantee Fund, PDAB = Regional (Bulk) Water Company, PDAM = Perusahaan DaerahAir Minum (local water company), PT. SMI = Sarana Multi Infrastruktur, SPV = special purpose vehicle.
Notes:
1. Assignment from Finance Minister to PT. SMI to do project preparation
2. Cooperation between provincial government and PT SMI to facilitate project preparation
3. Cooperation between provincial government and municipalities/cities
4. Build-operate-transfer contract between provincial government and SPV
5. Assignment from provincial government to regional water company (PDAB) to become off-taker
6. Bulk water supply contract between PDAB to local water companies (PDAMs)
7. Guarantee agreement between I IGF with SPV
8. Regress agreement between provincial government and I IGF
9. Provide viability gap funding
10. Support from municipalities/cities to PDAMs for bulk water payment
11. Support from the Ministry of Public Works in the form of partial construction, if needed
12. Support from the Ministry of Public Works to PDAMs

Source: F. Zen. ADB Economics. Working Paper Series No. 553. 2018. *Public-Private Partnership Development in South East Asia.* https://www.adb.org/sites/default/files/publication/444631/ewp-553-ppp-development-southeast-asia.pdf.

Implementation Timeline

1980-1999	• Early attempts to secure bidders and ensure financial closure are unsuccessful.
2010	• The government begins a consultative process with interested parties and considers fiscal incentives.
2015	• The government issues a Presidential Regulation, three Minister-of-Finance regulations and two Minister-of-Finance decrees.
2016	• All agreements are signed and financial closure attained.
2017	• Construction works commence.
2021	• Project is commissioned.

Stakeholders Involved

- Government of Indonesia
- PT Sarana Multi Infrastruktur
- Indonesia Infrastructure Guarantee Fund
- Perusahaan Daerah Air Minum
- Provincial Government of East Java
- Regional water supply companies

Benefits and Impact

- The pro-poor project provides clean drinking water to communities, leading to better health outcomes and a reduction in waterborne diseases.
- It has reduced the cost of water, thus making it more affordable for consumers.
- The project is a model for other PPP projects and has encouraged the government to create an enabling environment to attract private sector investment into large utility infrastructure projects.
- The project also implemented a water loss reduction program, cutting back on leakage and theft, toward a more sustainable and efficient water supply system.

Public-private partnerships can help to address the challenges associated with infrastructure financing by leveraging the strengths of both the public and private sectors. By working together, they can deliver infrastructure projects that are more efficient, cost effective and sustainable. Such partnerships can provide better value for money by introducing competition into the bidding process which can lead to lower costs and better infrastructure quality. They allow risks to be shared and help to improve service delivery by providing incentives to the private sector to maintain and operate the asset to a high standard. More importantly, PPPs can stimulate economic development by creating jobs and generating revenue for the local economy. They bring together the resources and expertise of both the public and private sectors as the private sector can provide innovative technical solutions while the public sector can ensure that the project meets the needs of the community.

12: Climate Risk and Catastrophe Insurance

Name of Project	Caribbean Catastrophe Risk Insurance Facility—Segregated Portfolio Company
Project Location	Caribbean and Central America
Sector	Various
Objectives	Climate and disaster risk insurance to countries
Year	2021–2023

Model Description

The idea of setting up the Caribbean Catastrophe Risk Insurance Facility (CCRIF) was driven by the large-scale damage wrought by Hurricane Ivan in 2004. The Caribbean Community (CARICOM) heads of government held an emergency meeting to discuss critical issues surrounding the provision of catastrophe risk insurance for its members. To design and implement a cost-effective risk transfer program for its member governments, CARICOM approached the World Bank for assistance.

The CCRIF was established with technical guidance from the World Bank and a grant from the Government of Japan. The organization was capitalized through contributions to a Multi-Donor Trust Fund (MDTF) made by various entities, including the governments of Canada, the United Kingdom, France, Ireland, and Bermuda; the European Union; and the Caribbean Development Bank. Participating governments also paid membership fees to fund the organization. In 2014, a second MDTF was established by the World Bank to assist with the development of new products for the CCRIF Segregated Portfolio Company's (SPC's) current and potential members, as well as to facilitate the entrance of Central American and additional Caribbean countries. Currently, the MDTF receives funds from various donors, including Canada through the Global Affairs Canada, the United States through the Department of Treasury, the European Union through the European Commission, and Germany through the Federal Ministry for Economic Cooperation and Development and KfW. The Caribbean Development Bank provided extra financing with resources supplied by Mexico, along with the Government of Ireland and the European Union through its Regional Resilience Building Facility, which is managed by the Global Facility for Disaster Reduction and Recovery and the World Bank.

The CCRIF SPC is a non-profit facility that pools risks and is registered, owned, and operated in the Caribbean. It was created as the first risk pool of its kind, covering multiple countries and perils. The CCRIF was also the first to introduce parametric insurance policies for catastrophes, which are part of a range of disaster risk financing instruments that governments can use to protect themselves financially in the wake of a disaster. Specifically designed to cover infrequent, high-intensity events, CCRIF's parametric insurance policies provide quick liquidity within 14 days of an event if the policy is triggered. This type of insurance aims to address the liquidity gap that occurs between a country's access to short-term relief supplies immediately following a disaster and the beginning of long-term reconstruction and redevelopment assistance.

The CCRIF SPC provides parametric insurance that is specifically designed to mitigate the financial impact of catastrophic tropical cyclones, earthquakes, and excess rainfall events on governments in the Caribbean and Central America. When a policy is triggered, the CCRIF provides short-term liquidity to its member governments. As the world's first regional risk-pooling fund issuing parametric insurance, it enables its members to purchase catastrophe coverage at a substantially lower price than what they could obtain through a non-pooled arrangement. At present, 19 Caribbean and 3 Central American governments are members of the facility. The CCRIF SPC currently offers earthquake, tropical cyclone, and excess rainfall policies to these governments, and is also planning to offer loan portfolio cover policies to financial institutions in Caribbean countries.[9]

Countries can purchase policies with coverage up to $150 million per peril, although the financial limitations of some countries constrain their ability to purchase optimal coverage consistent with the risk profiles of their countries, despite current discounts.

Since its inception in 2007, the CCRIF has made a total of 54 payouts to 16 of its member countries totaling $254 million. All payouts were made within 14 days of the event. Member governments purchased $1.2 billion in coverage for catastrophe risk insurance for 2022–2023 against climate-related and seismic hazards.

Implementation Timeline

2007	• CCRIF was formed as the first multi-country risk pool in the world. It was the first insurance instrument to successfully develop parametric policies backed by both traditional and capital markets. • It was designed as a regional catastrophe fund for Caribbean governments to limit the financial impact of hurricanes and earthquakes by quickly providing financial liquidity when a policy is triggered.
2014–2015	• CCRIF was restructured into a segregated portfolio company (SPC) to facilitate expansion into new products and geographic areas and is now named CCRIF SPC. • April 2015, CCRIF signed a memorandum of understanding with the Council of Ministers of Finance of Central America, Panama, and the Dominican Republic to enable Central American countries to formally join the facility.
2019–2020	• In July 2019, the facility, in collaboration with the World Bank and the United States State Department, introduced coverage for the fisheries sector for two member countries—Saint Lucia and Grenada. • In October 2020, CCRIF introduced coverage for electric utilities.
2022	• CCRIF offered its members the option to reduce the cost of their policy premiums, or to increase coverage, or both by approximately 11% for tropical cyclone policies and 24% for excess rainfall policies for the Caribbean and 15%–30% to Central American members. • CCRIF also provided discounts to its members as an incentive to increase coverage, including for tropical cyclone and earthquake policies.

Stakeholders Involved

- Nineteen Caribbean governments are currently members of the CCRIF: Anguilla, Antigua and Barbuda, Bahamas, Barbados, Belize, Bermuda, British Virgin Islands, Cayman Islands, Dominica, Grenada, Haiti, Jamaica, Montserrat, St. Kitts and Nevis, Saint Lucia, Sint Maarten, St. Vincent and the Grenadines, Trinidad and Tobago, and Turks and Caicos Islands.
- Three Central American governments are members of the CCRIF: Guatemala, Nicaragua, and Panama.
- One electric utility company is a member of the CCRIF: ANGLEC.
- In addition, the CCRIF also receives funds and other assistance from donors including the World Bank, European Union, Canada, Germany, and Mexico.

Benefits and Impact

- Climate risk insurance has the potential to reduce the catastrophic impact of disasters, enable a timely recovery, and contribute to sustainable, climate resilient development.

---

9   All content sourced from CCRIF SPC website. https://www.ccrif.org.

- By reducing vulnerability and incentivizing risk-reducing behavior, insurance contributes to increasing resilience to climate shocks.
- This risk transfer mechanism provides assistance to the most vulnerable communities and groups.

Climate risk and catastrophe insurance has become increasingly necessary given the frequency and severity of climate-induced events. This risk transfer mechanism safeguards and protects the interests of the most vulnerable communities by giving them the means to recoup some of their loss and restart their livelihood activities at a very low cost. The ASEAN+3 countries are highly susceptible to climate change impact and adverse weather events. Given the diversity of ASEAN+3 countries in terms of sustainability and resilience, the region would benefit from risk financing facilities like SEADRIF and CCRIF.

13: Crowdfunded Impact Investments

Name of Project	Music Securities Inc.—Securite
Project Location	Japan
Sector	Infrastructure and business operations
Objective	Post-disaster reconstruction, business revival, and new business support
Year	2009 to date

Model Description

Music Securities Inc. was launched in 2000 as a small fund to protect the creative and economic independence of artists by drafting contracts, signing artists, negotiating with investors, and producing and marketing compact discs. In 2009, it established Securite, a platform for crowdfunded investments. In the wake of the Great East Japan Earthquake in 2011, Securite Disaster Area Support Funds were set up to provide financial assistance to small and medium-sized enterprises (SMEs) in earthquake-hit areas. Recognizing that SMEs faced difficulties in accessing funds, Securite enables individual investors to undertake empathy-based investments by considering both financial and nonfinancial returns from the investment. Investors can choose the business in which they wish to invest and provide funding to local businesses by donating half of the investment and financing the other half. The investment unit is as small

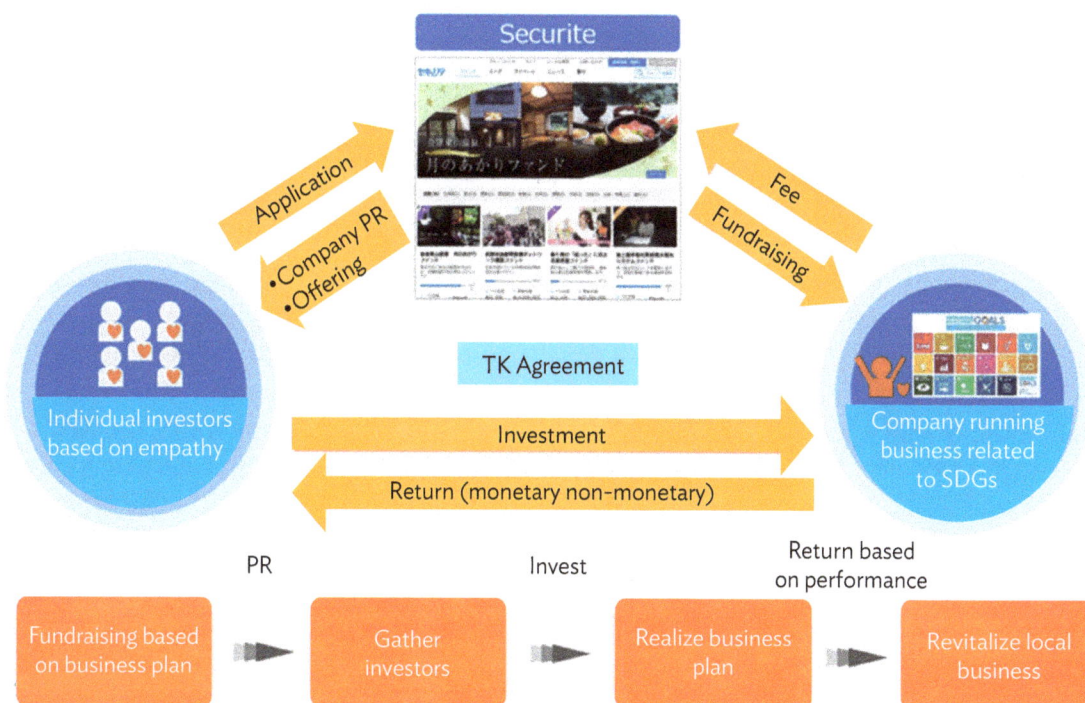

Figure A20: Securite Crowdfunding Investment Model

PR = public relations, SDG = Sustainable Development Goal, TK = *tokumei kumiai,* a Japanese bilateral contract governed by the Commercial Code of Japan.
Source: B. Huang et al. 2020. Crowdfunding with Music Securities: A New Approach to Impact Investing. ADBI Policy Brief. No. 2020-1 (March). Asian Development Bank Institute. Manila. https://www.adb.org/sites/default/files/publication/576091/adbi-pb2020-1.pdf.

as ¥10,500–¥10,800 ($91–$93), of which ¥500–¥800 is retained by Securite as an investment charge, ¥5,000 is donated to the business and ¥5,000 is financed as investment.

This innovative financing structure is neither equity nor debt, as investors do not have a share in the entity and the business is not obliged to pay back the investment. Based on the results of the business, investors receive a percentage return on their investment and are also compensated by gifts from the entity (Figure A20). Securite is an internet-based investment platform that provides functionality for payments and information through progress, due diligence, and audit and accounting reports. It provides potential investors an investment opportunity in vetted projects and entrepreneurs can raise capital for their businesses. The funds are compliant with the Financial Instruments and Exchange Act of Japan.

Implementation Timeline

2000	• Music Securities Inc. set up to ensure economic independence of musicians
2009	• Music Securities Inc. develops Securite—a platform for crowdfunded investment funds
2011	• Securite Disaster Support Funds launched; 39,200 individuals invested ¥1.1 billion in 38 companies
2021	• Securite created over 850 funds for more than 570 companies
2022	• Raised nearly ¥1.01 billion ($7.52 million); 29,282 investors*; raised ¥8 billion cumulatively.

* Source http://oen.securite.jp

Stakeholders Involved

- Securite
- Individual investors
- Entrepreneurs and local business units

Benefits and Impact

- The "half donation, half investment" financing mechanism provides SMEs with access to capital and offers fresh investment opportunities for small investors to support companies within their local area and beyond. This investment crowdfunding platform with a focus on empathy-based financial inclusion integrates both profit-driven and philanthropic objectives.
- The financing model creates a sense of responsibility and attachment through the flow of dividends, gifts, and entity-sponsored visits, thus leading to a greater commitment from both parties. It has assisted infrastructure reconstruction activities ranging from factories to shipyards and connected its beneficiaries to markets and suppliers.
- Securite offers financial mobility as potential investors can invest in their choice of entities and have the flexibility to invest with a small stake. All funding requests are supported by the company's business plan and a due diligence report to facilitate an informed investment decision. It has created an SME investment portal to facilitate networking and established partnerships with nearly 70 financial institutions to further assist businesses.
- Securite measures social and environmental impact using both qualitative and quantitative metrics and has adopted the United Nations Sustainable Development Goal targets to create a positive social impact. In May 2022, it joined the United Nations Sustainable Blue Economy Finance Initiative and established the

Fisherman Japan Blue Fund. The fund's investment objective is not limited to the fisheries industry as it includes marine resource management, marine environmental conservation, development of sustainable aquaculture food, and the collection and recycling of marine plastics, thus contributing to a circular economy.

The "half donation, half investment" micro-investment model has revived critically-affected industries and other small and medium-sized enterprises that cannot access traditional debt. It provides capital investment at low cost and enables companies to leverage the investment to become operational. Securite also supports entrepreneurs and research and development through assistance for new businesses and innovations.

14: Land Value Capture

Name of Project	Land Value Capture—Hong Kong, China Mass Transit Railway Corporation
Project Location	Hong Kong, China
Sector	Transport
Objective	Mobilizing funds for infrastructure expansion and long-term revenue streams
Year	1995 onwards

Model Description

Hong Kong, China is densely populated (7.3 million people)[10] and its transport network serves over 12 million journeys every day.[11] Real estate, both residential and commercial, is at a premium and their proximity to the Mass Transit Railway Corporation (MTRC) network dictates much of the value. Unlike most public transport entities, the MTRC is very profitable, does not depend upon government subsidies, and derives most (nearly 80%) of its profitability from real estate. Profit sharing with private developers in real estate residential sales and renting and managing MTRC-owned commercial properties, both property-related operations, have generated almost twice the revenue of the amount spent on railway infrastructure in the last 2 decades.

The MRTC adopts the following development process in the expansion of its transportation business (Figure A21).[12]

- When planning a new transit line, the MRTC, in conjunction with the government, assesses the cost of construction and then prepares a Master Plan to identify property development sites along the railway track.
- After obtaining all necessary approvals and negotiating terms, the MRTC purchases the right to develop property above and adjacent to the railway lines and depots from the government for 50 years. The payment made to the government does not include any increase in value resulting from the transportation project.
- The MTRC divides the land into smaller plots to make it more manageable and floats a public tender for allocating the development rights to private developers.
- The selected private developers pay for all development costs, including construction and land premium for acquiring exclusive development rights, as well as commercialization risks.
- Agreements with the private developers include profit-sharing mechanisms. If the private partner is able to sell all the units before the contractual deadline, the MTRC will receive an agreed portion of the profit generated. If the units are unsold, the MTRC will obtain them and decide whether to sell or lease them. For commercial units, the MTRC will lease them to generate long-term rental income
- The MTRC supervises the civil works construction and enforces technical control standards and requirements for interfacing between the railway premises and the property development.

The MTRC has developed around 33 stations, generating 100,000 housing units and more than 2 million square meters of commercial floor area in 2015. It manages more than 96,000 housing units, 13 shopping malls, and 5 office buildings that are equivalent to 764 thousand square meters of commercial and office space.[13] Though the property

[10] Hong Kong, China Census and Statistics Department. 2022. Provisional Figures. https://www.censtatd.gov.hk/en/.
[11] Hong Kong, China Transport Department. https://www.td.gov.hk/en/transport_in_hong_kong/its/introduction/index.html.
[12] M. Verougstraete, H. Zeng, and UNESCAP. 2014. Land Value Capture Mechanism: The Case of the Hong Kong MTR. July. https://repository.unescap.org/bitstream/handle/20.500.12870/3895/ESCAP-2014-PB-Land%20value-capture-mechanism-Hong-Kong-MTR.pdf?sequence=1&isAllowed=y.
[13] Franco Jauregui-Fung. 2022. Land Value Capture and Transit Oriented Development as a Way of Funding Railway Systems: The Case of Hong Kong Rail + Property Model. German Institute of Development and Sustainability (IDOS). Bonn. https://www.idos-research.de/uploads/media/Jauregui-Fung_Hong_Kong_MTR_IDOS.pdf.

development has been declining due to a lack of land grants and expensive land premiums, the MRTC's property-related activities are still a significant source of income (higher than its transport operations). Property-related activities have generated almost twice the amount of investment made by the MTRC to build the metro lines. The government also gains from the development by the sale of land at a premium, property taxes, and annual dividends by being the majority stakeholder in the MRTC.

Figure A21: Hong Kong, China—Land Value Capture Model

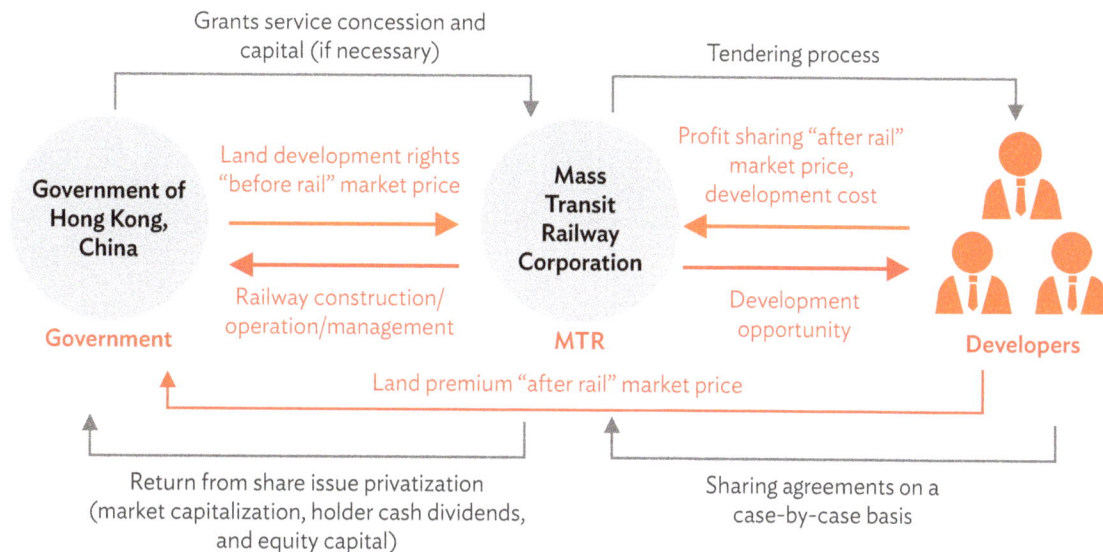

Source: F. Jauregui-Fung. 2022. Land value capture and transit oriented development as a way of funding railway systems: The case of Hong Kong Rail + Property Model, Report for the "Inclusive and sustainable smart cities in the framework of the 2030 Agenda for Sustainable Development" Project. Bonn: German Institute of Development and Sustainability (IDOS). https://doi.org/10.23661/r3.2022.

Implementation Timeline

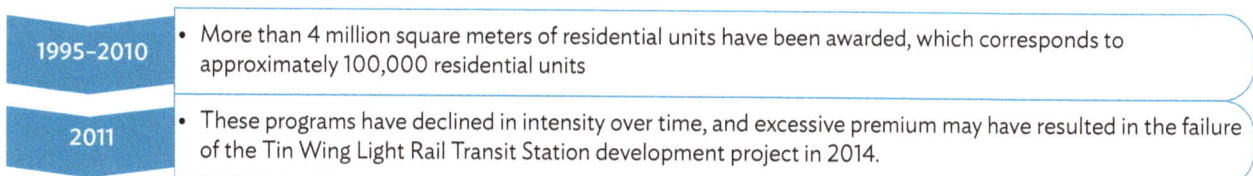

1995–2010	• More than 4 million square meters of residential units have been awarded, which corresponds to approximately 100,000 residential units
2011	• These programs have declined in intensity over time, and excessive premium may have resulted in the failure of the Tin Wing Light Rail Transit Station development project in 2014.

Stakeholders Involved

- Government of Hong Kong, China
- MTRC
- Private developers

Benefits and Impact

- Units located close to railway lines in Hong Kong, China command a housing price premium of 5% to 17%. If these properties incorporate transit-oriented design, such as pedestrian access to commercial amenities or pathways connecting with stations, the premium can exceed 30%.

- The "rail+property" model aligns with the government's goal to foster the development of local communities near railway lines.
- The relationship between the MTRC and the government, along with the land policy in Hong Kong, China, has streamlined the planning and allocation of development rights along railway lines. For private developers, partnering with the MTRC has also simplified the resolution of technical issues.

> *The Mass Transit Railway Corporation benefited from developing property along the railway lines by not only providing a stable and ample income but also by attracting residents to amenities and housing near the stations, which, in turn, led to increased use of the railway. This financing mechanism is a form of partnership in which a public entity works with private developers on infrastructure projects, such as real estate properties, with both parties sharing risks, costs, and profits. Typically, land value capture mechanisms are utilized to generate revenue for public infrastructure by capturing the future value of land (after development) through land sales, additional levies, and taxation.*

15: Debt-for-Climate/Nature Swap

Name of Project	Seychelles Debt-for-Nature Swap
Project Location	Seychelles
Sector	Marine conservation
Objective	Marine habitat protection and climate adaptation
Year	2017–2018

Model Description

The economy of Seychelles, being a small island developing country, is intrinsically linked to its coastal and marine assets. The 2008 financial crisis severely impacted the country's ability to repay its debts as well as commit funds to implement climate adaptation interventions to protect and preserve its marine assets. A series of discussions was initiated by the Government of Seychelles and The Nature Conservancy (TNC) with the Paris Club creditors to negotiate restructuring of the debt. In 2018, Seychelles became the first country to successfully undertake a debt-for-nature (DFN) swap aimed at specifically protecting the world's oceans and biodiversity. The debt restructuring mechanism used in this case is an innovative approach to debt relief that involves forgiving some portion of a developing country's foreign debt in return for a commitment or pledge to invest in domestic environmental conservation and sustainability initiatives. This debt-for-climate-adaptation swap involves converting some of Seychelles' foreign debt into local debt that is easier to manage. To facilitate this refinancing, TNC established the Seychelles Conservation and Climate Adaptation Trust (SeyCCAT) to secure grants and loans for the debt conversion, with the Seychelles government committing to improved policies and increased investment in marine conservation and climate adaptation (Figure A22).

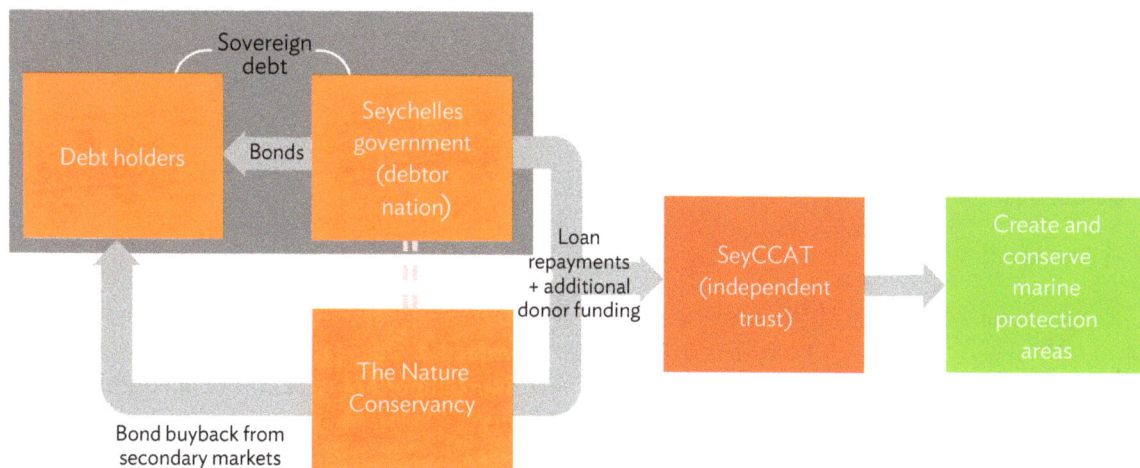

Figure A22: Seychelles—Debt-for-Nature Swap Model

SeyCCAT = Seychelles Conservation and Climate Adaptation Trust.
Source: Divjot Singh and Vikram Widge. 2021. *Debt for Climate Swaps: Supporting a Sustainable Recovery*. Climate Policy Initiative. https://www.climatepolicyinitiative.org/wp-content/uploads/2021/05/Debt-for-Climate-Swaps-Blueprint-May-2021.pdf.

To buy back its sovereign debt of $21.6 million at a discounted rate, SeyCCAT provided an impact capital loan including $5 million of grant funding to the government. The debt conversion effectively redirects Seychelles' debt payments from official creditors to SeyCCAT, and restructures debt payments to more favorable terms of 20 years (from 8 years), thus reducing Seychelles government's annual debt service liability by over $2 million annually and partial conversion to local currency. The trust will use debt payments to (i) repay the initial capital raised and (ii) fund ongoing marine conservation and climate adaptation programming through an endowment of $3 million. The government is committed to developing a Marine Spatial Plan to set up vast areas of protected marine parks for climate resilience, fishery management, biodiversity conservation, and ecotourism. In addition to the expansion of the Marine Protected Area (MPA), the fund will also improve governance of priority fisheries and support the development of the Seychelles' Blue Economy, with a particular focus on supporting small-scale fisheries. The government has provided a policy commitment to protect 30% of its seas.

Implementation Timeline

2012	• Seychelles commits to 30% marine protection at Rio+20
2013	• Proposed debt restructure discussed between Seychelles and the Commonwealth (23rd Commonwealth Heads of Government Meeting, 2013, Sri Lanka)
2014	• Seychelles delegation meets main bilateral creditors in London, Paris, and Brussels and plans to swap a portion of its external debt for funding for coastal/marine conservation projects
2015	• Government of Seychelles holds discussions with key local stakeholders about planning for the use of the country's marine economic zones
2015	• Government of Seychelles and Paris Club of Creditors announce the closing of the first-ever debt restructuring for climate adaptation
2016	• Government of Seychelles makes payment to creditors to buy back their debt via a loan from the SeyCCAT—funded by grants and a loan from TNC
2018	• SeyCCAT invests in local schemes to protect the offshore environment around the Seychelles island archipelago

Source: Divjot Singh and Vikram Widge. 2021. *Debt for Climate Swaps. Supporting a Sustainable Recovery.* Climate Policy Initiative.https://seyccat.org/wp-content/uploads/2019/07/SSCOE-Debt-for-Nature-Seychelles-Case-Study-final.pdf.

Stakeholders Involved

- Government of Seychelles
- The Nature Conservancy
- Paris Club of Creditors

Benefits and Impact

- Seychelles will increase its MPAs from 1% to 30% of its territorial waters—this area amounts to roughly 400,000 square kilometers. Half of this new marine protected area—approximately 200,000 square kilometres—will be classified as "no-take" zone to help protect important tuna feeding grounds, which will increase fish stocks and improve the Seychelles' tuna industry.
- Restoration of coral reefs and mangroves will buffer against rise in sea level and the force of severe storms. It will also develop and reform coastal zone management, fisheries, and marine policy and regulatory protection to cope with climate change.
- In addition to enforcing the terms of the debt restructuring agreement, SeyCCAT will manage the perpetual endowment to fund marine conservation and climate adaptation activities. It will also be responsible for distributing the proceeds of the debt conversion to the government and NGOs.

Debt-for-nature swap is an innovative mechanism for coastal nations as well as debt-burdened developing countries that have been severely impacted by the pandemic, climate events, and food and energy inflation. Most ASEAN countries are highly vulnerable to the impacts of climate change but lack the funding to adequately manage their natural resources and implement climate adaptation interventions and nature-based solutions. It has improved fiscal space by extending debt maturities and redirected external debt service to in-country investments, some proportion of which is payable in local currency.